Dan Hagedorn

The Curtiss-Wright AT-9
The Other Jeep

STRATUS

Published in Poland in 2019
by STRATUS sp.j.
Po. Box 123,
27-600 Sandomierz 1, Poland
e-mail: office@mmpbooks.biz
as
MMPBooks,
e-mail: rogerw@mmpbooks.biz
© 2019 MMPBooks.
http://www.mmpbooks.biz

ISBN
978-83-65958-30-3

Editor in chief
Roger Wallsgrove

Editorial Team
Bartłomiej Belcarz
Robert Pęczkowski
Artur Juszczak

Research and text
Dan Hagedorn

Colour profiles
Ted Williams

Scale plans
Robert Panek

Proofreading
Roger Wallsgrove

DTP
Stratus sp. j.

Printed by
Wydawnictwo
Diecezjalne i Drukarnia
www.wds.pl

PRINTED IN POLAND

TABLE OF CONTENTS

AT-9 Production List

http://mmpbooks.biz/assets/AT9/At-9-production-list.pdf

INTRODUCTION

Long-time friends, associates and fellow aviation history enthusiasts nearly all responded blinking and politely when I announced to them over the past few years that my next major monograph effort was to be devoted to the Curtiss-Wright AT-9. Some, I am reasonably certain, had to struggle to capture a mental image of the type while others, after some hesitance, eventually shaped the inevitable question: "Why on earth would anyone want to do a history of the AT-9 and, even if you did, would anyone be interested in reading it?"

We are about to find out.

Decades ago, the realization finally dawned on me that the Curtiss-Wright Corporation, St. Louis Airplane Division, lineal corporate descendant of the nearly legendary Travel Air aircraft series, and as distinct from the mammoth Buffalo Division, was woefully under-represented in the literature of the history of the first full century of manned flight. I subsequently made a concerted effort to address this for two reasons: first, because the product line seemed to provide manageable subjects for a series of articles on the CW- series following the merger of Travel Air for the wonderful *Skyways* journal, devoted to between-the-wars aviation and, secondly, because a sizeable number of their products were destined to end their days in Latin America, my professed sub-set of specialization in aviation history. That qualification has always been the 'bottom-line' qualifier for my attention and, I have to admit, the AT-9 series just barely qualified, and even then, somewhat tenuously, as will be seen.

Before *Skyways* wrapped-up conventional publication under the amazing editorship of friend Dave Ostrowski, I had finished the series from the CW-12 to the CW-23 and, intentionally skipping the CW-24 (which became the XP-55), which has been more than adequately investigated by other historians, I arrived at the CW-25 – which gave me pause.

During the inevitable literature survey, it became apparent that very little of a substantive nature had been done on the CW-25/AT-9 series, with the 1974 "Wings" article by Colonel Walt Boyne and the even earlier 1965 "Historical Aviation Album" coverage by Paul R. Matt, being unquestionably the best. Virtually every other word on the type was a repetition of the findings of these two esteemed historians and even these, on reflection, failed to adequately describe the wartime contributions of what was unquestionably an exceptional training aircraft series, although not without its vices.

Then, while all of this was simmering, I had the great fortune to be selected as the Curator and Director of Collections at The Museum of Flight at historic Boeing Field – the world's largest, non-governmental, private aviation and space museum. In this, I was fortunate enough to be empowered to collect aggressively – attempting to fill the known 'holes' in our understanding of the first century of manned flight – and one of the major collections we accessioned was that of Ken Crist, who had undertaken a long-term project to document, at the beginning, the history of WWII USAAF Air Training Command stations in the Southwestern United States. Ken's footwork supplied energy and comprehension to this study, as an overwhelming majority of the AT-9s built eventually migrated to stations within his initial area of study, which he necessarily broadened to include all ATC wartime stations. I believe he had found, as did the undersigned, that in order to understand the individual parts, it was necessary to understand the whole, as they were inextricably connected. My gratitude to Ken is boundless, as he saved me much footwork and made my subsequent research excursions to the National Archives and the USAF Historical Research Agency much more focused than they would have been otherwise. I am confident that Ken would be pleased that his efforts did precisely what he had hoped: they spawned additional, detailed investigations.

As I hope will be seen in these pages, the CW-25 and the definitive AT-9 series entered onto the historical stage at almost precisely the right moment for the U.S. Army Air Corps, and although many pundits even now still lash out at our military planners of the late 1930s for failing us and leaving us "ill-prepared' for what was to follow, the emergence of the AT-9 and similar, competent training and service aircraft designs at very nearly the same juncture was no accident. Planners and designers were doing the best they could in the face of rampant budgetary restraints and isolationist political dominance and, when the mosaic of service aircraft types that eventually won the war finally percolated to production, we can easily look back and point to what was little short of an amazing accomplishment in the space of five extremely frantic years.

This study will follow that historical curve. We will examine the genesis of the design, its competitors and, eventually, comrades-in-arms, with whom AT-9s were always literally the best and the brightest, and a detailed look at the fielding of the aircraft to the 24 initial stations as well as an astonishing number of unusual and special assignments – including assignment to line, tactical units.

After producing 791 aircraft between September 1941 and January 31, 1943 – a scant 16 months, and assigning every single one of them, and having served actively and continuously through to VJ-Day, exactly one complete AT-9 survives, and this solitary example is actually a composite of several aircraft. A large number survived the war to be passed, inevitably, to the clutches of the Reconstruction Finance Corporation (RFC) or War Assets Administration (WAA) for surplus disposal, and while a number were acquired by civil owners and a Supplemental Type Certificate issued – usually a sure-sign that at least one gained a civil identity – not a solitary AT-9 has been identified on the U.S. Civil Aircraft Register, one of the most enduring imponderables of this study.

There are some surprises to be found in these pages by those who have done more than average investigation into the wartime training miracle, while, hopefully, those who have largely ignored the contributions to victory of the vast ATC apparatus will come away with the same respect and admiration for that effort that I have come to via this project.

So now we come to the ultimate question: why the AT-9? In actuality, while this monograph is indeed dedicated to the evolution of that aircraft series, the real story here is to be found in the fact that the United States and its democratic allies forged air forces of overwhelming quality and numbers, with crews that were representative of their populations, and developed a comprehensive system to train those crews, from absolute novice to polished warriors, within a syllabus of training tools, lessons-learned and depth that the short-sighted and initially victorious Axis forces were never able to match. The Allies trained for victory; the Axis trained for conquest.

Finally, the ultimate fact that the overwhelming majority of long-suffering instructor pilots and Cadets who crewed this nearly extinct series of aircraft have now themselves made their final flights is not lost upon this writer, and more is the pity that their nearly forgotten contributions have nearly edged into oblivion as well. This is, therefore, a humble valedictory and salute to them, one-and-all, with the sincere hope that this study will at long last document their halcyon years.

As always, there are any number of open questions that remain, and some factoids that will probably be in dispute, but in all of this, these findings are the responsibility of the undersigned, while encouraging and, indeed, hopeful of additional input and clarification from any reader.

Dan Hagedorn
Maple Valley, Washington
2017

SETTING THE CW-25
AND AT-9 IN PLACE AND TIME

By the end of 1941, the huge Curtiss-Wright Corporation was totally engaged in producing a stunning variety of military aircraft, with just a very few civil types in the mix, for both the United States Army Air Corps, the United States Navy, Marine Corps and Coast Guard, and extensive foreign, export customers.

The Corporation's major facilities were Plants 1 and 2 at Buffalo, New York, while the new Plant 3 at Columbus, Ohio was just getting underway. Plant 4, usually described as at St. Louis (but actually in Robertson, MO), was also cited in corporate language as the Curtiss-Wright St. Louis Airplane Division, while Plant 5 was also at Buffalo and Plant 6 was at Louisville, Kentucky, often overlooked in the mix.

Curtiss was operating on an intensive production schedule against large orders for P-40B, P-40C, P-40D, P-40E and P-40F fighters for the USAAF and equivalent *Tomahawk I, Tomahawk IIA, IIB, Kittyhawk I, II* and H87 export variants from the Buffalo plants for the British Commonwealth and Allied customers. The Columbus plant was ramping up to production of the Curtiss SB2C-1 *Helldiver*, of which much was expected, while the SO3C-1 *Seagull* and ungainly O-52 *Owl* were sharing production space at Columbus and Buffalo as well. The St. Louis plant, which had always operated in a semi-autonomous manner, had developed a series of truly unique designs against announced service requirements, including the Curtiss-Wright CW-20, the prototype of the successful C-46 family, the all-wood C-76 *Caravan*, the CW-21 *Interceptor* for export, the CW-22/SNC-1 *Falcon* for export and the U.S. Navy – and the CW-25/AT-9.

For reasons that have never been fully articulated, the products of the Buffalo design bureau were invariably cited as simply Curtiss P-40s, etc, within their own Manufacturers Serial Number ranges, while those of the St. Louis bureau were cited as Curtiss-Wright products with their own, unique Manufacturers Serial Number ranges as well, which were invariably prefaced with a "CW-" designator. While on the surface of it, this difference may appear innocuous, in reality it reflected both administrative, philosophical and engineering separation.

To fully understand the historical setting in which the CW-25/AT-9 series emerged, it is instructive to examine exactly what Curtiss had on its plate in the decade spanning the lead-up to what we now know as World War II, and the end of that greatest of conflicts, and how the subject of this monograph was somewhere in the middle of it all.

Buffalo Plant Production 1936–1946

Curtiss Designation	Service Designation	Number Produced
Model 71	XSOC-1, SOC-1, SOC-2, SOC-2A, SOC-3, SOC-3A, SOC-4	261
Model 75	Y1P-36, P-36A, P-36B, P-36C, XP-36D, XP-36E, XP-36F, P-36G and multiple export variants	1,206
Model 75-I	XP-37, YP-37	13
Model 76 and 76A	XA-14, Y1A-18	14
Model 77	XSBC-1, XSBC-2, XSBC-3, SBC-3, XSBC-4, SBC-4	258
Model 81 to 87	XP-40, P-40, P-40A, P-40B, P-40C, P-40C, P-40D, P-40E, TP-40E, XP-40F, YP-40F, P-40F, XP-40G, P-40G, XP-40K, P-40K, TP-40K, P-40L, P-40M, P-40N, TP-40N, XP-40Q, P-40R and export variants	13,920
Model 84	XSB2C-1	1
Model 85	O-52	203
Model CW-20A	C-46, C-46A, C-46D, C-46F, R5C-1	2,711
Republic	P-47G	354
Total Buffalo Production		18,941

St. Louis (Robertson) Airplane Division Production 1936-1946

Curtiss-Wright Designation	Service Designation	Number Produced
CW-19	19L, 19R, A19R	28
CW-20	CW-20 and C-46A	29
CW-21	CW-21, CW-21B, CW-21B-1, all for export	56
CW-22	CW-22 export and SNC-1	487
CW-23C	CW-23 demonstrator	1
CW-24	XP-55	1
CW-25	CW-25 prototype	1
CW-25A	AT-9, AT-9A, (incl AT-9B, AT-9C)	791
CW-27	YC-76	5
Model S.84	A-25, SB2C-1A	900
Total St. Louis (Robertson) Production		2,299

Columbus Division Production to 1945

Curtiss Designation	Service Designation	Number Produced
Model 82	XSO3C-1, SO3C-1, SO3C-2, SO3C-2C, SO3C-3	795
Model 84	SB2C-1, SB2C-1C, XSB2C-2, SB2C-3, SB2C-4, SB2C-5, XSB2C-6	5,516
Model 97	XSC-1, SC-1, XSC1A, SC-2	576
Total Columbus Division Production		6,887

Louisville, Kentucky Division Production to 1945

Curtiss Designation	Service Designation	Number Produced
CW-20	C-46A, R5C-1	438
CW-27	YC-76, YC-76A	20
Total Louisville Production		458

Thus it can be seen that, altogether, the Curtiss-Wright Corporation produced an incredible 22,999 complete aircraft during that crucial decade, and the CW-25/AT-9 series emerged in St. Louis at almost precisely the right moment, both in terms of production capacity and engineering reach as well as meeting a very specific USAAC requirement in a timely and expeditious manner.

Enter Project P-253 and the Original CW-25

The very earliest known incarnation of the basic design which evolved into Project P-253 and, subsequently, the CW-25, was a Patent Filing by none other than Donovan Reese Berlin, on behalf of Curtiss, dated November 3, 1937, and issued December 17, 1940, as No.2,225,094. While recognizable in general layout, it inevitably evolved through a myriad of engineering tweaks and, by July 1, 1940, the project had been passed to St. Louis and assigned the general Curtiss-Wright Specification P-253-Z1. The changes reflected were, not unexpectedly, the result of design refinements and modifications necessary to produce what was described as a "...*harmonious assembly*" while also obtaining a guaranteed performance stipulated by the USAAC requirement for what was described at the time as a Transition Trainer. Although the specification described the Curtiss-Wright Model 25, the same report – for the very first time – also recorded the Model as "AT-9," a designator which would have had to be issued officially by the USAAC at Wright Field.

The United States fought a largely defensive war, following December 7, 1941, with aircraft which, for the most part, were either in-production or under advanced development prior to Pearl Harbor. Although in recent years, the gestation-to-maturity of a major aircraft system seems to stretch on into decades, during the 1930s the time-lag which existed between the conception of a requirement and its actual service use was often remarkably short, and this was usually dependent upon the relative complexity of the aircraft. This was especially true in the more advanced tactical aircraft types.

Of the aircraft produced by U.S. industry through August 1945, nearly 25% were trainers – all told some 55,000 of them. In contrast to the combat planes, their contributions and qualities were only very vaguely known to the U.S. public during the war but, in reality, their development and production in fact enjoyed the very highest priority during the early years of the post-Munich Crisis USAAC expansion. As a direct consequence, and usually coming as a surprise to disciples of the popular combat types, their

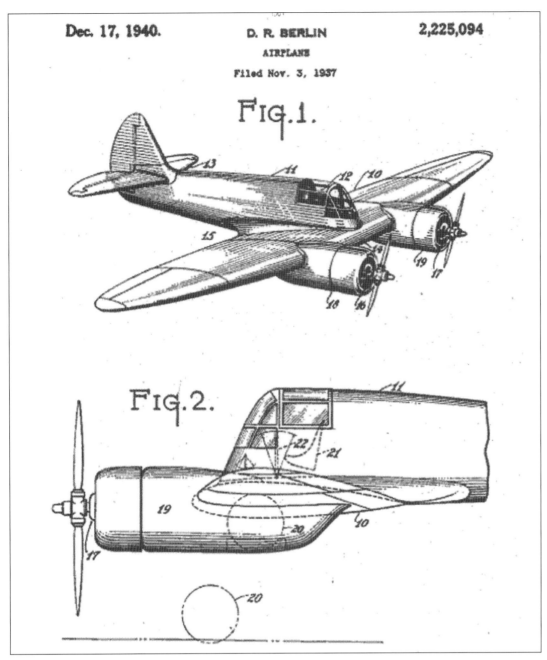

Dec. 17, 1940.   D. R. BERLIN   2,225,094

AIRPLANE

Filed Nov. 3, 1937

FIG.1.

FIG.2.

Dated November 3, 1937 and submitted by none-other-than Donovan Reese Berlin, U.S. Patent Number 2,225,094 dated December 17, 1940 bore more than a passing resemblance to the final general configuration of the CW-25 and AT-9. (U.S. Patent Office)

The one-and-only, very angular Curtiss-Wright CW-25 pictured at St. Louis on June 24, 1941. Cited as a "120-day project" and often erroneously as the "XAT-9," the ultimate fate of the aircraft after testing is a mystery. It wore no Experimental License nor USAAC serial number. (USAAC 76899)

9

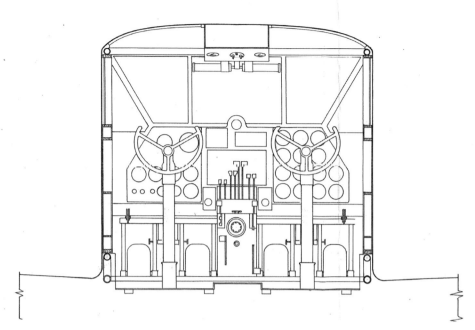

Very rare drawing showing the flight deck and cockpit of the original CW-25, looking forward, dated September 9, 1940. (Curtiss-Wright Data Book CW-25)

peak production was reached *long* before that of contemporary combat types: the very last AT-9A was turned over to the USAAF on 31 January 1943, for instance. Between November 1940 and February 1943, trainer types constituted at any one time *more than 50% of the total AAF inventory*, and only started a slow decline in 1944, as the Training Command started curtailing their work. It is the opinion of this writer that this phenomenon ranks as one of the outstanding – and unsung – planning achievements of General Henry H. "Hap" Arnold and his wartime AAF staff. In short, the aircraft acquired, and the anticipation of requirements, although not always perfect, turned out to be the right combinations at almost precisely the right historical moment.

The triad training system developed by the USAAC and Navy, consisting of a mix of pre-flight/primary, basic and advanced training, with an outstanding mix of capable aircraft in each category, proved to be the most glaring organizational difference between the air arms of the victors and the vanquished during the conflict.

Most of the trainers developed by U.S. industry during the war, on reflection, were versions of commercial or export types, which were then standardized to facilitate uniform training methods and procedures and, as well, to reduce maintenance problems. With but one exception, the classic Advanced Trainer series, running from AT-6 to AT-18 and beyond, were usually commercial or export models adapted for U.S. military purposes. The only exceptions were the Beech AT-10 – and the AT-9.

In their classic multi-volume series, *The Army Air Forces in World War II*, W. F. Craven and J. L. Cate, in volume VI, allude in this connection to the sturdy, adaptable Beech AT-7, and AT-11, all developments of the successful Model 18 transport, as well as the similar Cessna AT-8, AT-17 and UC-78 (often seconded to training units), which were, similarly, off-the-shelf developments of the Model T-50 *Bobcat*. Although the Beech AT-10 was also cited, as will be seen, this design was one which Wichita might just as well prefer to forget

But they devoted not a solitary word to the Curtiss-Wright AT-9.

Perhaps the best and most concise description of the entire AT-9 series was penned in 1974 by Colonel Walt Boyne in the sadly defunct *Wings* issue of February that year: "*When you come across a real inanimate tool like the humpbacked Curtiss AT-9, there is a decided temptation to look the other way. This isn't fair, for although the Jeep, a twin-engine knock propellered crew trainer, came into being as a tool, served as a tool, and retired with the moving ceremonies accorded a used hack-saw blade, its story still deserves telling. The hot little trainer from St. Louis did exactly what it was supposed to do for the people for whom it was supposed to do it, turning thousands of green kids into accomplished pilots in just a few months.*"

Testing the CW-25

As will be quickly noted by reference to the sole, known image of the original CW-25 (which was dated by Wright Field Image Number 76899 as 24 June 1941) included herein, the aircraft initially appeared to be a mid-western cousin of the Cessna T-50 with, essentially, steel-tube construction with fabric covering, other than the cowlings and a few miscellaneous components. It mounted two 295 hp Lycoming R-680-9 radials

Cited internally as CW-25 Airplane No.1 (but, significantly, titled as a Flight Test Report for type "AT-9" – it was in fact Manufacturers Serial Number CW-25-1) the very first trials were made on October 15, 1940 under the control of pilot H. Lloyd Child and observer Willis L. Wells, the latter on loan from Buffalo. Despite intensive research, so far as can be determined, this number one aircraft completed all tests from Lambert Field without benefit of a CAA Experimental License – which it surely probably should have been issued – or any form of USAAC serial, although it actually wears USAAC colors and markings in the sole photograph known to exist. This may probably be explained by the fact that the USAAC had, for all intents and purposes, funded this aircraft on Contract W-535-AC-15707 by March 12, 1941, and possibly earlier. Wright Field correspondence revealed that the Materiel Division was *not* happy with this arrangement, a letter dated mid-March 1941 stating that "...*it appears that, in the interest of expediting production, the Curtiss-Wright Corporation will have a free hand to furnish an airplane of which construction, arrangement and equipment will be unknown to the Government prior to the 75th article.*" This is the first of a number of enduring minor mysteries surrounding the development of this aircraft series.

The back-story to all of this may be apocryphal but, given the circumstances faced by "Hap" Arnold and his key leaders at the time, may be close to the truth. Apparently, Brigadier General K. B. Wolfe, Chief of the Materiel Division at Wright Field at the time, sent his personal representative, Captain William "Nelly" Morgan to Lambert Field with very specific instructions. Morgan, who eventually retired as a Major General, laid a series of very tough demands at the feet of C-W Chief Engineer George A. Page, Jr., usually credited as the father of the AT-9, amongst other St. Louis products. He described to Page what he repeatedly referred to as a "transition trainer" to help prepare maturing Air Corps Cadets at the Advanced stage for the high-performance, twin-engine combat aircraft which were just then starting to enter final development and fielding. This transition trainer was to embody, as nearly as possible, the flight characteristics of that coming generation of fighters, attack and medium bombardment aircraft – including the Lockheed P-38, Douglas A-20, North American B-25 and Martin B-26. He emphatically stated that the Air Corps *did not want* the aircraft to be easy to fly or to land.

Once again, according to Walt Boyne, when confronted with this specification, Page took Morgan at his word and, as noted, suggested initially that such an aircraft could probably be produced using non-critical materials. He set designers Herb Perkins and Carl Scott on detail design work, and the CW-25 came together in rather short order – and apparently too quickly.

Curtiss-Wright clearly understood that the rather angular features of the original CW-25 needed 'rounding and softening,' and this August 28, 1940 three-view drawing, labeled as the "CW-25 (Proto)", aside from the still "boxy" fuselage and cockpit area, reflects the mellowing of the eventual design. (Curtiss-Wright Data Book CW-25)

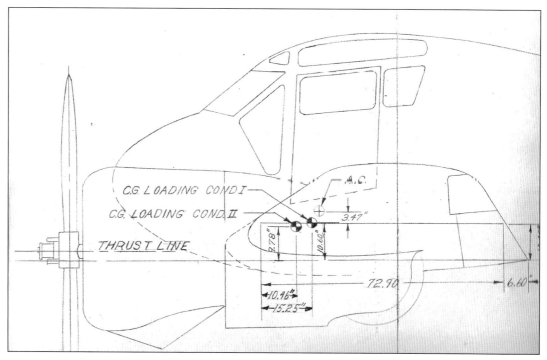

As usual with a brand-new type, problems very soon manifested themselves. During the first three high-speed taxi trials, very pronounced tail wheel shimmy set up, necessitating a return to engineering. On the fourth trial, with a 10.5 inch diameter tail wheel quickly installed (replacing a 12.5 inch wheel), the shimmy was completely gone and the aircraft actually got off the ground for about 10 minutes, and quick checks of ailerons, rudder and elevators proved effective.

On a second, longer flight that day, however, a "...*bad pitching*" set up just after take-off and it was found that the elevators could not hold the flight path and that it seemed like there was "...*bad longitudinal instability*" overall. Oddly, on subsequent flights, this over-control to correct longitudinal pitching was not present at all.

What was described as the first "real" flight was made on October 16, 1940, however. It proved to be anything but uneventful, however, with Edwin A. "Ned" Warren at the controls. During climb-out from Lambert Field, all of the controls seemed completely effective until, at 105 mph indicated, the left hand (pilots) window glass blew out completely. No sooner had the surprise of this event been appreciated, and while cruising at 1,500 feet at 2,000 rpm and 115 mph, serious stabilizer buffeting was experienced, which was not corrected by power reduction.

Maintaining control, Child entered into a low-power glide, with flaps partially extended – but the buffet continued, and seemed to be the same at all power settings and at both flap positions so long as the airspeed remained at 115. The elevators did not prove to be effective in slowing the airspeed and, significantly, it proved very difficult to fly slower than 115 because the elevators became almost totally ineffective.

Then, in the midst of all of this, the hydraulic line to the pressure valve burst, almost immediately drenching the hapless observer with hydraulic fluid.

Child remained in control, however, and somehow managed a landing at the minimum possibly airspeed – 100 mph – with the flaps up. The factory reported that, after fixes, on Flight 3, after modifying and reducing the stabilizer angle and adding a fuselage fillet, the results were still "...*not encouraging.*"

Prior to Flight 4, the fuselage was lengthened by a whopping 36 inches, and the entire empennage raised some 14 inches. However, even these measures did not cure the buffeting and, on Flight 5, tufts were attached to the upper wing surfaces – a relatively new test device – and it was finally determined that there was serious local stalling between the two engine nacelles and the fuselage.

Never reported before, Curtiss-Wright then went to the extreme measure of constructing a detailed wind tunnel model, which was shipped to Buffalo and tested in the Curtiss tunnel there. As a direct result, a fuselage/wing blister and fillet were then developed and changes incorporated into the actual aircraft. Finally, these changes solved the buffet.

But that wasn't all. As a direct result of the Buffalo wind tunnel tests, new engine cowlings were designed, and these were faired to direct the exhaust air backward instead of downward, and these were added to the aircraft just prior to Flight 17.

Just prior to Flight 19, an extension was installed on the horizontal tail which increased the span by not less than 28 inches, roughly 11%. At the same time, the rather angular lines of the lower part of the nacelles were also changed so that the fairing continued completely around the retracted main wheels, leaving only about 1/3 of the wheel exposed.

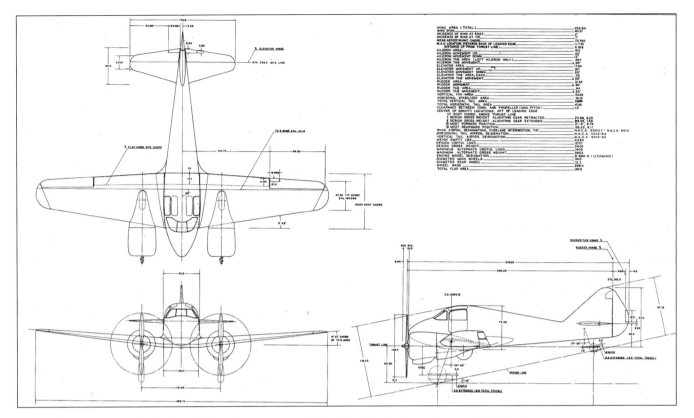

At the same time, the fuselage fuel tank was removed, limiting the fuel capacity to only 64 gallons. This, however, also reduced the empty weight to such an extent that a landing weight of 5,650 pounds could be attained.

A series of stability and climb runs were made just before Flight No.28, and briefly, the aircraft flew with the definitive engine cowl on the port engine, and the original cowl on the starboard side. Unfortunately, no photos seem to have survived showing this unusual configuration.

It has always been assumed that the entire tests series for the CW-25 were conducted in St. Louis. However, around August 27, 1940, correspondence found in RG342 at the National Archives indicates that the aircraft was at Wright Field, at least briefly, at which time it was referred to as, for the one-and-only time "...*the Prototype AT-9 airplane.*" It was there concurrent with the demonstration of the CW-21 *Interceptor* to Air Corps officers, and at the time, had Army-owned Lycoming R-680-9s (s/n 2206, AC40-1171 and s/n 2207, AC40-1178).

By March 25, 1941, many of the initial problems had been worked out, although recurring trouble with the configuration of the ram-air intake for the engines were "...*not too encouraging*" and, by Flight No.30, it was decided, finally, to use ground tests, instead, to develop a final scoop configuration. Somewhere in the midst of all of this, Curtiss-Wright management and Wright Field decided that the configuration of the definitive AT-9 would no longer be constrained by the dictates of non-essential materials (i.e., fabric covering and use of low-grade metal components insofar as possible) and that a truly modern, all-metal aircraft should constitute the actual production aircraft – a ruling which relieved the Curtiss-Wright management in Robertson, as they had vast experience with all-metal structures, having just finished building significant numbers of CW-19s, CW-21s and CW-22s, all of which contributed something to the definitive AT-9. Chief amongst these, unfortunately as it was to prove, was the undercarriage.

With those decisions in hand and final changes decided, the CW-25s Flight No.31 on March 29 was devoted almost entirely to checking the instrument plumbing on the aircraft. This revealed a number of weaknesses which would have been problematic in actual field, daily use, including a troublesome loose manifold gauge line fitting on the port (left) engine, and a cracked pitot tube line on the airspeed indicator. These minor corrections were made and, with that, testing was ruled complete after less than 50 hours total time (mainly because of the intentionally limited fuel capacity of the aircraft) and the decision was made to store the CW-25 until after the initial flight tests of the actual first production AT-9 which – for all intents and purposes – was a completely different airplane, benefitting from the refinements ironed out on the CW-25, and retaining the basic configuration and dimensions for the most part. It is interesting to note that the USAAC Curtiss-Wright Plant Representative, a Lieutenant Coupland (possibly 1LT Thomas D. Coupland) made at least two flights in the CW-25, although factory officials noted that there were "...*no release sheets*" for these excursions, being covered as "demonstration flights" by the Sales Department, and took place between Flights 27 and 28 – and were un-numbered!

Bearing all of the final characteristics of the initial production AT-9, this is actually the final General Arrangement Drawing for the definitive CW-25A dated November 24, 1941, rendered after the number one aircraft, AC41-5745, was delivered to Wright Field. (Curtiss-Wright Report 25-Z2).

The actual, ultimate fate of the CW-25 is unknown, but she was probably scrapped after being stored as no longer worth her valuable storage space, although as arguably USAAC property, she should have been Surveyed and disposed of following Army procedures. Although cited by at least one prominent aviation historian as USAAC type XAT-9, not a single official reference to such a designation has been located.

The AT-9 Prototype – The CW-25A

So far as can be determined, like the angular CW-25, the AT-9 Prototype, properly designated in the Curtiss-Wright series as the CW-25A, was nearly identical in most respects to the production AT-9, has never actually been identified as such before. This was in fact AC41-5745 (MSN CW25-3854 – but also described several times as MSN 25-X1), usually cited as the first "production" AT-9.

Strictly speaking, and had the Air Corps adhered to its own conventions in this case, the aircraft should properly have been designated as the XAT-9, but this did not happen.

It had been born as the direct result of the same Ned Warren traveling to Wright Field and selling Materiel Command on the proven sheet aluminum structure, instead of the tube-and-fabric expedient originally envisaged and embodied in the CW-25. Concurrently, another complete airframe (possibly MSN CW25-3853) was tested-to-destruction at Lambert Field, and has been largely forgotten. AC41-5745 probably owed more to the tested-and-proven features of the CW-21 *Interceptor* (no, not *Demon*) than has been appreciated, including most of the features of the tail surfaces, general wing planform and, again, landing gear retraction system.

Like the CW-25, this item was USAAC property, and was probably retrospectively covered by the original production contract for the AT-9, and thus accounts for the rather peculiar total of "straight' AT-9s procured – 491. However, as the actual language of that contract has not been located, this cannot be regarded as conclusive.

Warren himself was the test pilot for the definitive AT-9, and made the first flight on 30 July 1941. Although a quantum leap improvement over the CW-25, it still did not meet the performance specifications stipulated, nor did it possess the excellent control harmonization for which Curtiss had become known world-wide. In spite of this, however, Warren described the AT-9 as a great aerobatic aircraft – unusual in a twin – indeed, so much so that company test crews had to be cautioned about "beat ups" in it.

Like most new types, AC41-5745 was delivered to Wright Field, where she spent most of the war, being subjected to numerous test configurations and duties, including the fitting of a .30 caliber machine gun in the nose (about which more in Chapter Two) and the resolution of evolving propeller problems. Not less than 20 hours, alone, were spent on propeller tests by February 7, 1942.

Thus, via this sober and blunt response to the Air Corps' expressed guidance, Curtiss-Wright had, in the AT-9, achieved something of a first in aeronautical engineering and, in the grand scheme of things, this central fact has been largely overlooked. Stated simply, the AT-9 was built from the outset to be challenging, at a time when manufacturers were striving to produce predictable, vice-free designs that relieved crews from as much trauma as possible. As Walt Boyne stated so aptly, "...*Curtiss had achieved a design breakthrough by producing canine qualities in the prototype.*" As would be seen, these attributes were indeed carried on into the combat units by the pilots who mastered the AT-9.

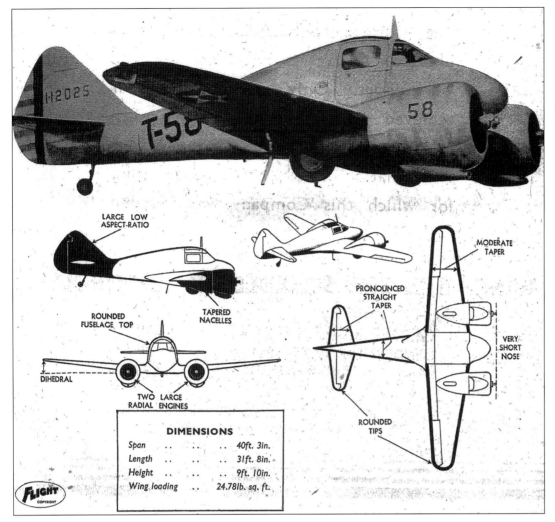

The first foreign notice of the AT-9 appeared in the long-running British periodical Flight for December 9, 1943 – by which time production had long since been completed. It illustrated a Mather Field example in-flight and useful recognition details for ground observers, although the likelihood of one being seen in Europe was zero! (Courtesy Flight Magazine)

Similar in description to the original CW-25, the CW-25A, as of November 24, 1941, was described as a twin-engine, low-wing, two-place, all-metal monoplane with retractable landing gear. It was powered, initially, with two Lycoming R-680-E3B engines and had constant speed props. It was specifically described as a "Transition" trainer (capitalization as it appeared in the detailed specification) and, it should be noted, included the information that "*...provisions are made to allow seating for two additional persons aft of the pilot and co-pilot. This space is also available for the mounting of a mapping or spotting camera,*" a capability which has not been noted publicly before.

First Appearances

Appropriately, the *St. Louis Star and Times* broke the news of the Army's first major contract for the first batch of 300 AT-9s in its Thursday evening, October 6, 1941 issue. The account included the rather questionable statement that "*...development of the AT-9 emphasizes a disclosure by the Star-Times at Washington last June 13 that as of that date there were fewer than 12 pilots in the Air Corps with sufficient training to be entrusted with a four-motored bomber, 500 of which the government hopes to produce monthly.*"

By almost any standard, the AT-9 was a good-looking airplane – with nearly art-deco curves and grace, one pilot, upon being introduced to the aircraft on the ramp for the first time, going so far as to relate that he was "*...struck by her deceptively innocent charm.*" It would be going too far to describe it as a beautiful aircraft, and it certainly wasn't lethal in appearance compared to its armed Curtiss cousins. Even the rather staid British periodical *Flight,* in its December 9, 1943 description of the type (the first substantive foreign account – by then no longer even in production) saying that "*...recognition does not present any difficulty as the 'Jeep' is quite distinctive in appearance, if not particularly beautiful by accepted standards.*"

One thing virtually all AT-9 trainees and crews remembered about the aircraft was that it was sure easy to mount-up and, if needed, to exit in a hurry.

But more about the actual flying qualities of the aircraft as we meander through the operational narrative. For now, there are a few more nuts-and-bolts details to be recorded herein.

Quality Control and Inspections: Model for an Industry-Wide Standard

The reader will find occasional references throughout this book alluding to so-called Unsatisfactory Reports (U/R's), a fairly well-developed system that the Air Corps had evolved during the 1930s to enable actual aircraft-operating units to report back to the Materiel Division on systems that were found to be faulty or sub-standard in actual day-to-day practice, and which has managed to slip by the rather comprehensive Acceptance and Testing phase that service types were routinely subjected to prior to even small orders.

The U/R system depended, however, upon an extremely diverse and rapidly expanding aeronautical industry which, itself, was self-regulating. The evolution of the so-called Army-Navy Standards (A/N Standards) and the rather arbitrary strictures of the Aircraft Manufacturers Association were "top heavy" and left to the actual prime contractors the critical role of ensuring that, when a finished aircraft tolled out of the factory, it was ready for service in every respect.

By early June 1942, it had become evident to the Inspection Section, Materiel Command at Wright Field that the avalanche of U/R's that were being received from the field, while at least in part attributable to the enormous and very rapid expansion program, indicated that more exacting quality control and inspection standards needed to be institutionalized at the prime-contractor, factory level.

The Materiel Command learned, via its Plant Representative at St. Louis, that the Curtiss-Wright Airplane Division there had already put into place its own internal Inspection and Inspector training establishment, consisting of not fewer than 432 inspectors, 105 of whom were being schooled two night each week in a special Inspectors' School. The classes consisted of a preliminary and basic inspection course during which full work days were spent working in the factory as understudies to experienced Inspectors to gain practical knowledge, and to qualify as Journeyman Inspectors. Curtiss-Wright took the unusual step of offering Army and Navy representatives the opportunity to attend this school, and the Resident AAC Representative was enthusiastic about the possibilities.

The basis of the Curtiss-Wright system for inspection rested on one bed-rock principle: all materials used in building the AT-9 (and other aircraft under contract) were purchased only from approved vendors. Materials received without express Army or Navy approval were subjected to physical, chemical, X-Ray and magnetic inspection and, even those which did have A/N approval were given spot chemical and physical checks. The subsequent Processing, Final Assembly, Flight Test and Shipping flow all had 100$ detailed contractor inspection control.

The Air Corps Materiel Command was so taken with the St. Louis system that they took the extraordinary measure of issuing an Air Corps-wide memo dated June 9, 1942 which stated that "...*it is recommended that all aircraft plants now delivering airplanes on Army contracts be surveyed for the purpose of determining to what extent the provisions modeled by the Curtiss-Wright St. Louis Airplane Division are being complied with by the AAF Factory organization.*"

AT-9
THE NUTS-AND-BOLTS

Peter M. Bowers' masterful book, *Curtiss Aircraft 1907–1947* (Putnam, London, 1979, ISBN 0-370-10029-8), which has long since become the definitive treatment of the convoluted Curtiss/Curtiss-Wright story, devoted precisely three brief paragraphs to the CW-25/AT-9, followed by some of the essential details describing the numbers built, USAAC serials and technical details.

That well-worn tome and several others containing even fewer words seemed to provide the essentials necessary to understanding this otherwise obscure aircraft series.

Unfortunately, during the course of primary source research leading to this volume, a number of errors in the data presented have since become clear and, perhaps inevitably, that same research revealed that there is actually quite a lot more to the AT-9 story than has been recorded previously.

First-and-foremost, it important that we get the numbers right. Every previous public source, for instance, mis-stated the USAAF serial number range for the second (and largest) batch of "straight" AT-9s, and the same sources erred in the unit costs for each aircraft by a rather substantial margin. Summarized below are the correct numbers:

Actual Designation	Was to Have Been	USAAC Serial Start	USAAF Serial End	First Delivery	Last Delivery	Unit Cost
AT-9	AT-9	41-5745	41-5894	9/1/41 Wright Fld, OH	2/22/42 Higley Fld, AZ	$32,382.00
AT-9	AT-9A	41-11939	41-12279	2/24/42 Victorville, CA	5/30/42 Valdosta, GA	$32,393.00
AT-9A	AT-9B	42-56853	42-57152	8/2/42 St. Joseph, MO	1/31/43 Blytheville, AR	$27,584.00

George A. Page, Jr., Curtiss-Wright's Chief Designer, standing proudly in front of one of the AT-9s from the second major batch, awaiting delivery to the Air Corps, April 30, 1942. Contemporary accounts suggest that the AT-9 was one of his proudest achievements. (F. Dale Smith Collection, No.30463, Missouri History Museum)

17

... another Curtiss-Wright FIRST

The CURTISS AT-9
...the quicker step from Trainer to Bomber

The Curtiss AT-9 is the most recent of a line of trainers whose history began with the famous Curtiss JN-4 in the days of World War I.

DESIGNED to save thousands of precious hours of advanced training, the new Curtiss AT-9 provides the United States Army Air Corps with a new and quicker step from single-engine trainers to speedy pursuit or multi-engine bombers. The new trainer simulates the flight and control characteristics of modern high-speed twin-engine military aircraft. Its design fortunately is such that it is ideally adapted to mass production, a vital factor in developing the equipment necessary for training the thousands of pilots needed for the nation's defense.

This Curtiss "Transition Trainer" is powered with two 280-horsepower radial engines and has a top speed in excess of 200 miles an hour. It has two seats side by side with provision for two additional observers' seats immediately back of the pilots.

CURTISS-WRIGHT
CORPORATION

Curtiss-Wright turned out 45 AT-9s for the AAC in 1941, a combination of 713 AT-9s and AT-9As in 1942 and 33 AT-9As in the first month of January 1943, completing the entire production run of 791 airplanes.

The announcement of the entry into service of this major new training aircraft was released to the public via the Chief of the Materiel Division, Office of the Chief of the Air Corps, on October 8, 1941, a little over a month after the 'official' delivery of the first AT-9 noted above – the Prototype, AC41-5745 – which in fact had been Air Corps property under test for some time.

Captain J. H. Van Cleve, Chief of the Technical Data Section at Wright Field, very carefully outlined to the Chief of the Materiel Division exactly what should be revealed about the aircraft. Besides the number one aircraft, he also reported that the second 'article' had also arrived at neighboring Patterson Field on October 5, 1941, and that it was already undergoing accelerated service testing, and it was to be followed by number three about a week later, and that it, too, would be the subject of accelerated service tests. The highly regarded monthly *Aero Digest* for October 1941 published the first known photo of the aircraft in the public domain on page 102 of that month's issue.

On October 13, Major N. R. Cooper, the Acting Chief of the Air Corps Public Relations Branch in Washington, formally advised T. E. Lawrence of Curtiss-Wright at Rockefeller Plaza that it would now be permissible for the manufacturer to release data on the aircraft, provided that it did not precede the Air Corps release, which was scheduled to hit the October 16, 1i941 Thursday afternoon papers.

The first public announcement of the new Transition Trainer appeared in, amongst other publications, Aero Digest for November 1941, barely two months after the first aircraft was accepted. In classic publicity department hyperbole, the verbiage attributed the AT-9 with a top speed "...in excess of 200 miles an hour," which must have made the engineers in St. Louis cringe! (Aero Digest)

Curtiss wasted little time, and had arranged a full-page advertisement describing the AT-9 for release to the aviation media, with the sub-heads "...*the quickest step from Trainer to Bomber,*" and the first to publish appears to have been *Aero Digest* in its October 1941 issue, in which it described the aircraft as the "Curtiss AT-9 Trainer" – with no other mention of any 'popular' name. *Western Flying* was next, with no less than a full-page color ad showing both the AT-9 Transition Trainer and the production-line partner, the Navy SNC-1. Even Lycoming, who provided the engines, got into the coverage, but a bit later, sponsoring a full-page ad in the February 1942 issue of *Flying and Popular Aviation*.

The prestigious British annual *JANE'S All the World's Aircraft* for 1941 also managed to squeeze in a crude three-view and brief specs before going to press.

Naming the AT-9

By the time the AT-9 debuted, U.S. aircraft manufacturers had come to appreciate the value of assigning some form of popular name to production aircraft – although this was often an on again/off again process.

There appears to have been a half-hearted effort within the Curtiss hierarchy to tag the aircraft as the *Fledgling,* a nickname with which the company had already been identified with its modestly successful biplane trainer for export and the Navy, as the N2C-1 and N2C-2 much earlier. This did not 'stick,' however, probably at least in part because the term did not convey the advanced nature or the intended utilization of the AT-9. In its early production releases and literature, the Company invariably tagged the AT-9 as the "Transition Trainer."

Since the USAAF did not concern itself with popular naming of aircraft until publication of AAF Regulation 200-3 dated 25 June 1943, and the appointment of a Board of Officers for the purpose, the practice had been to leave such appellations – provided they were at least socially acceptable to the public – in the hands of the manufacturers.

The number one AT-9, 41-5745 as she appeared June 28, 1943, complete with a .30 caliber machine gun mounted in her nose. Fitted as such, she was used for extensive tests at the Ajo Gunnery Range in Arizona. (USAAC 100412)

Historian Walt Boyne, after having conversed with George Page and others there at the time, probably arrived at the most accurate account of how this all came about. He recorded that, while not exactly handsome, and certainly not lethal in appearance, the AT-9 "*...did have the certain dopey élan possessed by the strange and wonderful animal of the Popeye cartoon strip, the Jeep.*" The fact that the Jeep was a Billikin, which just happened to be the mascot of St. Louis University – alumni of which abounded at the Curtiss-Wright St. Louis plant – almost certainly played a part as well. The story goes that some now-forgotten wag at C-W suggested the name jokingly and, as can only seem to have happened in late-1940s America, the name caught on and, before long, was being bandied about on the ramp, on the production line and, inevitably, to arriving ferry crews taking delivery of the brightly polished, spanking-new aircraft. Much later, Curtiss allegedly tried valiantly to dignify the name by suggesting that it was associated with the world-beating M38A1 Jeep ground combat vehicle, calling the AT-9 "*...the Jeep of the Air,*" but that story never gained credence. It was a Billikin.

Another source, however, tells a different story.

AT-9B? Or possibly AT-9C? Built as an AT-9A, 42-56889 was modified in response to experience in the field by engineers at Turner Field, GA, with added cockpit windows on either side to facilitate formation training sometime after April 1942. Although Wright Field approved and authorized similar modifications throughout the AT-9 fleet, this is the solitary image of any AT-9 showing the mods. (via Tom Heitzman)

1241A
83234

Wright Field had conducted extensive structural tests on an AT-9 airframe provided as part of the production contract, and the fuselage and empennage is shown here undergoing a 95% fuselage supporting U.L. in the second test. All other components were similarly tested. Early losses in the field called these tests into question, and resulted in 'fixes' to the existing fleet and new production example. (National Archives RG342, image 1241A/83234)

Supposedly during a press event in November 1941 at Ellington Field, Texas, a contrived 'christening' ceremony was staged, during which Cadet Martin Smith "broke" a bag of oxygen on the nose of a newly arrived AT-9, calling it "*...the Jeep of the Air.*"

Even at that, the name only crept into the vernacular slowly, and an extensive literature search revealed that the first known published use of the name appeared in the 1942 issue of *JANE's* by which time the total production was past the half-way point, and the aircraft had been in very intensive service for more than six months. Evidence seems to suggest that the name was seldom used out on the flight line, and never appeared a single time in training station reporting reviewed at the USAF Historical Research Agency at Maxwell AFB, AL. More recently, one widely-distributed U.S. aviation history journal published a vignette in which it was claimed that the aircraft was cited "in the ranks" as "The Humpback Hawk," but not a solitary source could be located to validate this proposition.

Variants

For internal, administrative purposes, Curtiss-Wright St. Louis inexplicably continued to use the root designator of CW-25 to describe the two initial production blocks of 'straight' AT-9s, even though these aircraft bore only lineal and configuration similarity to the angular, original CW-25.

Once the aircraft had been accepted for production by the USAAC and, following established protocol, been released for export potential, the company actively promoted the derivative CW-25A for both commercial, civil, and potential foreign military customers. In the event, none were actually built, as the wartime emergency precluded civil sales and the emergence of the Lend-Lease Act effectively ended any hope for direct export sales. Why would potential customers pay cash for state-of-the-art aircraft they could essentially acquire for nothing, with payment not due until the war was (hopefully) successfully concluded? Although unsubstantiated claims suggest that the CW-25A could be offered with several different engine options and with armament capability, to appeal to some long-standing Curtiss customers, little is known about these configurations.

When the USAAF came back to Curtiss-Wright with a large follow-on order for 300 slightly improved aircraft, incorporating lessons learned, different engines and hydraulic changes, these AT-9As were covered by company designation CW-25B.

But one of the imponderables that surfaced during the research for this monograph has surrounded the emergence of the apparently official use of the designations AT-9B and AT-9C. Setting aside the fact

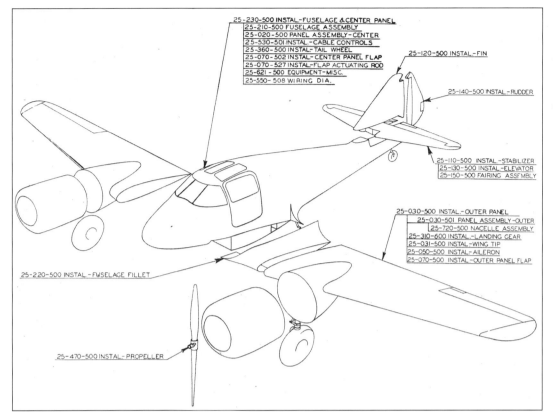

25-230-500 INSTAL.-FUSELAGE & CENTER PANEL
25-210-500 FUSELAGE ASSEMBLY
25-020-500 PANEL ASSEMBLY-CENTER
25-530-501 INSTAL.-CABLE CONTROLS
25-360-500 INSTAL.-TAIL WHEEL
25-070-502 INSTAL.-CENTER PANEL FLAP
25-070-527 INSTAL.-FLAP ACTUATING ROD
25-621-500 EQUIPMENT-MISC.
25-550-508 WIRING DIA.

25-120-500 INSTAL.-FIN

25-140-500 INSTAL.-RUDDER

25-110-500 INSTAL.-STABILIZER
25-130-500 INSTAL.-ELEVATOR
25-150-500 FAIRING ASSEMBLY

25-030-500 INSTAL.-OUTER PANEL
25-030-501 PANEL ASSEMBLY-OUTER
25-720-500 NACELLE ASSEMBLY
25-310-600 INSTAL.-LANDING GEAR
25-031-500 INSTAL.-WING TIP
25-050-500 INSTAL.-AILERON
25-070-500 INSTAL.-OUTER PANEL FLAP

25-220-500 INSTAL.-FUSELAGE FILLET

25-470-500 INSTAL.-PROPELLER

Although the AT-9 series consisted of a total of 30 production assemblies, the major assemblies are shown here with the corresponding part numbers. (USAAF T.O.No.01-25KB-2)

that, originally, the second (and major) production block was to have been designated AT-9A and the subsequent, final lot of 300 AT-9As were to have been AT-9Bs, as noted above, there appears to have been no connection between these very early administrative auto-corrections and what was reported from the field.

Between September 1942 and May 1943, at least nine aircraft were cited in official USAAF records as type AT-9B, and these were: 42-56856; 42-56857; 42-56869; 42-56880; 42-56882; 42-56888; 42-56896; 42-56897; 42-56931.

However, Technical Order No.01-25K-7, dated September 12, 1942, which described the installation of the Tail Wheel Lock Cable Fairlead, *specifically* addresses this issue to type AT-9B, and goes so far as to describe the aircraft impacted as "....AT-9B airplanes A.F. Nos. 42-56853 to 42-56877," going on to state that "...subsequent AT-9B airplanes will have this feature incorporated by the contractor prior to delivery." Yet in spite of this official pronouncements, not a single Individual Aircraft History Card records type AT-9B for this series. This T.O. remains the solitary official document citing the existence – and use – of this designation.

Since T.O. 01-25K-7 clearly covered the first batch of what we commonly refer to as AT-9As, this begs the question of whether the second production batch (AC41-11939 to 41-12279), known as 'straight' AT-9s, may at some point have in fact been designated AT-9As? No documentation has been located to support this obvious conclusion, however.

Additionally, and also inexplicably, one aircraft, 42-57138, was officially cited as type AT-9C and was at Patterson Field as of February 26, 1943, suggesting it was being used for some unspecified test purpose.

What makes all of this even more puzzling is that no corresponding entries or changes were noted for these aircraft on their Individual Aircraft History Cards (IAHCs) where, normally, such changes were almost invariably reflected. There may well have been more.

There are two possible explanations for these previously unknown suffix variants. The original AT-9, 41-5745, is known to have been modified at Wright Field to accommodate a .30 caliber machine gun, with appropriate linkage handling devices and gun sight, along with one other unidentified aircraft, and these were actively tested as dedicated gunnery trainers at the Ajo Gunnery Range, Arizona, before apparently being returned to their original configurations. Then, to the surprise of this researcher, it was learned while reviewing twin-engine flying training unit records at the U.S. Air Force Historical Research Agency (USAFHRA) that *at least 19 other AT-9s* (and as many as 30, total) were similarly modified and used intensively for gunnery training. Such a radical modification would almost certainly have had to be performed at the depot level, yet no trace of any official records, aside from frequent citation of the tantalizing Materiel Command Technical Instruction TI-1395, which governed the armament program, have surfaced. The AAF had in fact wanted to modify as many as 300 of the AT-9s for this purpose, but

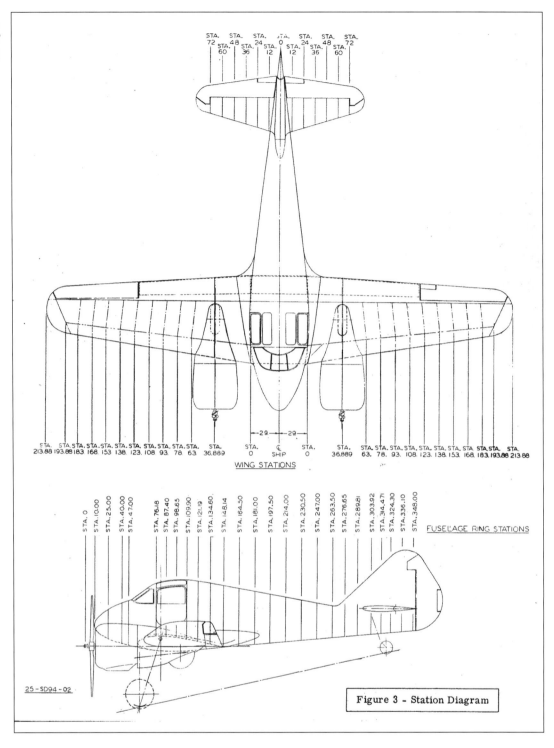

Figure 3 - Station Diagram

when this desire was communicated to Curtiss-Wright in St. Louis, the manufacturer rather pointedly reminded the AAF originator of this request that production of the type was near to ending, and any such program would involve either an additional production contract or rather considerable modifications to a large percentage of the existing fleet!

Then there were the obvious modifications which were carried out on AT-9A 42-56889, pictured here, which obviously involved fitting three small windows in the aft cockpit area for the benefit of two passengers who could be accommodated there (although it was probably best if they knew each other well), on both sides, which could possibly explain the AT-9C designation. According to one source, these were added on both sides to improve visibility during the frequent formation flying that was practiced in the type, but there is no known Materiel Command Technical Instruction covering this rather extensive modification, nor any corroborating documents, save two Memoranda dated May 23 and June 26, 1942.

Entitled "Permission to Alter AT-9 Airplane," the first of these originated at the Air Corps Advanced Flying School (TE) at Albany, Georgia (destined to become Turner Army Air Field shortly) on April 22, 1942, and was addressed to the Chief of the Experimental Engineering Section at Wright Field. In the

The windscreen and window arrangement of the AT-9 was, for its time, remarkably streamlined and adequate. Actual use in the field, however, revealed a weakness in visibility aft, leading to the addition of more window aft of the doors on either side, as described. (USAAF T.O.No.01-25KB-2)

letter, Colonel John B. Patrick, Commander at the ACAFS (TE) requested permission to add windows between stations 109.90 and 121.19 and stringers 5 and 6, not to exceed eight inches square while a second window, between stations 121.19 and 134.60 and stringers 6 and 7 was to be larger, at eight inches high by 10 inches long. They suggested reinforcing the entire area around the windows with a patch of 24ST Alclad sheet, in addition to the window frames themselves. The Memorandum explained that this modification would be applied to one aircraft only, but the Chief of the Engineering Section noted that, if the tests at Albany proved the effectiveness of the installation, that other aircraft be similarly modified. Colonel Patrick stated that the reasons for this rather radical field modification was, quite simply, to resolve "*...a definite need for this type window in order to eliminate blind spots which are particularly dangerous in the type formation flying done here.*"

These changes were in fact carried out at Albany and the aircraft was flown, following modification, to Wright Field by a Lt. Langon and Sgt. Tomlinson by June 26, 1942. Wright Field immediately noted that, although the work at Albany had been surprisingly well done, that the doubler plate to further strengthen the area modified had not been installed as Wright Field's Aircraft Laboratory had recommended. Wright Field, in evaluating the change, stated that the installation would be improved if the rear windows were slightly higher, and recommended moving them up about four inches.

These changes proved successful and Colonel F. C. Carroll, Chief of Experimental Engineering, issued instructions for "*...installing [similar] windows in other AT-9 airplanes.*" Thus, the alteration was in fact approved, and detailed instructions for carrying out the modification issued, but not a shred of information has been found which would reveal exactly how many such modifications were actually made and, perhaps more to the point, if these modifications resulted in a change to the suffix designation of the modified aircraft.

It is the hope of this writer that explanations for these anomalies might be revealed as a result of this publication.

Teething Problems and Right-Wing Panel Failures

Other changes came as a direct result of actual use in the field, and were similar to the experience of nearly every aircraft type accepted for production by the AAC.

One of the first of these involved a visit to St. Louis by Major E. J. Hale and Project Engineer Mr. F. M. Lasswell from Wright Field on January 3, 1942, to specifically investigate a report involving the malfunction of the 2B20 props installed on production AT-9s. Mr. Will Wells of Curtiss-Wright, joined by Chester Jadrewski from Hamilton Standard, reported to the officers from Wright Field that they had been experiencing hypersensitive control, erratic governing, hunting and, in some cases, a completely inoperative condition in the prop system. These engineers put their heads together and reportedly had resolved the problem by January 4th. The problem, as so often seemed to be the case, was due to a very inexpensive part – in this case, a light governor spring in the control linkage system, when attempting

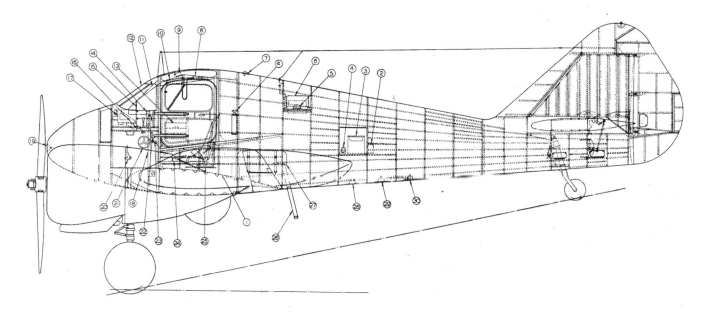

ITEM	DESCRIPTION	PART NO.
15	INSTAL.-INSTRUMENT PANEL	25-510-500
14	FLUORESCENT LAMP	AC94-32252 TYPE A-8
13	DATA CASE (RIGHT SIDE)	25-621-501
13	MAP CASE (LEFT SIDE)	25-621-503
12	WINDSHIELD, CENTER PANE	25-250-511
11	INSTAL.-BLIND FLYING HOOD	25-695-501
10	ELECTRICAL CONTROL PANEL	25-550-533
9	SPOT LIGHT	AC TYPE C-4
8	RADIO CONTROL PANEL	25-610-522
7	WHITE RECOGNITION LIGHT	AC32366 TYPE E-1
6	INSTAL.-RADIO EQUIPMENT	25-610-500
5	HORN	AC32223-A TYPE E-2
4	FIRE EXTINGUISHER	AC85-2 TYPE A-2
3	BATTERY	AN-W-B-152
2	SUMP JAR (BALL BROS. MFG. CO.)	6115
1	INSTAL.-FUSELAGE TO CTR. PANEL	25-290-500
ITEM	DESCRIPTION	PART NO.

ITEM	DESCRIPTION	PART NO.
30	AMBER RECOGNITION LIGHT	AC32374 TYPE E-2
29	GREEN RECOGNITION LIGHT	AC32374 TYPE E-2
28	RED RECOGNITION LIGHT	AC32374 TYPE E-2
27	INSTAL.-STORAGE BAG	25-621-510
26	STEP ASSEMBLY	25-210-678
25	INSTAL.-PILOT'S SEAT	25-561-500
24	INSTAL.-PILOT'S RELIEF TUBE	25-565-500
23	RUDDER TAB CONTROL ASSEMBLY	25-515-585
22	AILERON TAB CONTROL ASSEMBLY	25-515-520
21	ELEVATOR TAB CONTROL ASSEMBLY	25-515-528
20	RUDDER PEDAL ASSEMBLY	25-530-505
19	RED PASSING LIGHT	AC94-32118 TYPE B-3
18	CONTROL COLUMN ASSEMBLY	25-530-506
17	INSTAL.-AUTO-PILOT SYSTEM	25-5D52-01
16	PEDESTAL ASSEMBLY	25-515-500
ITEM	DESCRIPTION	PART NO.

25-SD94-04A-B

This cutaway of the AT-9 fuselage shows the location of all standard equipment other than instruments, as delivered. (USAAF T.O.No.01-25KB-2)

to meet the provision for positive high pitch control. A heavier governor spring and shorter spacer were the answer.

The "hunting" problem was attributed to the light counter-weight caps which were initially installed, which allowed the props to "hunt" about 20 to 40 rpm from the governed speed. This was eliminated by replacing the light counterweight caps with a medium-weight cap.

Several of the 2B20 props had also reportedly become inoperative and, when removed and inspected, were found to be overpacked with a lead-based thread lubricant known as "Lubriplate." After cleaning and flushing this lubricant, the props operated fine, so Curtiss-Wright issued an urgent shop process bulletin to eliminate the use of "Lubriplate."

The R-680-9 engines used contained prop hydraulic passages that were critical in size and any slight obstruction, which could be caused by sludge, foreign materials or even cold engine oil, could result in sluggish operation of the prop systems. This was fixed by changing the "low pitch" stop from eight degrees to 10 degrees. While this resulted in a slight decrease in take-off performance, it did result in an increase in range at altitude and also, as an added benefit, increased single-engine performance considerably.

Yet another structural problem required urgent attention around February 2, 1942. Several horizontal stabilizer failures at Turner Field on January 15th and 18th were traced to weakness in the stabilizers just forward of the piano-type elevator hinges. This was corrected by the installation of gusset plates at the trailing edge of each stabilizer in service, and then this was corrected on aircraft still on the production line. At the same time, several instances of buckling of the rear fuselage – a problem which had manifested itself on the structurally similar 'wasp waist' Curtiss-Wright 19R, CW-22/SNC-1 *Falcon* series as well – had also surfaced at Turner. This was attributed to the landing loads on the tail gear following 'hard' landings. This was corrected by the installation of additional stringers on the rear fuselage as well as narrower rivet spacing.

Wright Field made a service-wide recommendation March 21, 1942, for the installation of formation lights in a number of advanced trainer types, including AT-9s, in yet another attempt to address the problem of formation flying in these twin-engine types. It is unclear exactly how this was met.

But a potentially far more serious problem evidenced itself by mid-April 1942, by which time utilization at Albany, Georgia and Victorville, California, had reached a nearly feverish peak. Starboard (right)

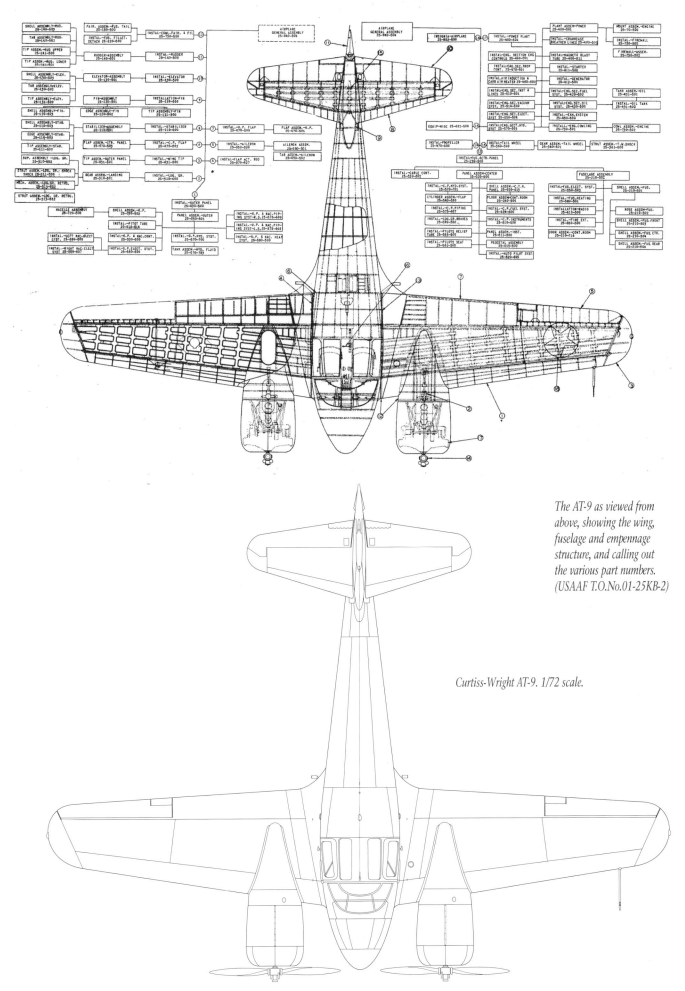

The AT-9 as viewed from above, showing the wing, fuselage and empennage structure, and calling out the various part numbers. (USAAF T.O.No.01-25KB-2)

Curtiss-Wright AT-9. 1/72 scale.

25

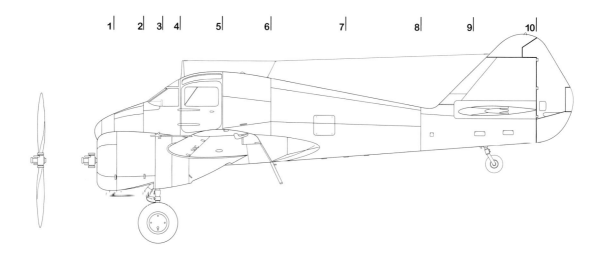

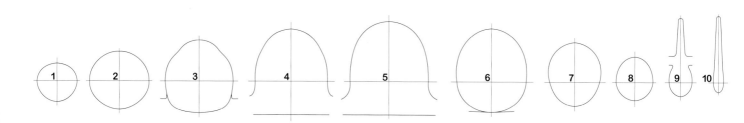

Curtiss-Wright AT-9. 1/72 scale.

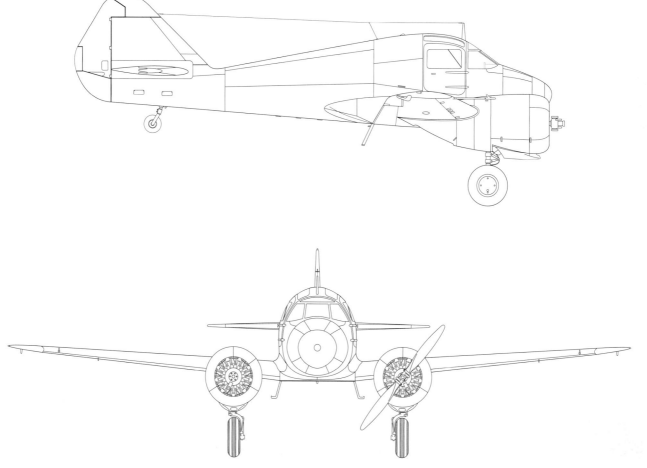

wing panel failures were discovered in three crashes, resulting in five fatalities. The three aircraft at the center of the investigation were AC41-5757, AC41-11961 and AC41-12013.

Wright Field had full confidence in the structural stress tests they had performed on the AT-9 – to virtual destruction – and in concert with Curtiss-Wright urgently sough to understand and rectify any hidden issues. As a result of this exemplary cooperation under wartime conditions, Wright Field issued urgent recommendations for reinforcements for both wing panels, even though tests had shown only an eight percent difference in strength between the original right and left wing panel construction techniques. Even with these changes on aircraft already delivered and those still under construction and contract, they were considered satisfactory only for a gross weight of 5,850 pounds – unless subsequent destruction tests proved the reinforced wings to be satisfactory for a gross weight of 6,000 pounds. The subsequent installation of stiffeners, much to the relief of all, fixed the problem and the aircraft never suffered a similar failure again.

AT-9 AC41-11961 had crashed March 9, 1942 near Victorville, California while being flown by 2LT Knox Parker, following the failure of the right wing midway between the root joint and the nacelle. The pilot, who used his parachute safely, reported as follows: *"I was on instruments for about 10 minutes, making right turns. The ship started to dive, but the needle and the ball were in the center. I tried to pull back on the stick, with no apparent results. I started to come from under the hood and had the hood about half-way off when the wing came off, knocking off my door. I bailed out. The plane was completely demolished."* The angle of the dive was approximately 45 degrees when the wing came off. The other pilot onboard, the identity of whom was not reported, was killed.

AT-9 AC41-12013 and 41-5757 both crashed near Turner Field, GA, the first on March 31, 1942 and the second on April 2, 1942. In both instances, the right wing had again failed between the wing root joint and the nacelle. Both aircraft were engaged in routine instrument flights at the time; AC41-5757 was on a night training flight. AC41-12013, according to the report of a witness, was making a spiral and was banked almost vertically when first observed. After completing a 360 degree turn with some loss of altitude, the plane was coming out of the banked and diving attitude and had reached the position of level flight when the wing came off. Two fatalities occurred, including Cadet Paul W. Kingston. In the case of AC41-5757, the position and condition of the wreckage and the craters made by the various parts of the aircraft on impact indicated that the right wing had failed about seven inches outboard of the root joint at a low altitude and that the aircraft at the time of impact was diving almost vertically. Two fatalities resulted, including Cadet E. W. Kaler.

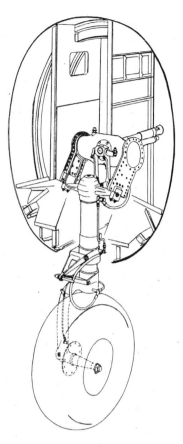

L. H. LANDING GEAR

The principle source of accidents throughout the service life of the AT-9 involved the main undercarriage members, which were developments of the gear used on the Navy's SNC-1s and the CW-23. In fairness, the positioning of the undercarriage retraction levers in the cockpit was the primary culprit, not the gear design per se. This drawing shows the port-side (left hand) main gear. (USAAF T.O.No.01-25KB-2)

The AT-9 was refueled in its sole main tank, located in the center section, via the fuel filler neck at the forward end of the wing-walk on the port (left) side near the wing root. The ground crews were enjoined to remain with the nozzle at all times during refueling, and not to let the nozzle simply stand in the filler cap without support. (USAAF T.O.No.01-25KB-2)

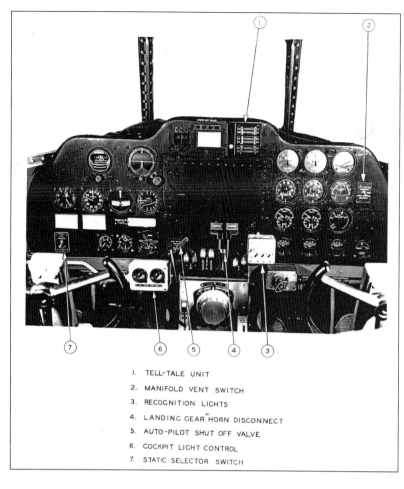

1. TELL-TALE UNIT
2. MANIFOLD VENT SWITCH
3. RECOGNITION LIGHTS
4. LANDING GEAR HORN DISCONNECT
5. AUTO-PILOT SHUT OFF VALVE
6. COCKPIT LIGHT CONTROL
7. STATIC SELECTOR SWITCH

The instrument panel standard on most AT-9s and which changed only slightly during the war. Note the unique Curtiss-Wright "Tell-Tale" unit prominent at the upper right, center. (Curtiss-Wright 25-SD51-10)

Air Corps Materiel Division concluded that, in all three instances, the failure was the result of a bending failure of the right wings, which just happened to be identical to that obtained during Materiel center static testing, and they concluded that it appeared to be the result of very high airloads on the wings. The Materiel Center observed that, in the static tests which precipitated the same phenomenon, the right wing had failed only after supporting more than 90% of the ultimate design load for a period of more than 15 minutes, something in the order of a limit load factor of 5g at 5,850 pound gross weight, without reinforcement.

In fact, Wright Field had recommended reinforcements in the wings on Memorandum Report No.EXP-M-51/TR329-17, and that this had not been incorporated into any of the three aircraft lost. Significantly, after these reinforcements were made on the fleet, not a single instance of wing loss was ever reported again.

Around mid-May 1942, another series of odd failures manifested themselves, and these involved, of all things, the inadvertent opening of the crew access doors while in flight! Operating units in the field could not figure out whether these were occurring due to mechanical or aerodynamic characteristics – or by actual accidental openings by the crews.

Wright Field observed that the unusually streamlined design of the fuselage did, indeed, result in unusually heavy air loads on both doors, which defeated the effectiveness of the rather conventional door latch built into the design.

Since the elimination of these air loads would have required a complete redesign of the aircraft, Wright Field quite properly concluded that what was in fact a mechanical problem should be corrected by mechanical means, and that is what happened.

More mundane changes followed. Tech Order 01-25KA-54 was issued July 1, 1942, almost certainly as a direct result of the large numbers of raw recruits who were being pushed into Air Corps units for On-the-Job-Training, and who had no previous experience working with aircraft. The TO directed that all AT-9s then in the inventory have stenciled "No Step," "No Push" and "Push on Walkway" markings applied to the trailing edges of the wings and near the edge of the walkway. A rash of minor damage had been experienced due to rough handling, and the addition of these stencils is an easy way to identify when a photo may have been taken. Other minor stenciling details followed.

An odd Memorandum was issued by the Wright Field Engineering Section August 24, 1942, and was directed specifically to all AT-9B aircraft then in service, advising that the Type M-2 generators installed on these aircraft were not generating sufficient capacity and advised that Curtiss-Wright was installing type O-1 generators in all subsequent production aircraft to rectify the problem. This Memo was followed by another on September 2, 1942, referring to these aircraft as AT-9A-2-CU aircraft – the solitary known instance of a reference to Block numbers on any AT-9 series aircraft – and a possible clue to the apparently short-term use of the suffix AT-9B.

The last known change directed towards the AT-9 fleet in being at the time came on February 17, 1944, when Type E-1 Recognition Lights were directed to be installed in all AT-9 and AT-17 aircraft then in service. This apparently originated, of all places, at the San Bernardino Air Service Command in California, and related to Type E-1 (Upward) and Type E-2 (downward) recognition light assemblies. Wright Field advised that the aircraft were already supposed to have these installed or, alternatively, the Type B-3 passing light. These installations apparently required a wing modification in the AT-17s. These were all necessitated by the continuing need for better recognition during night formation flight training.

By July 12, 1944, all remaining AT-9s in the inventory were reclassified as Category 1A which, essentially, meant that they were no longer regarded as priority, first-line advanced trainers (Category 1), but rather as second-line types which could be seconded to other duties, and required less stringent maintenance procedures.

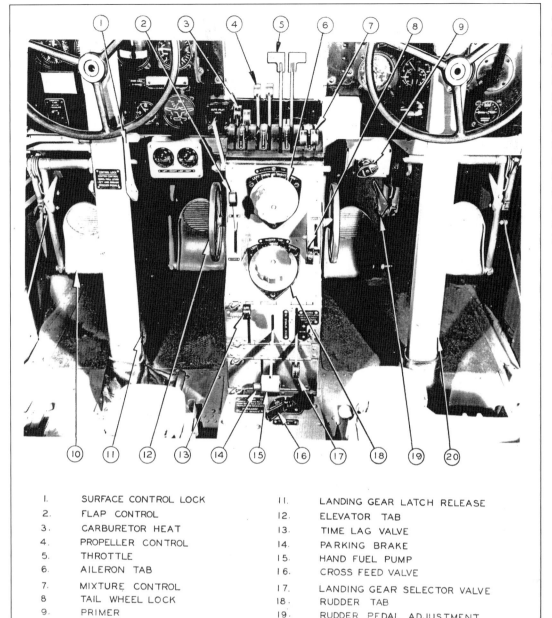

A view of the central control pedestal between the forward seats in a standard AT-9. Although they appear separated by some distance, items 17 (Landing Gear Selector Valve) and 15 (Hand Fuel Pump) were apparently often confused by the Cadet or student in the left-hand seat, resulting in an inordinate number of 'gear up' and inadvertent retraction accidents. (Curtiss-Wright 25-SD51-11)

1.	SURFACE CONTROL LOCK	11.	LANDING GEAR LATCH RELEASE
2.	FLAP CONTROL	12.	ELEVATOR TAB
3.	CARBURETOR HEAT	13.	TIME LAG VALVE
4.	PROPELLER CONTROL	14.	PARKING BRAKE
5.	THROTTLE	15.	HAND FUEL PUMP
6.	AILERON TAB	16.	CROSS FEED VALVE
7.	MIXTURE CONTROL	17.	LANDING GEAR SELECTOR VALVE
8	TAIL WHEEL LOCK	18.	RUDDER TAB
9.	PRIMER	19.	RUDDER PEDAL ADJUSTMENT
10.	RUDDER PEDAL	20.	CONTROL COLUMN

The AT-9 Described

The production AT-9 and AT-9A aircraft consisted of 30 production assemblies, consisting of:

Fuselage Center Section	Fuselage Fillets (2)	Vertical Stabilizer
Rudder	Horizontal Stabilizer	Elevators
Engine Mounts (2)	Engine Cowlings (2)	Engine Nacelles/outer wings
Ailerons (2)	Wing Tips (2)	Inner wing flaps (2)
Outer wing flaps (2)	Flight Controls (2)	Wing flap controls (2)
Engine controls (2)	Fuel controls and lines	Control cables
Main landing gear (2)	Tail wheel	Instrument panels
Electrical wiring & conduits	Aircrew seating (2)	Elevator trim tabs (2)
Engines (2)	Propellers (2)	Misc. fixed equipment
Engine oil tanks (2)	Fuselage nose section	Fuselage aft section

The Fuselage Structure: The fuselage contained a fully enclosed cockpit arranged for side-by-side seating for the student and instructor and, seldom mentioned, a space sufficient for two passengers was provided behind the pilot's seats. A safety-glass windscreen, Plexiglas side and top panels, provided adequate vision. The fuselage was constructed in three assemblies: a rear section, a center section and a nose section. During manufacturing, the three assemblies were rigidly and permanently joined together to comprise an integral assembly. A small part of the nose section could be quickly removed for service – which became important later on, as we shall see. Aft of the entrance doors, the fuselage was of a stressed-skin construction of circumferential ring formers and extruded angle stiffeners. The lift and static loads were distributed to the fuselage by doubler plates and structural rings. Cutout holes for access plates were heavily reinforced to maintain structural strength.

The nose section of the fuselage was constructed of formed aluminum alloy skin with circumferential rings but no stiffeners. It was attached to the fuselage structure by flush fasteners to facilitate removal for servicing of interior components.

Entrance doors were comprised of a bulkhead frame covered with aluminum alloy skin. The two front hinges had a release mechanism, normally safetied, which permitted the doors to be quickly released for emergency exit. The door latch itself was at the aft jamb and was safetied in flight. The vision panel was of Plexiglas, sealed in the doorframe. A diagonal, continuous hinge at the forward part of the window supported a small window, which was not sealed to the frame, but was secured by a latch at the forward side. The small hinged window opened inward for cockpit ventilation. The doors and frames were padded with felt and rubber seals to make an airtight seal. The door was provided with a cylinder lock, but this was apparently seldom used in field service.

These doors – a boon to Cadets and instructors, compared to struggling, with a parachute and various clipboards, into the AT-10s, AT-17s or UC-78s found inhabiting the ramps at most twin-engine flying training schools, were not without initial problems, however. As early as May 1942, it was found that the factory-installed latches for the doors were failing under certain flight conditions, leading to the doors opening in-flight. While it was determined that this posed no immediate threat to the airworthiness of the aircraft – unless it happened to be engaged in formation flying – it was, to say the least, unsettling to crews and a fix was quickly organized.

The Windscreen: The main windscreen consisted of three formed panels of laminated safety glass. In addition to the windscreen and the entrance door windows, two formed Plexiglas panels were built into the top of the cockpit roof. The few surviving wartime color images of AT-9s seem to suggest that these upper windows were tinted green. The windscreen and vision panels were sealed into the structure.

The Engine Nacelles: The engine nacelles were of stressed skin, constructed as a stressed skin structure reinforced by transverse formed rings and longitudinal stiffeners. They were located in the wing outer panels outboard of the splices and are supported by heavy structural ribs in the wing when assembled. The nacelle was permanently attached to the wing, being bolted and riveted to structural match angles to comprise an integral part of the wing structure. The bottom of the nacelle was cut to comprise a well for housing the retractable main landing gear. Besides carrying an engine, the engine nacelles also housed and supported the retractable landing gear. The landing gear fitting was attached to supporting brackets on two parallel vertical beams aft of the nacelle firewall bulkhead.

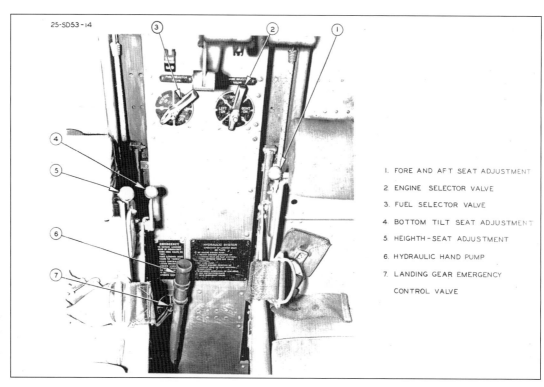

This view shows the space between the pilots' seats looking forward. (Curtiss-Wright 25-SD53-14)

25-SD53-14

1. FORE AND AFT SEAT ADJUSTMENT
2. ENGINE SELECTOR VALVE
3. FUEL SELECTOR VALVE
4. BOTTOM TILT SEAT ADJUSTMENT
5. HEIGHTH-SEAT ADJUSTMENT
6. HYDRAULIC HAND PUMP
7. LANDING GEAR EMERGENCY
   CONTROL VALVE

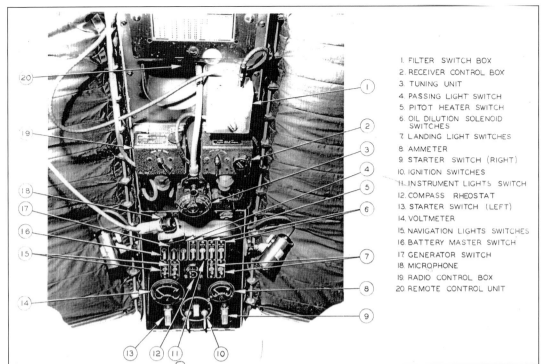

1. FILTER SWITCH BOX
2. RECEIVER CONTROL BOX
3. TUNING UNIT
4. PASSING LIGHT SWITCH
5. PITOT HEATER SWITCH
6. OIL DILUTION SOLENOID SWITCHES
7. LANDING LIGHT SWITCHES
8. AMMETER
9. STARTER SWITCH (RIGHT)
10. IGNITION SWITCHES
11. INSTRUMENT LIGHTS SWITCH
12. COMPASS RHEOSTAT
13. STARTER SWITCH (LEFT)
14. VOLTMETER
15. NAVIGATION LIGHTS SWITCHES
16. BATTERY MASTER SWITCH
17. GENERATOR SWITCH
18. MICROPHONE
19. RADIO CONTROL BOX
20. REMOTE CONTROL UNIT

Like many of the service types they would experience following graduation, the AT-9 had controls in the overhead area of the cockpit, too, including radio controls. (Curtiss-Wright 25-SD55-58)

The Engine Mounts: The two engine mounts were identical and interchangeable, which made maintenance on the AT-9 much easier. The mounts were a welded configuration of high strength steel tubing with reinforcing gussets and attachment fittings. The complete engine mounts were a single integral structure. They were attached to eight lugs on the mount ring through rubber vibration absorbing bushings. The engine mounts also had three brackets to support the nose cowl ring. Two lugs near the top of the mount provided attachment points for hoisting the engines.

The Engine Cowlings: The engine cowlings were constructed of 24 S.T. sheet reinforced with channel and hat-section stiffeners. The cowls consisted of three parts, each covering approximately 120 degrees of the engine periphery. The two upper segments were joined to each other by two hinges located above the engine in the plane of symmetry. The lower segment of the cowlings attached at the front to a supporting structure welded to the engine mount ring and at the rear of the firewall bulkhead. Each of the upper sections could be swung open for access to the engine compartment. In the closed position, the upper segments could be swung open, permitting access to the entire side of the engine compartment. In the closed position, the upper segments fastened to the lower by means of flush cowl latches on each side, which were held in place by Dzus fasteners. The two upper segments were fitted tight to the nacelles at the aft end of the cowl. Cooling air entered the front of the engine compartment evenly around the periphery of the engine. It was exhausted at the underside of the cowling. The engine cowls on the AT-9 were essentially identical in design to those developed for the earlier CW-21 *Interceptor* and CW-23 Basic Combat trainer.

The Propellers: Besides the issue of the props as of January 1942 mentioned earlier in this chapter, one of the lesser-known stories surrounding the subsequent AT-9 entry into service was the sudden and urgent decision by the AAF to issue, on 14 August 1942, Technical Order No. 01-25KA-64. As a direct result of extensive flight tests both at the plant in St. Louis and at Wright Field as early as May 11, 1942, this directed that stations equipped with AT-9s serials 41-5745 to 41-5894 and 41-11939 to 41-12194 (in other words, every aircraft that had been delivered by that date) must change the hub assemblies, Part No. 2B20-241-6135A-6, each 8 feet, 6 inches in diameter and replace them with Hub Assembly Part No. 2B20-229-61 35A-15 (with Blade Design 6135A-15, Counterweight Cap 50284 and Clevis AN 392-47), which were 7 feet, 9 inches in diameter. The problem had actually manifested itself as early as January 5, 1942, very early in the production run, and could not be laid at the feet of Curtiss-Wright, as they had installed props that had been stipulated by the Air Corps, and over their objections. To their credit, the Air Corps complimented the Curtiss-Wright staff on their cooperation in resolving the issue, and in particular Chief Engineer Wells himself. In service, the props specified in the original Specification had displayed hypersensitivity in their control linkage, hunting of between 20 to 40 rpm, erratic governing and super-critical blade angles. What this order did *not* say was that these new prop blades were the same as those installed on Beech AT-10 series aircraft at those stations. So, what in effect happened is that maintenance crews were sent out on the line to switch the prop blades out from every AT-9 and put them on AT-10s, and vice-versa! One can only imagine the flight-line banter that accompanied this Army SNAFU! The order resulted in some 31 AT-9s, then still at St. Louis awaiting delivery to train-

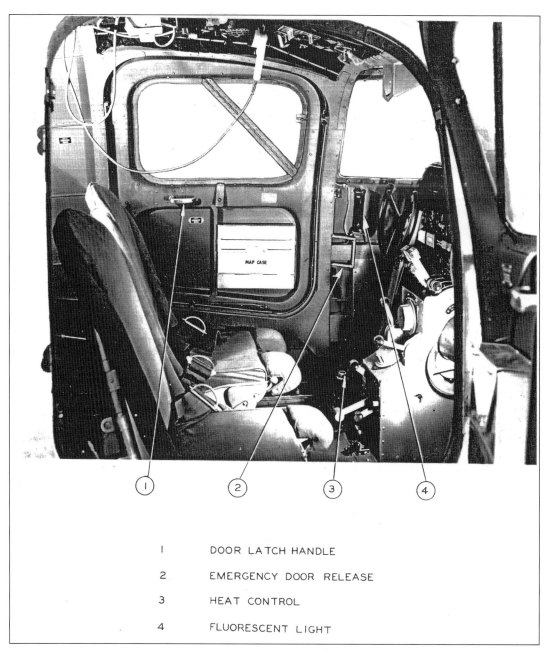

1	DOOR LATCH HANDLE
2	EMERGENCY DOOR RELEASE
3	HEAT CONTROL
4	FLUORESCENT LIGHT

ing stations, being grounded until such time as the correct prop assemblies could be made available from the manufacturers. At the end of all of this, and not later than July 20, 1942, all AT-9s thus were equipped with Blade Design 6135A-15, Hub Assembly 2B20-229, Counterweight Cap 50284 (although S-8475 was also acceptable) and Clevis AN 392-47

The above account of this curious series of events is based on actual Curtiss-Wright and AAF documents. However, there is a different version of how this all transpired and, while possibly apocryphal, is related here in the interests of posterity.

Curtiss had been taken-to-task by the AAF because the aircraft simply could not be made to achieve its "guaranteed" maximum speed in level flight, which was published as 200 mph. It seemed to invariably max-out at 197 mph which, while only slightly under the guarantee, had vexed the Curtiss staff. Then, they received a curious report of a "field modification" from a Ferry Command squadron which claimed to have resulted in a level flight maximum of slightly over 200 mph. Curtiss dispatched a small team to investigate and they apparently learned that an AT-9 being ferried west had nicked one of its standard, factory-installed props while landing at an intermediate field, apparently near Wichita in Kansas. The maintenance folks there had no AT-9 props on hand, but did have numerous Beech AT-10 props, which they supported and which, as noted above, shared the same basic hub, but which had 7'9" blades. The flight line wrenches pulled the damaged Curtiss props, substituted the smaller Beech blades, and cleared it for a test hop.

The Curtiss team then returned to St. Louis, verified the 'fix' to their satisfaction, and then sold Wright Field on a fleet-wide exchange.

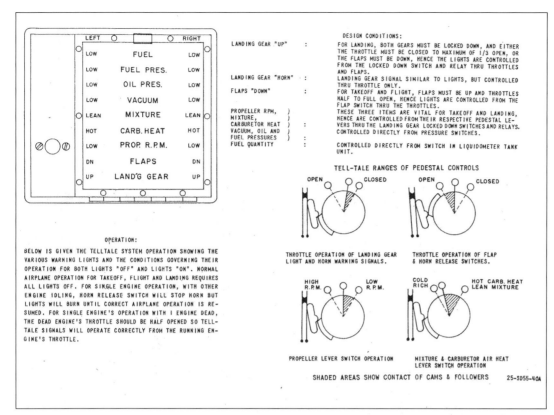

A description of the unique, Curtiss-Wright proprietary "Tell-Tale Indicator," installed on the upper, center instrument panel console of all AT-9s. Some training stations disabled this device, the instructors reasoning that the graduates would be unlikely to encounter such an aid in actual service aircraft. Ferry Command crews found it helpful, however, when flying alone long distances. (USAAC T.O.No.01-25KB-2)

The truth of all of this is probably somewhere in the middle but the truly amazing part of it all is that this was the solitary fleet-wide AT-9 major modification stipulated by Wright Field during the war, the other two having involved the wing stiffeners and a small equipment change in only a certain number of aircraft.

The Wing Structure: The wing structure was of aluminum alloy, full cantilever, internally braced neo-geodetic construction, employing two main spars and three main panel assembles as the primary structural components. The outer wing panels had integral engine nacelles. The wing tips were removable. Even within the company, the wing design was described in numerous documents as "unusual" and, as a result, as early as 3 December 1941, strain gauges were installed in a number of aircraft to specifically record the chordwise variations experienced by the spanwise stiffeners, on both the tension and compression surfaces – at a location as far as possible from a full rib. In actual service, this method of construction, while unique, soon manifested some problems. As early as April 1942, following extensive static tests on an AT-9, and contrary to Curtiss-Wright's predictable position on the matter, and after the catastrophic loss of three AT-9s (and five fatalities) as an apparent failure of the starboard (right) wing in high stress maneuvers (as detailed earlier), Wright Field demanded reinforcement of both wings with stiffeners, involving no fewer than 13 in the starboard wing and 11 in the port (left) wing. These apparently proved satisfactory, as no subsequent losses were attributed to wing failure per se.

The Undercarriage: The two main gears were retractable, Cleveland Aerol Oleo shock struts hydraulically operated with positive action fairings covering the landing gear when retracting. The tail wheel unit was not retractable. The main gear was essentially re-engineered from earlier Curtiss-Wright designs, notably the CW-22 and CW-23, and as noted elsewhere, proved to be the source of recurring problems. Oddly, some AT-9s have been noted in late-war photos as appearing to have had longer tailwheel struts than standard early production examples. However, no Tech Orders have been located dictating such changes.

The Fuel System: The AT-9 fuel system was of the cross-feed type, and included an integral center panel fuel tank of 145-gallon capacity. A direct-reading fuel quantity indicator was located on the instrument panel. Indicating lights on the unique Curtiss "Tell-Tale" instrument unit warned of low fuel pressure.

The Fuel Hand Pump: The fuel hand pump was located on the engine control pedestal. All fuel valves were manually controlled.

Recognition Lighting Equipment: Although on the surface of it not a critical item of equipment, in actual service the initial lack of Type E-1 (upward) and E-2 (downward) recognition lights, as well as the Type B-3 passing lights on both AT-9 and AT-17 series aircraft in service, turned out to result in a number of serious accidents. Since both aircraft types were often engaged in both day and night-time formation training, and visibility for the Cadet pilots was marginal to begin with on both types, the

installation of these additional lights became an important modification – but in fact wasn't addressed by Wright Field until March 1944, long after the greatest number of Cadets and attendant accidents had already been through the Training Command syllabus. However, photographic evidence indicates that the nose passing light was clearly installed in quite a few aircraft well before that date.

Standard Fuselage Equipment: When new, each AT-9 and AT-9A was equipped with two pilot seats, a blind-flying hood for the port (left) seat area, a storage bag, two crew relief tubes, a flight report holder, a check-list holder, a data case, a windscreen glare hood, and a map case.

Vital statistics: Both the AT-9 and the AT-9A were dimensionally identical at a wing span of 40 feet 3.7 inches, a length of 31 feet 8 inches, and a height of 9 feet 10 inches. They weighed 4,494 pounds empty, and had a 1,270 pound disposable load, with a loaded weight of 5,764 pounds. The wing loading was 2,478 pounds per square foot and the power loading 10.29 pounds per horse power. The published maximum speed was 200 mph, cruising 175 mph and landing speed 65 mph, and endurance or range was 750 miles.

The AT-9s Achilles Heel:
The Main Landing Gear Problem

During the research leading up to publication of this monograph, a careful review was made of every single Air Incident and Accident Report relating to AT-9 series aircraft. As a high – performance twin, and considering the demands placed on the training establishment and the Cadets in the cockpits, the experience of the series – especially when compared to that of its AT-twin peers – was really quite good. A summary of these investigations will be found in the Annexes to this monograph.

One recurring theme surfaced over-and-over again however, and that was the surprising incidence of accidents involving the main, retractable landing gear system.

By the time the AT-9 had been in the field for about six months, the Air Corps Liaison Group to Curtiss-Wright St. Louis had amassed sufficient data to request that the manufacturer conduct extensive tests to isolate the cause of the problem.

As a consequence, a series of very thorough tests were conducted to determine the cause of landing gear failures which had followed a Service-wide T.O. to remove the secondary down-lock from the landing gear retract cylinders.

A special item of equipment, made in accordance with SK-40829, was installed on the main gear of a recent production aircraft that was intended to indicate ½ inch of retracting piston travel, but which would also not allow the gear to collapse.

With the test aircraft up on jacks, the landing gear was kicked with the selector valve in the 'down' position, and then in the 'up' position. The aircraft was dragged with a shop mule over rough ground near Lambert Field in such a manner that high drag loads were imposed on the main gear and, again, with the selector valve in the 'down' position and then in the 'up' position – with residual pressure on the system. The aircraft was then taxied, with engines on, over rough ground with the selector valve in the 'down' position. These taxi tests were then followed by a series of intentional 'hard' landings, to try to dislodge the gear with the selector valve again in the 'down' position. The aircraft was allowed to sit on the ramp for a very extended period of time, then jacked up and the gear kicked again with the selector valve in both the 'down' and 'up' positions.

As a result of these tests, which were obviously intended to replicate, insofar as possible, actual use at the training stations, it slowly became evident that in aircraft which had already seen extensive service the geometric lock of the landing gear linkage was simply not satisfactory when the hydraulic pressure had gone down. It did not seem to matter whether the selector valve was in the 'down' or 'up' position.

Curtiss-Wright recommended that a definite secondary 'down' lock be installed, and this urgent operational requirement started to be implemented starting around 23 June 1942.

This change certainly helped, as evidenced by accident data, but the proximity of the gear retraction selector valve to the flap control handle could not be changed, and this continued to manifest itself throughout the service life of the AT-9 – both in the hands of flight crew as well as ground crews.

Export, Foreign Interest and Foreign Use – the CW-25A and Others

The Curtiss-Wright St. Louis Division had enjoyed a very successful history of export sales of its several designs, ranging from the obscure CW-14 *Osprey* to the hot-rod CW-21 *Interceptor*, and had extensive foreign contacts as a direct result – plus the very considerable good offices of the allied Curtiss-Wright Export Corporation in New York.

As noted earlier, the design team had specifically set aside a designation (CW-25A) to cover such an eventuality. Although, like its other export series, the CW-25A could be modified to an extent to cater to specific customer demands, including engine choice, equipment and fuel capacity, these considerations were usually factored into the derivatives once a firm set of specifications was received from a potential customer. It appears clear that, in keeping with the prior C-W experience, the CW-25A was also anticipated to be offered as a tactical aircraft with armament capability, but precisely what these may have been has not survived.

As early as December 3, 1941, the Joint Aircraft Board, Division of Exports and Defense Aid in Washington had received a formal inquiry from the British regarding the CW-25A, and had approved release of data on the aircraft to the British Purchasing Commission, although it is not clear how they evaluated that data.

The fact is, however, that by the time the AAC accepted the type for service as the definitive AT-9, combined with other projects on the line such as the CW-20, SNC-1, C-76 and others, the St. Louis staff was at or beyond capacity, and no known firm foreign overtures arrived. In reality, even had such interest materialized, it would almost certainly have originated via some major foreign user, such as the British Commonwealth or France, as few other possible foreign end-users could have afforded or promoted a specific requirement for such an advanced, twin-engine type.

But there was one tantalizing follow-up overture. As the final AT-9A production line closed and the last one was handed over to the AAF 31 January 1943, RAF Squadron Leader Chris Clarkson, the resident British Air Commission test pilot in the U.S., arrived at St. Louis in mid-June 1943, and on the 18th, made a 1:20 test flight of an AT-9A that happened to be at the factory for last minute tweaks. By that juncture, however, the British Commonwealth Air Training Scheme had more than enough Avro *Ansons* and Cessna T-50 *Cranes*, amongst other types, to meet twin-engine conversion tasks and nothing more materialized of the visit.

An extensive review of the records of the Lend-Lease Administration and the Munitions Assignment Board (Air) revealed not a solitary instance of a requisition or even an inquiry regarding the availability of AT-9 aircraft which, in itself, is noteworthy, since virtually every other type accepted for mass production was mentioned at some juncture.

Quite aside from these considerations, the fact is that a significant number of Allied air arms benefited directly from the AT-9 – and, indeed, several of them did in fact end up on foreign soil, although not via conventional means.

Numerous British Commonwealth Cadets trained on AT-9s at several Air Training Command stations, as did Cadets from the Chinese Nationalist Air Force and the Royal Netherlands Air Force in exile, most of these preparing themselves for conversion to North American B-25s being provided under Lend-Lease.

And finally, as a small additional inducement (and the solitary justifying Latin American connection for this writer!), no fewer than four AT-9s (one AT-9 and three AT-9As) ended their useful lives in neighboring Mexico, but under rather unfortunate circumstances. These aircraft, stationed at Williams and Douglas Fields in Arizona, had become hopelessly lost and exhausted their fuel, and crashed in Mexico with varying degrees of damage and harm to their crews. Given the extremely remote locales of their losses, the USAAF made no attempt to recover them and so, to this day, at least some of their remains are probably still scattered in the wilds of Sonora and Chihuahua, Mexico.

Those AT-9As

As the delivery of the final AT-9 of the second major tranch was approaching in March 1942, the Air Corps realized that additional aircraft would be needed to supply the rapidly expanding Air Training Command units devoted to advanced, multi-engine schooling.

While this was the predominate reason for the continuation of production of the 300 AT-9As, it was not the only motivating factor. The AAF had conducted a study of the overall production situation at the Curtiss-Wright St. Louis plant, and was concerned with respect to the rate at which the plant could bring the A-25 *Helldiver* onto the production line. They determined that, in order to maintain a steady and unbroken rate of skilled employees on the line, to achieve the highest rate of A-25 production, that a production rate of 60 AT-9As per month would be ideal. Thus, the first 10 AT-9As were finished in July 1942, 45 more in August and then 60 per month through the end of the year, with the final five in January 1943. Spare parts for the entire AT-9 fleet was factored into the equation and these were produced at a rate that was proportionate to and concurrent with aircraft deliveries. There was actually a plan to increase the total number of AT-9As from 300 to 475, but as tooling for the A-25 was accelerated, this turned out to be unnecessary.

Thus, the contract W535-ac-26982, for 300 additional aircraft – Curtiss-Wright CW-25Bs – was issued with sufficient lead-time to enable deliveries to commence in August 1942. The design was first described 12 February 1942 and, once again, was cited as "Air Corps Type Designation: Transition Trainer," with the major difference being slightly different 280 hp (295 at take-off) Lycoming R-680-13s and minor improvements that had resulted from actual field experience with the initial two major production batches. As noted above, on the original, hand-written USAF Ledger for these deliveries, they were initially to have been designated as AT-9Bs, but this was crossed out and "AT-9A" penned in.

AT-9
CONTEMPORARIES

Looking back at the incredible expansion of the Army's training establishment that unfolded between about 1937 and 1945, it is possible to trace that experience through the parallel historical events that obliged U.S. planners, both within the Army and the aviation industry, to anticipate the demands that would be placed upon them.

The factors involved were, of course, convoluted and complex, and had as much to do with advancements in the state-of-the-art as with geopolitical considerations. But the fact is that the Army Air Corps staff and the process they employed that settled upon requirements and specifications was actually quite small and, in the case of training aircraft, decidedly low on the food chain. Yet, to the credit of the "A" team procurement Boards who dealt in pursuit, bombardment, attack, observation and cargo aircraft – in almost precisely that hierarchy – it was understood that achieving world-class aircraft in those combat categories was going to require a logical array of increasingly challenging, world-class training aircraft to take relatively raw recruits from the realm of 40 hp Taylor J-2s to Republic P-43s of 1,200 hp which, as of about 1939, was as far into the future as the best thinkers could see.

Urgency was indicated. Japanese depredations in China, the brutal Spanish Civil War – which witnessed the use of 'modern' airpower on a wide scale for the first time – the German invasion of Austria, rejection of the Treaty of Versailles, the rape of Czechoslovakia and, frankly, imperfect foreign intelligence, all swirled around those planners as they struggled to grasp what the coming years would demand of them.

One thing that seemed clear was that combat aircraft would grow ever larger and more complex, and that, in particular, the use and rapid development of multi-engine aircraft, for employment in pursuit, bombardment and attack tasks, was almost certainly going to accelerate. The Lockheed P-38, North American NA-40 (to become the B-25 *Mitchell*), Douglas DB-7 (to become the A-20 *Havoc*) and the Martin Model 179 (to become the B-26 *Marauder*) were going to require pilots with skills that simply could not be provided via the single-engine trainers on hand at Randolph Field, Texas, as of the cusp period of 1938-39 which, for the most part, were represented in their most advanced form by North American BT-9s.

Although a contemporary of the AT-9, the larger and heavier Beech AT-7 series were really not competitors, as they were designed for very specific training functions, notably navigation and radio and not pilot transition. This trio, including AT-7A AC41-21174/N-74 nearest, were assigned to the 391st School Squadron at Randolph Field as of September 12, 1941. (Norm Taylor Collection)

Indeed, the very term "Advanced Trainer," had not been used by the Air Corps since 1928, when Curtiss AT-5As, trainer versions of the sleek *Hawk*, had been acquired in modest numbers. It was not until the acquisition of the first of 517 AT-6s – the immortal *Texan*, itself a development of a short-lived series of "Basic Combat" aircraft – in 1940, that the genre was resurrected.

It is significant to note that, following large-scale procurement of initial lots of single-engine AT-6s, the very next aircraft in the series were variants of the Beech AT-7, with an initial order for 577 in 1941 – which itself was essentially a modified version of the very capable Beech Model 18 commercial twin. Another 566 AT-7A, AT-7B and AT-7Cs would follow by 1943. These, however, were highly specialized trainers, outfitted in the first instance as dedicated navigation trainers, and were very seldom employed as pilot trainers.

The AT-7s were procured almost concurrently with another off-the-shelf civil design adopted to Air Corps requirements, the Cessna AT-8, 33 of which were acquired, differing only slightly from their civilian T-50 origins. Of mixed construction, it is significant that they differed from the T-50 in the selection of engine, being fitted with Lycoming R-680-9s – the same engine as the definitive initial production Curtiss-Wright AT-9. While these 33 aircraft were described, like the AT-9s procured at the same time, as 'transition trainers', almost all were assigned initially to Key Field, Mississippi, Stockton Field, CA, or Barksdale Field, Louisiana, although a few ended up at Columbus, Mississippi where they served briefly alongside some AT-9s, and their primarily wood-and-fabric structures suffered grievously from the combination of student induced indignities and the hot, humid and insect infested station.

As their designation suggests, the 33 AT-8s were contracted for ahead of the AT-9, with the first one – as usual with a new design – arriving at Wright Field, Ohio 3 February 1941 on Contract W535-ac-15155. Although the first aircraft, for reasons unknown, cost the Air Corps $56,510, the remaining 32 production aircraft came in at $32,361 each. Besides their rather fragile construction, the AT-8s suffered from a chronic series of tail-wheel assembly failures and, between the time of initial deliveries in February 1941 and November 1942, at least 23 of the 33 aircraft had been involved in accidents of varying severity. For all intents and purposes, by the end of 1942, few remained. Although they provided adequate utility as transition trainers, both Cadets and instructors worried about the difficulty of exiting the aircraft in an emergency through the single, aft port-side door and, perhaps inevitably, they were the first of a long series of essentially similar AT-17s and UC-78s to follow that gained the nickname "Bamboo Bomber" (although eventually officially named the *Bobcat*). They were not sufficiently durable to sustain the rigors of the training syllabus, and failed to mimic the characteristics of the modern, high-performance twins that they were intended to simulate for the benefit of trainees.

The AT-8s were followed by 1,199 essentially similar Cessna AT-17 (450), AT-17A (223), AT-17B (466) and AT-17C (60) *Bobcats* which, however, were markedly inferior in performance to even their earlier AT-8 siblings, as they were fitted with twin 245 hp Jacobs R-775-9s. Even these numbers were not sufficient to keep ahead of Training Command attrition, however, and as a result, significant numbers of essentially similar UC-78 variants were also transferred to ATC to take up the slack. It was thus not at all uncommon to find AT-9s, AT-10s, AT-17s and UC-78s on the same flight line and ramp at the various stations. The first AT-17 (AC42-2) was handed over 24 November 1941, and went to Wright Field, and the AT-17s were acquired at an average unit cost to the AAF of $30,128.00 – the cheapest of the bunch.

By September 1944, the high-point in the Training Command contributions to the war effort had peaked and was starting to ebb, and the Historian of the Central Flying Training Command, where the majority of the surviving AT – series twins had been concentrated, decided to interview Lieutenant Colonel J. M. McAuliff, who had been the Chief (A-3) of the Command's Pilot Training Section, about the experience the command had encountered with regard to the twin-engine training program.

Amongst other things, Colonel McAuliff revealed that, as late as June 1944, the Command had experimented with combining twin-engine with single-engine aircraft in the Basic training phase, and thereby mixing the huge numbers of Vultee BT-13s and BT-15s, Cessna AT-17s, UC-78s, Beech AT-10s and AT-9s, as well as adding North American AT-6s to the mix. While approved in theory, it failed to gain legs for the pure and simple reason that there simply were not enough AT-6s to go around, and the solitary twin that met all requirements, the AT-9, was not available in sufficient quantities either.

He had some very candid things to record with regard to the AT-17 and UC-78 series, however. He said "...*we had considerable trouble with the AT-17 and UC-78. The planes were made of wood and fabric. There was no training value in the aircraft. We called them "Mahogany Marauders" or "Bamboo Bombers" and had never-ending trouble with the wings rotting out at the spars, caused by the aircraft being left out in the open and rain and from fuel overflows. After several hundred hours of flying each, the leading edges of the wings became weak and had to be locally reinforced. The AT-17 and UC-78 were simply never designed for the constant take-offs and landings required when used by students. They were used, quite simply, because they were available and rather inexpensive compared with others.*"

Colonel McAuliff also revealed an interesting selection criteria that was engaged when selecting students advancing to twin-engine advanced from Basic training. He said "...*the only assignment procedure used for twin-engine students was that we picked the largest men for twin-engine. They had to be 150 pounds or more and at least 5 feet seven inches tall. What determined the twin-engine student was his size.*"

He also revealed that instrument training in the twin-engine advanced phase "...*hadn't been solved for the UC-78s and AT-17s. The situation was plenty serious. Several times in my own experience during 1943, the supply of instrument instructors was so short we had regular instructors substitute to at least give the students a ride on instruments.*"

But earlier, Air Corps planners decided to hedge their bets by contracting with Beech, also of Wichita, for yet a third 'transition trainer' design, planned from the outset to be built almost entirely of various plywood, non-critical products. Ironically, this was the Beech Model 25, which gained the Air Corps designation, on Contract W535-ac-15580, of AT-10 at a unit cost of $30,226.00 each (although it was originally to have been designated AT-7A, according to some sources) and the Beech-assigned popular name *Wichita*. That initial contract was for a whopping 1,771 aircraft and, like its brethren the AT-8s and AT-9s, the AT-10s mounted twin Lycoming R-680-9s – the clear intention being to simplify maintenance on station with common engines, if not common structural repair challenges. Before Beech com-

It seemed like a good idea at the time. The more than 1,700 Beech AT-10s produced, built almost entirely from wood, was extremely maintenance intensive, and Air Training Command roundly disdained the aircraft, but made use of them nonetheless due to the pressing need. This trio, part of the initial production batch of 149 aircraft, bear early wartime colors and markings. Ironically, AT-10s outlived AT-9s and a number gained U.S. civil registrations post-war. (Beech)

pleted its large production run, an additional 600 examples were ordered from Globe Aircraft of Dallas, TX. Contrary to popular belief, the AT-10 was *not* a variant of the successful Model 18 series but, rather, an entirely unique design which took advantage of a few Model 18 parts. Like the initial AT-8 and AT-9, AT-10 AC41-1711 was delivered to Wright Field for Accelerated Service Test 14 November 1941 but had been wrecked by 1 August 1943. Subsequent deliveries saw the overwhelming majority assigned to Air Training Command Twin Engine Flying Training Squadrons at the same stations as the AT-8s, AT-9s and AT-17s, mainly in Illinois, Arizona, Texas and Alabama.

From the very outset, the ATC units commenced submitting a blizzard of Unsatisfactory Reports (U/Rs) on the AT-10s which, gradually, became maintenance nightmares. As noted, the aircraft was made almost entirely of wood products, with the exception of the three largest metal parts – the two engine cowlings (and engines, of course) and the cockpit enclosure. Even the fuel tanks were made of wood, with a covering of neoprene rubber. Beech had subcontracted with a number of furniture manufacturers to supply various components, with the result that some parts were exquisite, while others were crude in the extreme. This mode of construction, when new and as yet not saturated with moisture or dried-out from extended exposure to the sun, resulted in a fairly light aircraft with decent performance – as long as both engines were turning. One of the economies employed in the aircraft was the propellers – also wood with metal hubs – that could not be feathered in case of engine failure. If the aircraft thus lost an engine in flight, it almost invariably did not end well. The many, many Unsatisfactory Reports (U/Rs) submitted by operating stations varied widely, but recurring themes surrounded moisture absorption (especially in Alabama) and, at the opposite end of the spectrum, accelerating dry rot and delamination at the very hot Texas and Arizona fields, where the aircraft could not be sheltered from the merciless sun and heat. Crews reported that the aircraft absorbed sound and "...*turned it into endless creaking and groaning, with the occasional electrifying sharp crack, like a firecracker going off.*" Although the AT-10s offered perhaps the easiest escape of any of the trio – out the top of side-by-side sliding top panels – it was employed far too often, and the AT-10s suffered, by far, the worst accident rate of the Cessna/Curtiss-Wright/Beech triumvirate. In fairness, many of the accidents suffered were *not* the fault of the aircraft or design but, rather, fundamental errors by Cadet pilots, with not a few the direct result of mock combats with "dissimilar" types, hot-dogging and fuel exhaustion when lost.

Indeed, the shortcomings of the AT-10 had been the subjects of intensive study by none other than the Southeast Air Corps Training Center at Maxwell Field as early as May 15, 1941. An Acceptance Board had been convened to "...*pass upon the merits of the AT-10*" at Wichita, at which time the Board reported "adversely" on the aircraft for the purpose for which it was intended. That consensus had been arrived at even before the unfortunate death of Major Moody, himself one of the members of the Training Center, in the fatal crash of the prototype aircraft. Ironically, an early variant North American B-25 *Mitchell* had been dispatched to Wichita for consideration by the Board. The Board found that "...*the AT-10 was in no way suitable as a transition ship to the B-25, one of the primary objections being that the AT-10 was designed along the conventional lines of the past, while the B-25 was designed with the tricycle gear and, accordingly, had vastly differing landing characteristics.*" The lengthy report was brutal, and in fact recommended that the AT-10 not be procured *at all, for any purpose*. To be fair, the Board also chastised the AT-9 for not having tri-cycle gear, but allowed that it at least incorporated performance and handling characteristics that actually prepared crews for what they would experience in line B-25s, B-26s, P-38s and A-20s.

But the story of the hapless AT-10 did not end with that. By July 1944, AT-10s had completely supplemented AT-17s and UC-78s at the Lubbock Army Air Field twin-engine school and the instructional cadre contributed what, in retrospect, and with the foregoing in mind, was an astonishing testament. They said that "...*the flying personnel at this station were glad to receive the AT-10 airplanes. The instructors believe that the AT-10 is a better training airplane than the AT-17s and UC-78s. This is the general consensus of opinion among the flying instructors, who believe that the AT-10 is a more difficult airplane to fly; that it handles more like a tactical airplane* [emphasis added by the author] *and that it is a stronger and sturdier built airplane; that it has metal propellers instead of wooden propellers in most of the AT-17s and UC-78s, and that more proficiency is required to fly an AT-10 than an AT-17 or UC-78. It was also pointed out that more proficiency was required to fly an AT-10 than an AT-17 or UC-78. It was also observed that it was difficult to get precision flying in an AT-17 because of the low wing loading, which caused the AT-17 to react more readily to wind currents than the AT-10.*"

Significantly, Lubbock had said goodbye to the large numbers of AT-9s which had been stationed there between February and May 1943, and the attributes bestowed upon the heretofore chastened AT-10s, emphasized above, were the exact qualities that had been derived from the AT-9s while stationed there! Apparently, the institutional memory of the AT-9s had essentially evaporated in less than 12 months elapsed time since the last of them had departed for other stations.

Readers with some background in the development of the twin-engine Advanced Trainer series will have by now have noted that the outstanding Beech AT-11 series has been omitted from this study, and it should be understood that this was intentional. The AT-11s, like its AT-7 and F-2 brethren, were highly specialized aircraft utilized for most of the crisis period of 1942-43 as dedicated bombardier trainers – for which they were designed – and were only engaged in 'transition training,' as practiced by the AT-9, in isolated and very late and post-war instances

It should be understood that the vices among its contemporaries notwithstanding, they are not intended to represent the AT-9 as without fault. They certainly had their own problems but, by 1943, ATC and its widely dispersed operating stations had conclusively established, in repeated reports, that the AT-9s were "...*by far*" the best of the three types, and they wished they had more. Besides their sprightly performance and handling characteristics, one instructor actually reported that, unlike the AT-17s and AT-10s, which seemed to manifest their accelerating age on a daily basis, "...*the AT-9 seems to improve with use; it actually seems to be 'self-tightening'.*" Indeed, if the entire AT-9 series could be said to have had one major fault, it was found in the fact that it could perform one function well and one function only: transition training. Although it will be seen later in this narrative that AT-9s also became highly prized in 1942 and early 1943 as high-speed personnel transports and communications aircraft, especially by units of Air Transport Command and the Ferry Command, the Air Training Establishment vigorously protested these diversions and, with only a few exceptions, they did not last long.

By the fall of 1944, however, the demands placed on the surviving fleet of dispersed AT-9s, in order to make up for the shortcomings of the AT-17, UC-78 and AT-10 had started to manifest itself. AT-10s, even with their warts and blemishes, were the most common type at Blackland, Ellington and Lubbock, Texas while the AT-17 and UC-78 dominated at Pampa and Frederick. Prior to June 1, 1944, most of the AT-9s remaining in Central Flying Training Command had been concentrated at Altus alongside AT-17s and UC-78s, but crews were starting to encounter considerable difficulties with the AT-9s. They were, for the most part, simply worn out. There had been an increase in accidents as a direct result and most were attributed to materiel failures. A conference was held at Altus on May 31, 1944 and, as a result, it

The USAAF acquired a large number of Cessna AT-17s, including this early example, AC42-62, to supplement the AT-9s and AT-10s. Like their cousins the AT-8s, they proved extremely fragile in service and, according to one Air Training Command senior officer, possessed "no training value." However, they were available and were utilized extensively throughout the crucial war years. (USAFHRA)

was recommended that the surviving AT-9s should not be used further for student pilot training and, in a supreme irony, they were replaced by late series UC-78s

While the AT-17/AT-9/AT-10 trio provided platforms to train pilots, they were not configured to train complete crews – especially for bombardment and attack types – which the USAAF soon realized, as a result of the crucible of combat in Europe and the Pacific – was perhaps just as important as having competent hands in the front end. Thus, Wright Field commenced a major effort in 1942 to solicit manufacturers to provide dedicated crew trainers to take the value of the Beech AT-11 series one step further. This resulted in the experimental Fairchild XAT-13 and XAT-14, the rather large Boeing XAT-15, the so-called "Reverse Lend-Lease" Federal AT-20 (a license built variant of the Avro *Anson Mk.II*) and the unfortunate Fairchild AT-21 series. The progress of the war and time overtook these experiments, however.

For as the war started turning towards the Allies in late 1943, and as U.S. aircraft manufacturers production attained ever new heights, the ultimate pilot and crew training solution was obvious and, by the autumn of 1944, dedicated Advanced Training variants of actual tactical aircraft (Lockheed AT-18s, Martin AT-23s, North American AT-24s, as well as 'war-weary' early variants of these types) rapidly replaced the vast remaining fleets of AT-9s, AT-10s and AT-17/UC-78s, which were then amongst the very first aircraft types to be consigned to the War Assets Administration (WAA) and Reconstruction Finance Corporation (RFC) sales locations for surplus disposition. They had done their job.

Wartime USAAF Non-Combat Type Twin-Engine Trainers*

Builder	Designation	Popular Name	Number Built	Gross Weight	Wing Span	Length
Beech	AT-7, A, B, C	*Navigator*	1,142	7,835-8,009 lb.	47'8"	34'3"
Cessna	AT-8	*Bobcat*	33	5,100 lb.	41'11"	32'9"
Curtiss-Wright	AT-9	*Jeep*	491	6,062 lb.	40'4"	31'8"
Curtiss-Wright	AT-9A	*Jeep*	300	6,065 lb.	40'4"	31'8"
Beech	AT-10-BH	*Wichita*	1,771	6,465 lb.	44'0"	34'4"
Globe	AT-10-GF	*Wichita*	600	6,465 lb.	44'0"	34'4"
Beech	AT-11	*Kansan*	1,582	8,195 lb.	47'8"	34'2"
Fairchild	XAT-13		1	12,401 lb.	53'0"	37'7"
Fairchild	XAT-14	*Gunner*	1	10,526 lb.	53'0"	37'8"
Stearman (Boeing)	XAT-15		2	12,061 lb.	59'10"	42'0"
Cessna	AT-17	*Bobcat*	450	5,303 lb.	41'11"	32'9"
Cessna	AT-17A	*Bobcat*	223	5,100 lb.	41'11"	32'9"
Cessna	AT-17B	*Bobcat*	466	5,196 lb.	41'11"	32'9"
Cessna	AT-17C	*Bobcat*	60	5,200 lb.	41'11"	32'9"
Lockheed	AT-18	*Hudson*	217	19,300 lb.	65'6"	44'4"
Lockheed	AT-18A	*Hudson*	83	22,300 lb.	65'6"	44'4"
Federal	AT-20	*Anson*	50	7,660 lb.	56'6"	42'3"
Fairchild	AT-21-FA	*Gunner*	106	12,183 lb.	52'8"	37'0"
Bellanca	AT-21-BL	*Gunner*	39	12,183 lb.	52'8"	37'0"
McDonnell	AT-21-MC	*Gunner*	30	12,183 lb.	52'8"	37'0"

*NOTE: Combat type conversions such as the Douglas B-18 and B-18A, Martin AT-23A and AT-23B *Marauder*, and North American AT-24A, AT-24B, AT-24C and AT-24D *Mitchell* are not included, as they were in a distinctly different class.

FLYING THE AT-9
THE SCHOOL SOLUTION

As with any aircraft, it seems, there were those who recall the AT-9 with fondness and a chuckle, and those who cursed the day they first encountered the type. On balance, it all seems to boil down to the individual experience level of the pilots exposed to the type, and whether they were seasoned veteran instructors or Cadets right out of advanced, single-engine training.

Cadets found both AT-9s and AT-9As on the same ramp and, as they were dimensionally identical (with a span of 40 feet, 3 and ¾ inches; length of 31 feet, eight inches and height at the 3-point position of nine feet, 10 inches) were informed that the two variants were identical from the operational standpoint. They differed somewhat in the arrangement of the hydraulic systems and minor accessory items. They mounted either Lycoming R-680-9 or R-680-13 engines although they quickly learned that, in actual practice, either engine type might be installed in either the AT-9 or AT-9A, but that the R-680-13s were about 30 pounds heavier, each, than the R-680-9s.

They were equipped, as usual, with the Flight Restrictions common to all trainer aircraft. In the case of the AT-9 and AT-9A, they were to observe a Do Not Exceed Speed of 230 mph IAS, they were not to lower

Two Curtiss-Wright employees, almost certainly in the first AT-9, AC41-5745, demonstrate student and instructor positions in the relatively roomy cockpit in this October 13, 1941 view. (Curtiss CF-5666)

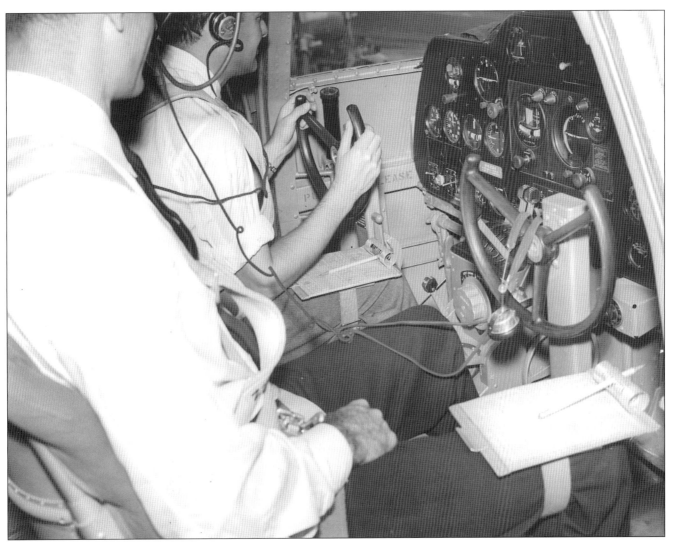

Students and instructors alike all agreed on one thing: of all of the two-engine advanced trainers, the AT-9 was by far the easiest to mount-up. Here, a Curtiss-Wright test pilot (with nifty oxfords!) demonstrates the mounting procedure. (Curtiss via Mark Nankivil)

the flaps, landing gear or landing lights above 140 mph IAS; and they were under absolutely no circumstances to allow the engine speed to exceed 2,640 rpm in dives.

For starters, and to be fair, let's take a look at how the Air Training Command (ATC) described handling and flying the aircraft from a Tech Manual, and purely didactic, viewpoint.

The Take-off

The very first instruction that the pilot was given – as with every single training and service aircraft in the inventory – was to *complete the checklist and check-off prior to take-off.* They described the AT-9s take-off procedure as "normal" and stipulated that the Pilot in Command (PIC) should retract the main undercarriage members "*...as soon as convenient after take-off,*" a stricture that was occasionally violated by a number of hot-shot Cadets who pulled up the gear before the aircraft was ready to fly.

The manual insisted that the PIC attain a minimum air speed of 105 mph (indicated) "*...as soon as possible*" for the pure-and-simple reason that it was possible to maintain control of the aircraft at that speed in the event that one of the two engines failed. The props were to be immediately placed in full high-pitch on the dead engine were this calamity to occur, and then trim the aircraft for single-engine flight and continue the climb at an indicated 100 mph at 2,200 rpm, with full throttle on the "good" engine. The PIC also needed to cut the switch and turn off the fuel flow to the dead engine in the midst of all of this and somehow keep the dead engine on the "high" side of all subsequent turns. Needless to say, Instructors frequently invoked this condition – and for good reason – as the sweating Cadets at the controls would almost certainly be facing similar conditions in service aircraft, if they survived training.

Cadets were also trained in so-called Emergency Take-offs, in which case they had to clear obstacles and, for this, 1/3 flap could be selected along with full take-off power. The best climb-out under such conditions had to be achieved at not less than 85 mph which, perhaps needless to remind the student, was "dangerous" in the event of an engine failure, and this procedure was to be engaged only in extreme emergency situations. If they in fact had to do so, they were instructed to level-off as soon as the "obstacle" was cleared and to raise the flaps only very slowly after an air speed of 110 mph had been reached.

Cadets were instructed to keep the tail-wheel locked except when making turns while taxiing and, even then, to assist the turns by the use of engine power rather than being dependent on the brakes. They usually taxied with the minimum engine rpm required to keep moving and, again, to use the brakes sparingly. The tail wheel was to *always* be locked for take-offs and landings, and an oversight of this fundamental injunctions led to any number of otherwise avoidable accidents – no fault of the aircraft. One of the most important instructions in the manual, similarly, was in actual practice one of the primary faults of the AT-9 cockpit layout. The instruction was deceptively simple: *use care that the tail-wheel locking lever is not confused with the landing gear retracting lever!*

For high-speed touch-and-goes, a very frequently practiced maneuver, full take-off power was to be selected as soon as the "touch" was achieved, and flaps were to be raised *slowly* after 110 mph indicated had been achieved, and trimming out tail-heaviness, which almost always appeared as the flaps came up.

In Flight

The USAAF manual described the stall characteristics of the AT-9 as "*normal for this type of ship.*" It went on to declare that the stall characteristics were about the same in virtually all conditions, gear up or down, flaps up or down and with or without power. The stall was preceded by very noticeable buffeting, which was more pronounced in the power-on mode and the tendency was for the nose to fall *straight down* with either wing dropping only slightly, in some cases. Even with this, there was ample aileron authority to "pick-up" the wing, and the rudder was very effective in these cases. The stall was also preceded by considerable "mushing," but the AT-9 had zero tendency to fall into involuntary spins. Normal indicated speeds for the power-off stall were 85 to 90 mph with the flaps and gear up and 75 to 80 mph with the flaps and gear down – higher than most Cadets had been accustomed to up to this point but, again, appropriate for a Transition Trainer to high-performance service types. Indeed, Cadets were drilled repeatedly that the AT-9 was *specifically* restricted from spins (by T.O.01-95KA-1), although,

perhaps by way of reassurance, the manuals stated rather blandly that "...*the AT-9 has been spun repeatedly in tests and recovered normally.*"

The diving speed of the AT-9 was red-lined at 230 mph indicated, a factor which came into play when the aircraft was selected as an attack gunnery trainer (q.v.), but that trim changes to deal with such a condition were normal and that the aircraft was stable at all speeds, with ample trim control for high-speed and single-engine flight.

The Front Office" on a Yuma-based AT-9, U-115. Taken May 29, 1943, the cockpit is showing signs of wear-and-tear, and a copy of the checklist has been taped to the central instrument panel. Note the different style control wheels than on the earlier series aircraft. (USAAF 42649AC)

Take-offs Are Optional, but Landings are Mandatory

Cadets discovered one of the key flight characteristics of the AT-9 very quickly indeed. The manual stated it very matter-of-factly: *It will be found that the angle of approach will steepen precipitously when the flaps are lowered.* The rate of descent was, in fact, quite rapid in a power-off, full-flap approach, a characteristic that many Cadets found thrilling, once the initial surprise had passed. They were reminded, perhaps unnecessarily, that "...*it has been demonstrated that the AT-9 can be safely landed in every possible combination of conditions: flaps full-up to full-down, with or without power, three-point or 'wheel' landings*" and with considerable variation in landing speeds.

Single-engine approaches were a key training element at most of the Twin Engine Flying Training Schools, and resulted in inumerable accidents. In these instances, the Cadet had to quickly trim the aircraft for single-engine flight and, as the power on the remaining 'good' engine was retarded, the trim actually had to be overcontrolled by use of the control surfaces, rather than retrimming. During the landing roll-out, there was a resultant tendency for the aircraft to "...*deviate from a straight course due to the thrust from the good engine,*" but this could be compensated for by the use, in this case, of the brakes and the locked tail wheel. Once again, the cause of numerous accidents

Cross-wind landings were also high on the "pucker factor" during the average Cadet's training cycle. Here the partial use of flaps, depending on the wind angle and velocity, coupled with the locked tail wheel and some power, with practice, became routine and predictable.

Flying the AT-9 – In Actual Practice

At the beginning, it has to be noted that any account of the actual day-to-day use of the AT-9 series by ATC has to be tempered by factors that are not usually taken into account in historical narratives.

For starters, the training cadre and the cadet crews who welcomed the first large numbers of brand-new AT-9s at Albany, Georgia (soon to become officially Turner Army Air Field), Randolph, Mather and others in late 1941 and early 1942 were faced with not only acquainting themselves with a brand-new type, but working through its initial teething troubles and adapting to a new training syllabus all at the same time. Their experience was rather different than that of instructors and trainees after the mass shift of the surviving AT-9s to Arizona, Oklahoma, and Arkansas by late 1943 and 1944.

Not mentioned at all in the ATC description of the AT-9 was the unique Curtiss-Wright "Tell-Tale" system (although it was covered in detail in the Flight Manual for the aircraft) – probably because, while a handy thing to have on-board if you didn't have other things to worry about, it was unique to the AT-9 (although several other sister and contemporary Curtiss-Wright aircraft also mounted similar devices) and the other advanced training twins on the line had nothing else remotely like it. This device, which in current avionics vernacular would probably be described as an annunciator panel, was mounted on the upper-right center of the instrument panel and, in truth, reported to a pilot familiar with the system what was going on with his airplane. If all was well, it was unlit. But, if anything was amiss, it started to light up. It monitored oil temperature in the engines, oil pressure and control coordination – such as retarding the throttles too far if the gear was not down. The actual AT-9 T.O. AN-01-25K-1, "*Pilot's Flight Operating Instructions*" for both the AT-9 and AT-9A described it as an "automatic warning indicator" with not less than 17 different lights. It seems clear that some stations incorporated the use of the "Tell-Tale" into their orientation to the AT-9 and others did not, preferring to train cadets to rely on their primary panel instruments and controls, just as they would have to do in an actual service type. Curtiss-Wright had pioneered the "Tell-Tale" on a number of their pre-war export types, and it had been a key component in "selling" the Air Corps on the aircraft as an advanced transition trainer.

Instructors and ground crews, contrary to some accounts, overwhelmingly accepted the AT-9s and, indeed, extolled its virtues, especially in comparison with its Cessna and Beech stable-mates. They described an aircraft that was comparatively easy to maintain and, perhaps more to the point, gave the overall impression of a "finished" and well-thought-out design, as opposed to the AT-17s and AT-10s, which were almost universally recognized as expedients. It was really as simple as first impressions: imagine a Cadet approaching the flight line for the first time for twin-engine advanced instruction. Arrayed before him could easily be one of each type, side-by-side, AT-17, AT-10, AT-9. Guess which one his eyes moved to.

The instructors, of course, invariably had a far different set of opinions of the AT-9 than their hassled Cadets who either completed their required cycle or not. One very junior Second Lieutenant instructor, who had taken his own training on AT-17s, 2LT Don J. Armand, reported the sentiments of many of his peers: "*As my time built up in the plane, I liked it more and more. It demanded my full attention, but as long as I stayed ahead of it, the AT-9 was a joy to fly.*" Throughout this narrative, the voices of other Cadets and instructors will be heard – both the good and the bad – as well as accounts of accidents and incidents that appear to have contributed to the 'bad rap' that the AT-9 seems to have received in the few accounts published to date.

THE CUSTOMER
ARMY AIR CORPS AIR
TRAINING ESTABLISHMENT

Viewed in retrospect, one of the greatest United States contributions leading to Allied victory in World War Two was found in the evolution, organization and eventual output of the vast aviation training establishments of both the Army and Navy.

In the case of the USAAC, the experience of the inter-war years had resulted in the creation of a selection, screening and three-tier training syllabus that – with but fairly minor adjustments – served as the model for the enormous expansion necessitated by the worsening world situation after 1938.

The progressive system of pilot training, in particular, from Cadet to basic combat entry lay in a pattern of Primary, Basic and Advanced stages, usually followed by operational training in a tactical unit. Although the Axis nations evolved rudimentary structures similar to this in some respects, the fact is that none approached the effort and investment manifested in the U.S. system. Indeed, and at least to some extent, the Axis failure to develop comparable and competent systems was due largely to deliberate choices and geographic restrictions. Germany, Italy and Japan had planned for fairly short conflicts in which forces committed consisted in the main of highly trained crews who, it was believed, would require only occasional replacements due to attrition. Likewise, none of the three Axis nations enjoyed the comfort of a remote 'rear area' in which to conduct intensive training of every description such as that afforded by the vastness of the U.S. south, mid-west and western (as well as, for British Commonwealth crews, Canadian, Rhodesian and Australian) reaches. Quite aside from the aircraft, the actual training systems and instructional methods, these two factors unquestionably contributed to the nearly inevitable Allied triumph and have seldom received the recognition that they deserve.

Until 1939, the USAAC training system focused overwhelmingly on a combination of the output of Randolph Field (the often cited "West Point of the Air") near San Antonio, Texas, and the semi-operational 'club' style training afforded by the rather casual state National Guard air units. Both of these afforded what amounted to nearly personalized pilot training, yet between them provided the USAAC and the hugely expanded USAAF with a central cadre that stepped up to provide leadership and well-trained 'first responder' crews during the extremely difficult months following Pearl Harbor – before the training establishment could commence churning out new crews.

By 1940, the USAAC found itself, despite having a solid foundation and training formula, in the unexpected position of having far too many men to train and, with world-wide demands on previously trained crews, far too few instructors to instruct them effectively. In effect, as the official history of the AAF in World War II expressed it, *"training shifted in production methods from piecework to production line"* methods.

While the active duty establishment was commencing a huge metamorphosis, yet another, seldom heralded set of programs significantly impacted the ultimate success of the active duty efforts. The Civilian Pilot Training Program (CPTP), for all intents and purposes, largely supplemented the formal Primary Training Phases of both Army and Navy training establishments, although the quality and standards achieved by the many schools varied significantly. The truth was that the Air Corps never really cared very much for the CPTP, and which knew full well that it was largely a New Deal economy-boasting measure with only isolated instances of genuine military value.

But seldom mentioned at all was a second and collaterally organized system created under the aegis of the Civil Aeronautics Authority (CAA) known as the War Training Service (WTS). Similar in most respects to the CPTP, the WTS aided selected civilian flying schools in financing and acquiring appropriate aircraft, and set basic instructional and curriculum standards. Relatively short-lived, the accomplishments of the WTS have been shrouded since, for reasons that have never been fully explained, the National Archives directed the destruction of all records pertaining to the WTS in 1986. The brief assumption by those civil contractors of responsibility for primary flight training left the Air Corps free to concentrate on more advanced training. One of the chief impediments of both the CPTP and the WTS, in the view of the Air Corps, was that there was no requirement to actually enter the service after graduation – although, as events transpired, many in fact did do so.

Although the "process" of selecting, classifying and pushing candidates for aircrew positions changed during the course of the war, this early schematic prepared by the first of the major AT-9 operating Training Centers, the Southeast, reflects the scheme as of early 1942. (USAAC)

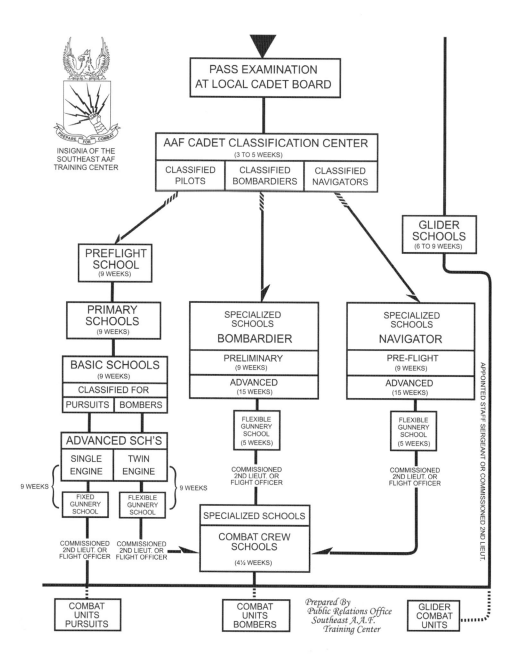

INSIGNIA OF THE SOUTHEAST AAF TRAINING CENTER

PASS EXAMINATION AT LOCAL CADET BOARD

AAF CADET CLASSIFICATION CENTER (3 TO 5 WEEKS)

CLASSIFIED PILOTS | CLASSIFIED BOMBARDIERS | CLASSIFIED NAVIGATORS

GLIDER SCHOOLS (6 TO 9 WEEKS)

PREFLIGHT SCHOOL (9 WEEKS)

PRIMARY SCHOOLS (9 WEEKS)

BASIC SCHOOLS (9 WEEKS) — CLASSIFIED FOR — PURSUITS / BOMBERS

ADVANCED SCH'S — SINGLE ENGINE / TWIN ENGINE — 9 WEEKS — FIXED GUNNERY SCHOOL / FLEXIBLE GUNNERY SCHOOL — 9 WEEKS

SPECIALIZED SCHOOLS BOMBARDIER — PRELIMINARY (9 WEEKS) — ADVANCED (15 WEEKS) — FLEXIBLE GUNNERY SCHOOL (5 WEEKS) — COMMISSIONED 2ND LIEUT. OR FLIGHT OFFICER

SPECIALIZED SCHOOLS NAVIGATOR — PRE-FLIGHT (9 WEEKS) — ADVANCED (15 WEEKS) — FLEXIBLE GUNNERY SCHOOL (5 WEEKS) — COMMISSIONED 2ND LIEUT. OR FLIGHT OFFICER

APPOINTED STAFF SERGEANT OR COMMISSIONED 2ND LIEUT.

COMMISSIONED 2ND LIEUT. OR FLIGHT OFFICER / COMMISSIONED 2ND LIEUT. OR FLIGHT OFFICER

SPECIALIZED SCHOOLS COMBAT CREW SCHOOLS (4½ WEEKS)

COMBAT UNITS PURSUITS

COMBAT UNITS BOMBERS

GLIDER COMBAT UNITS

Prepared By Public Relations Office Southeast A.A.F. Training Center

The massive Air Corps expansion program directed by the Roosevelt administration came not a moment too soon for USAAC staff and leadership, who almost immediately, as a first measure, directed that the pre-emergency training syllabus be reduced from twelve to nine months, start-to-finish. By May 1940, even this wasn't sufficient, and all three phases – Primary, Basic and Advanced – were reduced from 12 to 10 weeks each, with fresh classes entering the cycle every five weeks.

USAAC Flying Training Command was formally established as such only on January 5, 1942 after extremely hectic organizational shuffles in the scant 30 days since Pearl Harbor. Until Hitler ran rampant over most of western Europe in the spring of 1940, Randolph Field had ample, permanent facilities to provide Basic and some Advanced flying training, initially, to the graduates of the nine approved civil Primary schools. Both the nearby legacy Kelly Field and Brooks Field aided this process, and things seemed to even out for a brief time. With the *Blitzkrieg*, however, the Training and Operations Division of the Office of the Chief of the Air Corps (OCAC) rushed to completion studies that had already been under way for a huge increase in training objectives, and the new goal – to the astonishment of all – was set at a rate of not fewer than 7,000 pilots per year. Additionally, with new units and aircraft on the near horizon, it was concluded that the supply of dedicated bombardiers and navigators would also need to be drastically increased, initially to a rate of 3,600 per year.

It became obvious quickly that the established schools around San Antonio could not possibly meet these demands. The OCAC thus directed the priority creation of two additional Training Centers. Under this plan, the Continental United States was to be divided into three geographic zones. All flying schools located arbitrarily east of the 92nd meridian were to fall under a new Southeast Air Corps Training Center headquartered at the permanent Maxwell Field, Alabama; those situated between the 92nd

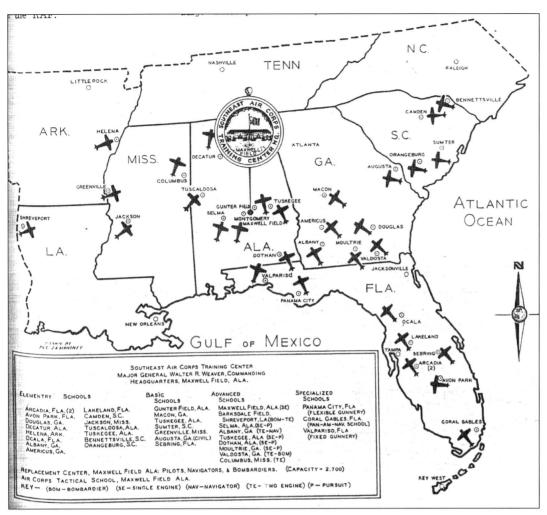

This early-war map showing the locations and functions of the comprehensive Southeast Air Corps Training Center included five of the initial, major AT-9 operating stations located at Maxwell, Barksdale, Albany, Valdosta and Columbus. The other Centers to the West were more geographically separated, but similarly well-rounded with a mix of school types to facilitate movements. (USAAC)

meridian and the 108th were to become the Gulf Coast Air Corps Training Center (headquartered at Randolph) while those west of the 108th came under the West Coast Air Corps Training Center located at Moffett Field, CA. These were all activated on July 8, 1940 and, interestingly, came under the direct supervision of the OCAC – an untenable situation, despite the cache which it implied – and these were all placed under Flying Training Command after it was formed in January 1942, as noted above.

With the stunning and unexpected fall of France June 22, 1940, Congress authorized the USAAC to expand even further and the objective to train 7,000 pilots a year was suddenly increased to 12,000, along with the funds necessary to construct eight new pilot training schools and associated infrastructure. Most of these came into being by June 1941 and, pertinent to our story, made ready for the arrival of appropriate training aircraft, including the brand-new Curtiss-Wright AT-9s.

Before the dust had settled on the 1940 authorizations, however, the USAAC's Second Aviation Objective was announced and, to the astonishment of nearly everyone in the Air Corps, a goal of not less than 30,000 new pilots per year was announced. This resulted in the addition of 20 more new flying training schools. Perhaps to no one's surprise, very few of these were ready by December 7, 1941 but, to the eternal credit of all concerned, by June 1942 all were up and running.

At the Plans Division of USAAC Headquarters, the AT-9 figured prominently in what the Chief of that Division saw as the minimum numbers of dedicated training aircraft which would be required to meet the objective of 30,000 graduated pilots. In a memo dated March 28, 1941, the Division set down with precision the four priorities of equipment and types which would be needed to meet this objective, and it is illuminating to note the order in which these were listed:

PRIORITY	TYPE	NUMBER REQUIRED
1ST Priority	North American AT-6	530
2nd Priority – 1	Curtiss-Wright AT-9	791
2nd Priority – 2	Beech AT-10	1,409
2nd Priority – 3	Beech AT-11	350
2nd Priority – 4	Beech AT-7	120
3rd Priority	Vultee BT-13 and BT-15	1,000
4th Priority	Primary Trainers (a mix)	500

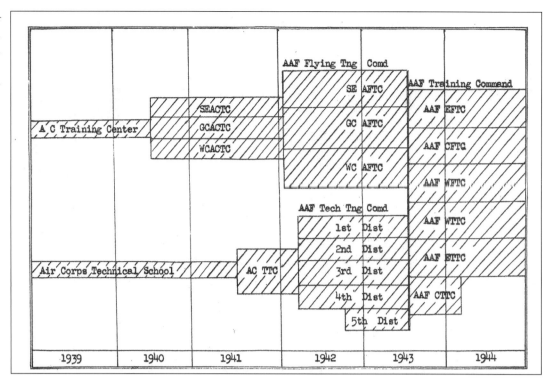

Although a seeming exercise in semantics, for the purposes of this study, it is worth noting that the AAF Training Command was the lineal successor to the Air Corps Flying Training Command and which was established as a major command January 23, 1942 – and yet again redesignated as the AAF Flying Training Command a month later! On July 7, 1943, the Flying Training Command merged with the Technical Training Command to become, simply, the AAF Training Command, and the actual schools which will be enumerated in this narrative which had AT-9s assigned were grouped into three regional flying training commands. The achievements of this organization were astounding. Regardless of the official name they carried, between July 1, 1939 and August 31, 1945, these organizations produced 193,440 Army and Allied pilots[1], although it must also be noted in considering this figure that an astonishing 40% more who had actually entered that elite group as Cadets had failed to make it through to "wings" status and were "washed out," usually being diverted to other specialties such as bombardier track, navigator or ground officers.

Although the various training stations and regions formulated their own curriculum based on AAF Training Command strictures, the fundamentals of the entire three-stage training system did not change greatly during the course of the war. In general, cadets had to perform certain specified maneuvers satisfactorily as well as demonstrate familiarity with controls, engines and instruments on the sometimes puzzling array of aircraft put before them, before moving on to the next stage successfully.

Transition Training

It is vital to complete understanding of the Curtiss-Wright AT-9 and its service to know that, from its very conception, it was intended as what was then termed a *transition trainer*. The USAAF and Navy training system – which differed markedly in this regard from that of the Axis forces – held that a less-than-fully trained Cadet was simply incapable of handling high-performance combat aircraft, so was obliged to move step-by-step through simpler to more complex aircraft.

Due to the availability of significant numbers of North American AT-6 variants, Training Command frequently used some of these in the Basic training phase, alongside Vultee BT-13s and BT-15s. This has led to some confusion amongst historians studying these units, and is cited at this juncture to caution readers that some training units used a mix of aircraft types, rather than standardizing on one type, which would seem optimum under most circumstances.

---

1   In fairness, it must also be recorded that more than 20,086 bombardiers, 18,805 navigators, 107,218 gunners and 555,891 ground and air combat crew members were also trained. Seldom mentioned, the Command also trained more than 3,491 glider pilots, 2,348 liaison (NCO) pilots and 444 women pilots.

But What About the Aircraft?

While the structure and objectives of the training establishment were being committed to paper and, rapidly, into reality in that blizzard of planning leading up to Pearl Harbor, a concurrent struggle was taking place to propose, describe, select, build and field the dedicated aircraft to carry out the plan.

It is seldom recognized that, between 1940 and August 1945, nearly 25% of the eventual grand total of aircraft accepted by the USAAC and USAAF were purpose-built training aircraft – all told, more than 55,000 of them.

In contrast to the celebrated exploits of our combat aircraft in the active theaters, the contributions and qualities of these training aircraft were generally unknown – and remained unknown – to the American public. But ironically, their development and production held the very highest priorities during the early years of the AAF's extraordinary expansion.

The peak period of production of these trainers was reached long before that of comparable combat types and, from about November 1940 well into the spring of 1943, trainers of every type constituted at any one time more than 50% of the total USAAF inventory!

As the war progressed and the march towards victory commenced after Normandy in 1944, the Training Command very rapidly cut their program and, gradually, the percentage of trainers to combat types moved downward.

Ironically, the official AAF history specifically cites the contributions of the principle Primary, Basic and Advanced trainers by type, describing the Boeing-Stearman PT-13, PT-17, PT-27 series, the Fairchild PT-19 and PT-23 in the Primary Trainer category. It also described the venerable Vultee BT-13s and BT-15s which held almost an exclusive on the Basic Trainer series; and in the Advanced Training category quite rightly extolled the enormous contributions made by the North American AT-6 and *Harvard*, the Beech AT-7, AT-10 and AT-11, and even the fragile Cessna AT-8 and AT-17 series.

But only seven words and one citation was devoted to the only twin-engine advanced trainer specifically designed and acquired by the USAAC for both Transition and Advanced Training from the outset– the Curtiss-Wright AT-9 – but it spoke volumes. The exact quotation read as follows: "*No suitable training plane became available for advanced two-engine flying until late in the war, when the B-25 was modified for the purpose. Therefore, the Cessna AT-17 and UC-78, the Beech AT-10, and the Curtiss AT-9 were used, <u>with the last considered the most satisfactory</u>*" [emphasis added by the author].

Before the majority of the dedicated, purpose-built Advanced Trainers were fielded, however, the Air Corps had recorded that "*...an acute shortage of planes suitable for advanced training [is] seriously jeopardizing our ability to carry out our pilot training objectives.*" At the outset, the expansion program had compressed even the critical advanced phase. Actual flying time was reduced from 111 to 75 hours and the number of hours of equally vital ground instruction dropped from 77 to 68. Specialization in attack, bombardment, pursuit and observation aviation thus shifted from the advanced phase to tactical units. Under the 7,000-pilot program noted above, the Air Corps had planned a separate five-week course of specialized training, but even this scheme did not materialize before the advanced course once again – out of necessity – absorbed specialized training.

Pertinent to our story, however, twin-engine pilot training took unquestioned precedence (on paper), even though it barely existed in fact until the delivery of the very first Beech AT-7s, Cessna AT-8s and Curtiss-Wright AT-9s in the same month as Pearl Harbor. Indeed, the only school which had actually produced *any* new multi-engine pilots was Barksdale Field, LA, and this only by dint of having employed Douglas B-18s, together with a few

The dreaded Grade Slip used, in slightly varying forms, by every Two-Engine Flying Training Squadron. As the Cadet advanced through the course, the slip was amended to include 12 more criteria, including Leadership, Judgment, Responsibility, Military Bearing, Initiative, Self-Confidence, Force of Character, Alertness, Comprehension, Cooperativeness, Attention to Duty and Professional Proficiency. The last entry, on the bottom reverse side of this form always stated "Use pink form for below passing grade" – the origins of the "Pink Slip!"

GRADE SLIP

Squadron _____   Flight _____   Element _____

Student's Name   Initials   Rank   Date _____

Type Ship Mission (Dual Solo)   Pilot   Co-Pilot

1. Vis. Insp.-Cockpit Ck.	REMARKS
2. St. Engs. Run-up, Stopg.	
3. Radio Procedure	
4. Taxiing	
5. Take-off	
6. Climb	
7. Trimming	
8. Stalls	
9. Slow Flying	
10. Single Engine Drill	
11. Single Engine Turns	
12. Single Engine Stalls	
13. Single Engine Landings	
14. Traffic Pattern	
15. Pre-landing Check	
16. Cross-wind Landings	
17. Power Appro. Landings	
18. Gliding Appro. Landings	
19. Short Field Landings	
20. Short Field Take-offs	
21. Simulated Fcd. Landings	
22. Go-around Procedure	
23. Formation (Lead)	
24. Formation (Wing)	
25. Navigation Preparation	
26. Day Navigation	
27. Night Navigation	
28. Night Landings	
29. Low vis. Pattern Appro.	
30. Cloud Flying	

Instructor _____   Rank _____

bFTF #2   (Over)

51

venerable Martin B-10s and B-12s. The few other schools which had received a few rare AT-7s, AT-8s or AT-9s used their time to train instructors, which was even more critical in the grand scheme of things – while being exceptionally unpopular with the students, who wanted to get at the enemy. The good news was, however, that the majority of the methods developed at Barksdale helped shape the curriculum at nearly all of the twin-engine schools for the rest of the war.

Throughout this narrative, we will make frequent reference to the actual students who occupied both of the front seats of nearly all AT-9 aircraft. In as many instances as possible, we have cited them (especially in the Detailed Production List) by their status as it was described, for instance, in the numerous Accident Reports. It was not until June 3, 1941, however, that an actual Congressional action changed the old designation of Flying Cadet to the new Aviation Cadet designation. For our purposes, aside from occasional Royal Air Force (RAF), British Commonwealth, Dutch, Chinese or Latin American trainees, we have more often cited them as either AC (Aviation Cadet) or merely Cadet.

Although it would be illuminating to chart the ebb and flow of aircraft used by Training Command through the crisis period of the war, such an exercise would easily exceed the bounds of this volume. However, the following chart, which illustrates aircraft strength by type in the Command during the months of the final apogee and then rapid decline, provides a snapshot view of how things had progressed to that point. Although other, more advanced types were by then entering the stream, after almost four years of continuous and unbroken service, nearly 25% of all AT-9s produced were still in first-line, twin-engine advanced training daily use.

Training Aircraft by Training Phase, as of June 30, 1944 and August 31, 1944

Training Phase and Aircraft Type	At June 30, 1944	At August 31, 1944
Primary		
Fairchild PT-19	1,880	1,566
Boeing-Stearman PT-17	-	90
Boeing-Stearman PT-13	-	90
Vultee BT-13A	57	44
Basic		
Vultee BT-13A and BT-13B	1,739	1,405
North American BT-14	178	178
Vultee BT-15	116	4
Cessna UC-78	62	90
Cessna AT-17	24	38
Advanced Single-Engine		
North American AT-6 thru AT-6D	823	979
Curtiss P-40 (mixed variants)	143	114
Advanced Twin-Engine		
Cessna UC-78	815	631
Beech AT-10	305	538
Curtiss-Wright AT-9	197	140
Cessna AT-17	197	124
North American AT-24 (*Mitchell*)	67	-
Fairchild AT-21	43	45
North American B-25 (mixed)	41	47
North American TB-25	11	167
Bombardier Schools		
Beech AT-11	552	555
Beech AT-7	24	24
Navigation Schools		
Beech AT-7	551	583
Lockheed AT-18	77	76
Transition Schools		
Martin B-26 (mixed)	150	144
Consolidated RB-24	102	95
Vultee BT-13A and BT-13B	30	33
Consolidated B-24 (mixed)	58	57
Martin TB-26	-	55

Glider Schools		
Boeing-Stearman PT-17	171	153
Taylorcraft L-2	114	99
Lockheed C-60A	22	21
Douglas C-53	19	16
Douglas C-47	17	24
Liaison School		
Taylorcraft L-2	119	116

Accidents – they Were, After All, Students

At the peak of Training Commands efforts in 1943, it was turning out 15 times more graduates than the comparable Japanese system but, with the density that this represented, and in an effort to attain the 'right' balance during wartime between thoroughness and speed, there was inevitable tension between realism and safety.

The AAF did a very good job of documenting accidents involving aircraft which, after all, were regarded as 'non-expendable, expensive government equipment.' In the detailed examination of every single Individual Aircraft Record Card and Accident Report involving AT-9 series aircraft which provided the statistical documentation for this study, the casual observer could very quickly gain the overall impression that it was far easier to identify AT-9s which did *not* suffer some form of accident than those which did.

In that detailed analysis, no fewer than 98 status codes were identified which were used to describe the causes of individual accidents – including those which resulted in fatalities to crew members. These were, perhaps inevitably, reduced to descriptive military style acronyms ("BOMAC" for instance indicated that one or both crew had Baled Out due to a Mid Air Collection – three such instances, almost certainly resulting in the total loss of those aircraft).

Although obviously a posed image, this Ellington Field-based AT-9, Field Code 21 reveals the early 1942, low-number codes and relatively clean, yellow-cowled aircraft preparing for a dual flight. Note the unusual half-wheel cover on the port main gear. **Colour photo see page 166.** *(NARA RG342-FH-K-150 via Stan Piet)*

But perhaps to no one's surprise, 10 criteria accounted for the overwhelming majority of all accidents and, perhaps more importantly, the majority of these (a) resulted in no injuries or deaths and (b) were completely repairable, with the aircraft returned to service.

The number one culprit was "LAC" – Landing Accidents, with a total of 220 having been recorded. Second were "TAC" – Taxiing Accidents, which accounted for 112. This was followed by "LACMF" – Landing Accidents Due to Materiel Failure in fourth place at 96 instances. Fifth was "LACGL" – Landing Accidents due to Gear Not Lowered at an interesting 61 experiences. Take Off Accidents ("TOA") only accounted for 47 incidents.

Amongst other accident data, it is important to remember that in many instances, the aircraft were recoverable and completely repaired and returned to service. A prime example is " – Forced Landing, Exhausted Fuel" – a very frequent sin for Cadets, especially on long, cross-country flights for navigational training, an important part of their curriculum. A total of 36 such accidents occurred, but nearly all of them witnessed the aircraft recovered and repaired. Similarly, the Training Command was religious about reporting a surprising number of ground accidents involving aircraft being handled – whether being taxied locally or towed – by the long-suffering ground crews. The large hard-standings found at most of the training stations were dangerous places, crowded with moving aircraft, tow-vehicles and taxiing aircraft, and just a moment of distraction could ruin a "wrenches" day, and probably cost one or two stripes as well.

It was also illuminating to study the accident rate as the type progressed through the war years. Perhaps to no one's surprise, those received at the first four or five training stations as a brand-new type, straight from the factory, where the learning curve was high for both instructors and students, the rates were correspondingly higher. However, rather odd anomalies were found. For instance, at some stations, more than 90% of AT-9s assigned suffered some form of accident during their assignment tenure while at others, the accident rate was very low. Some of this could of course be attributed to the discipline of the station records staff and the extent of rigor that the local commander assigned to safety. However, the urgency of the training cycle and the overwhelming need to produce graduates for the combat units surely also played a part and, as the war progressed and these tensions eased, and experience on the type became routine, the corresponding accident rate dropped.

The long-suffering ground crews assigned to Training Command activities often worked in pooled or centralized organizations to meet the extremely hectic training cycles and keep the aircraft serviced, clean and ready for their exertions. Here, Field Code 66 at Ellington, an AT-9 from the second major production batch, is starting to show hard use, and has her wheel covers, and the shielded passing light aperture in the extreme nose painted red as well as the cowls. Colour photo see page 167. (NARA RG342-FH-K2231 via Stan Piet)

Although the temptation to conduct a similar analysis of the overall accident experience of the two basic AT-9 contemporaries, the Cessna AT-17/UC-78 and Beech AT-10, would probably have resulted in a worthwhile study, the overwhelming reports from operating Twin-Engine Flying Training Squadrons precluded the need to do this, at least for now. A careful examination of the unit histories of every single operating squadron that could be found showed that they overwhelmingly and independently concluded that the Cessna AT-17/UC-78 series was far too fragile for the demands being placed on them by very high utilization rates, while the Beech AT-10 as a type, at least initially, was scathingly ridiculed (see a summary of a report on the AT-10 further on).

But perhaps the most significant accident related statistic, covering all categories, was for those which resulted in the death of the Cadet, Instructor or both, which totaled 64, of which two categories predominated: "KMAC" (Killed Due to Mid Air Collision) with 21 fatalities and "KCRGC" (Killed in Crash When Collided with the Ground) at 16. It is worth noting that there was only one known accident involving an AT-9 in which the aircraft was operating at its theoretical maximum crew capacity of four; the overwhelming majority involved two crew members. This tragic number, considering that 791 aircraft were produced and operated continuously throughout the war, is actually remarkably low. When it is also appreciated that the AT-9 was the preferred twin-engine advanced type at nearly every training station which employed it, and usually in concert with AT-17/UC-78 and AT-10 aircraft, and thus was in greater demand than the other two types, the conclusion is obvious: the AT-9, even with its teething problems and occasional flight limitations, did what it was designed to do – and did it well. When the fact that it was, as a design, far more durable and robust than the AT-17/UC-78 and AT-10 series, while performing and handling more like the actual combat types that the Cadets would be migrating towards, it becomes an even more compelling conclusion.

In the Detailed Production Listing which is available as a free down-load with this monograph (it may also be obtained, as well as updates, at our web site, www.thehagedornhouse.com), every known accident – no matter how mundane or tragic – is noted, together with the operating unit at the time, the names of the crew members involved (whether aircrew or ground crew), location, date, and cause.

A detailed breakout of all of the 98 accident status codes, and the actual experience in each category, is appended to this monograph.

Another flight-line view at Ellington Field, TX, these AT-9s all have Field Codes in the 900s and recall the anticipation and anxiety of young Cadets approaching their mounts for another day filled with challenges. Colour photo see page 168. (USAAF)

MAJOR OPERATING
STATIONS AND UNITS

As production AT-9s, followed by AT-9As, rolled off the production line at St. Louis, they were dispatched to their duty stations as rapidly as possible, given the urgency of those first hectic months following Pearl Harbor.

In this chapter, the reader will find a station-by-station summary of these assignments, arranged chronologically as they were first assigned, directly from the manufacturer. A total of no fewer than 25 stations received AT-9s and AT-9As for training or evaluation purposes direct from St. Louis, which may come as something of a surprise to some readers. While this arrangement may seem awkward, at first, as the successive stations came up to strength and commenced intensive training and entry-into-service tasks, it will reveal itself to not only support a better understanding of the rapid expansion of Training Command, but the ebb-and-flow in the structure of that organization as it unfolded.

This chapter is perhaps best understood by an examination of the detailed Production List which has been prepared to accompany this volume, in which a tabular format examination aids both chronological as well as lineal interpretation through the service lives of the individual aircraft, some of which were remarkably well-travelled!

While every effort has been made to link dates with actual known assignments, a number of unexplainable anomalies have manifested themselves, and these are discussed within the individual station sections.

It should be noted that an effort has been made to identify AT-9 operating units at each station by the designations that were current at different stages of the war. Likewise, some of these were wholly equipped with AT-9s, while others operated a mix of types and others may have found AT-9s in the minority. If an AT-9 series aircraft is known to have been assigned, however, the unit has been included, regardless of how many or for how long. Where known and appropriate, comments in the text for each station will expand on known assignments.

A word about the training and associated units which have been identified as AT-9 operators is also in order.

Although there were variations in the constitution and Table of Organization and Equipment (TO&E) of these units during the course of the war, and the evolution of Training Command, most School Squadrons – and those which either morphed into Two-Engine Flying Training Squadrons (TEFTS) or were formed as such – consisted of an average of about 50 Cadets per class or cycle and usually about 15 qualified instructors. These were all under the command of a Squadron Leader and his Operations Officer. Each instructor was usually assigned between three and five cadets to carry through, this group being referred to as an Element. Each Squadron usually, but not always, enjoyed its own building, with offices for the Squadron Officer, desks and lockers for the instructors, and lockers and a Ready Room for the cadets. Each Training Squadron was, in effect, a small flying school.

The Cadet's schedule fell into the familiar pattern of his earlier training. They spent half of each duty day in some form of ground school or athletics, the other half flying. Operated on a six-day-a-week basis (Cadets usually, depending on performance, getting two evenings each week to go off post) the Cadet was usually flying every day. If he was behind schedule, he might fly as much as four hours (maximum) per day. As in Primary and Basic, the instructors maintained a day-to-day loose-leaf record on each student, and examples of some of the performance forms are included in this study. A white sheet was used for a satisfactory day; a pink sheet for an unsatisfactory day; a green sheet for any day not flown; and a yellow sheet for progress checks by the Squadron Leader or designated check pilot. Solo in the AT-17, AT-10 or AT-9 usually followed after only a few hours of dual, and four hours was usually required as the maximum allowable to achieve solo.

Now, let's take a look at the breadth of AT-9 assignments, starting with the 25 stations that received AT-9s 'brand new' from the factory, in the order that they were assigned, chronologically. And of course, as was the case with every production aircraft type to enter Army Air Corps service, our account begins with Wright Field, Ohio.

Wright Field, Ohio (1)

Station Field Code: None Known
Known Unit Markings: None Known
Known AT-9 Operating Units: ★ Various Branches of the Materiel Command

A portion of the former Fairfield Air Depot and the original Wilbur Wright Field was acquired by the city of Dayton, Ohio, in 1924, along with about 750 additional acres and was jointly named Wright Field to honor both of the Wright Brothers. A permanent Air Corps facility with handsome brick facilities was constructed and formally dedicated October 12, 1927, and essentially assumed all of the functions of the former and pioneering McCook Field.

Home of the Materiel Command, and described by many as the "heart of the Air Corps," the station has often been confused with its sister installation just to the Northeast, Patterson Field (see next), which was aided by the eventual merger of the two stations to become Wright-Patterson Air Force Base.

It was common practice during the pre-war years, and clear through WWII, for newly developed aircraft, whether considered for full production or simply as experimental designs, to make the pilgrimage to Wright Field for intensive service tests and evaluation – tasks which were soon shared with the expanded, neighboring Patterson Field.

And so it was with the first AT-9, sometimes cited as the "prototype," but in fact, perhaps more accurately described as a "production prototype."

That aircraft, AC41-5745, arrived at Wright Field sometime in September 1941, and then migrated, administratively, to Patterson Field in a series of purely local transfers, between then and September,1942, to Patterson Field. It was assigned to the Flight Detachment of Headquarters, Air Materiel Command, where it was subjected to extensive flight tests and other tests of various descriptions. Aside from a brief period, commencing on April 11, 1942, when the aircraft was bailed back to the manufacturer at Lambert Field, St. Louis, MO (it returned to Wright on May 8th) the aircraft spent its entire existence at Wright or Patterson Field, surviving the war to be assigned to Altus Field, OK, January 8, 1945, probably for surplus action.

The aircraft suffered two accidents during its assignment at Wright Field. The first was at 1153hrs on Wednesday, November 25, 1942, while being flown by none other than Lieutenant Colonel Edward J. Hale, who had been a rated Air Corps pilot since July 1935. Ironically, the flight was a 'pilot proficiency' excursion, and Colonel Wright had some 9:35 on the type, which by this time, into its 14th month of existence, had amassed 1915:55 total time, indicating extensive utilization in Ohio. The cause of the repairable accident was one of the teething bugaboos of the AT-9 series: the port (left) main gear would not go into the 'down and locked' position, and Colonel Hale put the aircraft down very nicely in a grass area at Wright Field with only slight damage to the left aileron and prop. Colonel Hale earned the doubtful distinction of thus becoming the highest-ranking Air Corps officer to ever prang an AT-9!

The aircraft suffered one other incident on April 6, 1944 while being flown by 1LT George L. Wales, another landing accident, but was repaired and returned to service.

The first AT-9, AC41-5745, spent nearly her entire service life at Wright Field, OH. In this view, we see the results of a landing accident experienced by LTC Edward J. Hale of Materiel Command Headquarters at 1153 hours November 25, 1942, when the left main gear would not fix in the locked and 'down' position. Colonel Hale had 9:35 time on AT-9s. (USAAF 103668)

Strictly speaking, the aircraft should have worn the distinctive "Wright Field" arrow on the fuselage at some point but, in fact, it maintained a rather spartan, standard appearance throughout its existence.

The initial aircraft was followed on January 10, 1942 by another, also for accelerated service tests, AC41-5804, but this one was returned to Curtiss-Wright on March 25, 1942 and further assignments.

Likewise, the 20th production AT-9A, 42-56871, was assigned to Wright Field from Columbus AAF, MS, January 22, 1943 briefly, but returned to Columbus January 31st. The reason for this brief assignment has not been discovered.

Patterson Field, Ohio (2)

Station Field Code: None Known
Known Unit Markings: None Known
Known AT-9 Operating Units: ★ Accelerated Service Test Unit (A.S.T.U.) ★ Training Film Production Laboratory

Patterson Field, just to the northeast of Wright Field, was named for an Air Corps martyr and designated as such July 6, 1931, encompassing an area east of Huffman Dam and including the former Fairfield Air Depot, and the historic Huffman Prairie area. It became the site for the Materiel Division branches and, by 1935, the key logistics center for the Air Corps. Development was slow, however, and the station did not even have hard-surface runways by 1939, making landings there for heavier aircraft somewhat dicey. The nearby Wright Field complex, as noted earlier, retained the area west of the Huffman Dam.

As noted, the very first AT-9, AC41-5745, was first logged as being posted to Patterson Field October 16, 1941, where it was subjected to the comprehensive Accelerated Service Test Program. These involved flight tests over a triangular course from Patterson Field to Findley, Ohio, thence to Newark, Ohio and return. A number of line Air Corps officers, most of whom had been involved in the Air Corps preliminary efforts at twin-engine transition training with B-18s, B-10s and B-12s at Barksdale Field, LA, were detailed to take part in these accelerated tests, in order to amass experiences over a wide range of backgrounds, and were formed into a short-lived Accelerated Test Unit (A.S.T.U.) for the purpose. A total of 14 officers reported for this program between October 17th and 20th, 1941. These included Major Daniel S. Campbell and 1LTs Ray W. Osborn, Chester L. Sluder and Andrew D. Moore, all from Brooks Field, TX; 1LT Russell C. Reeves and 2LTs Robert L. Kooley, Jack J. Catton, Ernest L. Blackmore, Dayton W. Countryman and Robert L. Jackson, all from Barksdale Field, LA; 1LT Hertbert A. Von Tungeln from Luke Field, AZ; 2LTs Burnhill C. Davis and Ernest Mann from Kelly Field, TX and 1LT Ralph L. Merritt, Jr., from Mather Field, CA.

By November 27, 1941, these officers had thoroughly wrung-out the first three production AT-9s, AC41-5745 having been joined in September and October by AC41-5746 and AC41-5747. Totaling more than 150 hours of flight time, the tests did not pass without incident: On November 4, 1941, two of the least experienced officers in the test group, 2LTs Countryman and Blackmore, flying 41-5746 had taken off at 1400hrs from Patterson Field when, mimicking the experience had by LTC Hale on 41-5745, the port (left) main gear "...*seemed to give way*" and the port-side prop hit the ground. The Pilot in Command, 2LT Countryman, immediately cut the throttles and the aircraft bellied in. 2LT

Blackmore, Co-Pilot, admitted to the review board that he did in fact have his hand on the landing gear handle as the aircraft bounced on take-off and that he may have accidentally hit it into the "up" position, thus retracting the main gear. The Board agreed, and cited "pilot carelessness" as the cause, and no fault of the aircraft. It had a total of only 168:05 hours total time, and was repaired and returned to service, returning to Albany, GA to the tender mercies of countless Cadets on December 8, 1941, the day after Pearl Harbor.

The Service Test Unit was not easy on the aircraft, and cited six specific criteria in which the 14 officers all concurred. Considering that the tests were being conducted during the midst of an Ohio winter, the first finding is significant:

- Insufficient cabin heating
- Weak, flimsy doors which would not close tightly [a Change Order was immediately originated, resulting in Curtiss-Wright redesigning the doors and installing an additional door latch pin, which allowed the doors to be closed tightly]

The A.S.T.U. recommended that the main fuel tank, which was in the center section, be modified to permit rapid refueling – especially of the last 15-20 gallons. Curtiss-Wright complied, and altered the design, including a new filler neck design, in subsequent production aircraft

A problem which has been discussed elsewhere in this narrative was first discovered during these tests, namely, the extreme prop governor sensitivity and prop surging. As noted, this was corrected by coordination with Curtiss-Wright and Hamilton Standard

The Test Unit specifically addressed the need for what were, at the time, called Passing Lights, and highly recommended installation of Type C-1 or C-2 Passing Lights at the earliest possible juncture

It was also the opinion of the Test Unit that both the Ignition and Master Switches were positioned in the instrument array in such a manner that could easily result in either being accidentally shut off. This was, indeed, the source of a number of subsequent accidents, and was never satisfactorily corrected

But in summary, the A.S.T.U., even with the deficiencies noted, concluded their report with words that must surely have been sweet to the ears of the Curtiss-Wright team in St. Louis. Their concluding recommendation closed with the words, "...the AT-9 is a superior transition training aircraft."

As noted, both 41-5746 and 41-5747 ended their part in the Service Tests on December 8, 1941, and hustled on to Albany, GA, but the original prototype, 41-5745 remained behind. A surprising array of experiments were carried out using this aircraft over the next four years, and helped resolve many of the teething problems with the design, including the door latch solution, the prop governor control issue, installation of a .30 caliber machine gun (and distant tests with the gun in Arizona). Rather strenuous structural tests in March 1942 proved that the AT-9 could sustain in excess of 135% of her design load in the three-point landing position, this apparently in response to Unsatisfactory Reports (U/Rs) from the field indicating that the rear fuselage was too weakly constructed. By October 27, 1943, after a brief detachment to Vandalia, OH, for unspecified reasons, the aircraft was used to test the mock-up of the Type SCR-269-F Radio Compass and the Type RC-193-A Marker Beacon. Unfortunately, no images have been found showing this dual installation, but they must have been very distinctive. AC41-5745 was finally released from her seemingly endless indignities, as noted, and dispatched to Altus Army Air Field, OK, following her last tests in June 1944.

There was one other puzzling AT-9 assignment to Patterson Field, around February 2, 1943, which has eluded identification. A single AT-9B, apparently direct from the factory, was assigned to the Training Film Production Laboratory on Training Film Project No.465, but no Individual Aircraft Record Card entries match this assignment or sub-variant!

Patterson Field did not see any additional AT-9s, other than the occasional transient, until October and November 1943, when the first of no fewer than 66 AT-9s and 10 AT-9As started arriving, at least on paper, from Turner, Moody, Blytheville, Columbus and Ellington Army Air Fields. This was apparently a purely administrative series of assignments, however, for Property Book action, and all of these aircraft in fact ended up at Hat Box Field, Muskogee, OK for surplusing by September and October 1944. It is possible that some of them may have in fact been temporarily stored at Patterson during the interim, but this cannot be verified.

Chanute Field, Illinois (3)

Station Field Code: None Known
Known Unit Markings: None Known
Known AT-9 Operating Units: ★ **Flight Detachment (3502nd Base Unit)** ★ **Air Corps Technical School**

Like Wright and Patterson Field in Ohio, when new aircraft types were introduced into the active Air Corps inventory, at least one brand-new and pristine example was almost invariably supplied to the Air Corps Technical School, which had been located at Chanute since 1926.

And so it was with the AT-9 although, in the case of the *Jeep*, the School acquired three examples, AC41-5748, 41-5749 and 41-5755, between November 4 and 28th, 1941. Of these, the first two gave instruction to untold hundreds of AT-9 maintainers until around August or September 1942, when the first two moved to Goldsboro, NC, while the third, 41-5755 passed to Scott Field, IL December 28, 1941.

One other AT-9 (41-12010) and one AT-9A (42-56934) were assigned to Chanute in February 1945 and December 1943, respectively, but for only brief periods and probably incident to special projects or repairs, prior to passing on to surplus via the Reconstruction Finance Corporation (RFC). Strictly speaking, the AT-9s at Chanute were probably assigned to the resident 3502nd Base Unit for administration.

Scott Field, Illinois (4)

Station Field Code: None Known
Known Unit Markings: None Known
AT-9 Operating Units: ★Headquarters and Headquarters Squadron ★Air Corps Training School

Scott Field was also home to a branch of the Air Corps Technical School although, as the war progressed, the schools at Scott tended to specialize in training for radio and communications specialists.

Almost certainly the best-maintained AT-9 in the entire USAAF, AC41-5750 was assigned direct from the factory to the Technical School at Scott Field, IL November 4, 1941, where it remained until going to surplus in Oklahoma October 8, 1944. Here, she is seen at the Curtiss-Wright factory, for some reason, in early 1944 and is rare in that AT-9s with the late-war U.S. National insignia are rarely illustrated. (USAAF)

Thus, it is somewhat surprising that Scott also received an early AT-9, AC41-5750, on November 4, 1941, and which remained at the station through August 19, 1944, when it was finally sent to Rome, NY for surplus processing. Another, AC41-5755, which had been at Chanute Field, was also briefly assigned, on loan, December 12, 1942 before suffering an accident there January 23, 1942, when the undercarriage collapsed on landing – possibly due, once again, to pilot error. The damage sustained was so extensive that the aircraft was returned to St. Louis for rebuild by the manufacturer.

Three other AT-9s and one AT-9A were also assigned to Scott Field. AC41-5825 arrived from Randolph Field, TX February 6, 1942 and suffered an accident on February 14, 1942, when it made a forced landing at the CAA Emergency Field at Rolla, MO due to what the pilot described as an "...*error in the fuel gauge.*" It was recovered and repaired, and moved on to Ellington Field, TX by May 5, 1942. It was followed by 41-11987 on May 30, 1942 but was wrecked and reported as a total loss at Adairville, KY March 7, 1942, the remains becoming an Instructional Airframe under Class 26 thereafter. It was apparently replaced by 41-12001 on February 28, 1943 (formerly at George Field) but this was a short-term assignment, ending on April 20, 1943. AT-9A 42-56948 arrived January 31, 1943, also from George Field, but may have only been there TDY, as it returned to George on February 22, 1943.

It is not clear how the AT-9s were used at Scott Field, as they certainly did not seem to lend themselves well to in-flight radio training duties.

Albany (Turner Field), Georgia (5)

Station Field Code: "T-"
Known Unit Markings: T150, T251, T568; (728th School Squadron (SP) used Field Numbers T-700 to T-799 inclusive with royal blue engine cowlings)
AT-9 Operating Units: ★82nd School Squadron ★84th School Squadron ★85th School Squadron ★86th Two-Engine Flying Training Squadron ★89th School Squadron (Sp) (89th TEFT Squadron by 12/17/1942) ★94th School Squadron (94th TEFT Squadron on 10/20/1942) ★95th School Squadron (Sp) (95th TEFT Squadron on 11/20/1942) ★96th School Squadron ★98th School Squadron ★556th School Squadron (556th TEFT squadron by 6/7/1943) ★558th School Squadron (558th TEFT Squadron by 6/7/1943) ★559th School Squadron (559th TEFT Squadron by 3/24/1943) ★727th School Squadron (727th TEFT Squadron by 2/9/1943) ★728th School Squadron (SP) (728th TEFT Squadron by 6/5/1943).

During the summer of 1940, the permanent cadre at Maxwell Field, Alabama had commenced research into the expansion of Air Corps training stations and activities in the Southeastern United States, and had contacted the Albany Chamber of Commerce regarding a possible site there.

At first, the existing Albany Municipal Airport was considered but, instead, while a Primary Contract School was eventually located there, the Air Corp settled instead on a totally new site about four miles northeast of Albany in Dougherty County – and understanding the potential impact on the sleepy economy of Albany, the Chamber managed to raise some $95,000 not only to acquire 4,700 acres for the main cantonment, but land for four Auxiliary fields in Lee County as well. When the Army indicated it might need an additional 200 acres at the main site, the City purchased the land outright – and then leased the entire area to the Army for $1 per year.

Construction got under way at the brand-new airfield March 25, 1941, and this included runways, hangars, three concrete runways, taxiways and a very large hard-standing apron, as well as a central control tower. The first contingent of Air Corps troops arrived June 25, 1941, the first aircraft landed there on July 17th and the first pilot class graduated October 31, 1941 – although clearly not having trained on AT-9s at that date.

Initially known informally as Albany Army Air Field, it was officially renamed Turner Army Air Field July 21, 1941 – although the overwhelming majority of AT-9s dispatched there direct from St. Louis listed as their destination "Albany, Georgia," rather than Turner Field – as the official name took some time to be entered into the Army Station Index, a rapidly revised and ever-expanding document in 1941.

Although originally intended to have four utilitarian Auxiliary Fields as satellites, ultimately there were a total of nine, and many of these became very well known to Cadets flying AT-9s. They included Leesburg (No.1), West Smithville (No.2), West Leesburg (No.3), Albany (near the main station, No.4), No.5 (a small turf field, also close to the mother station), North Smithville (No.6), Cordele (No.7), Vidalia-Lyons Field (No.8) and Tifton (No.9).

The station became known within the Army lexicon as the Southeast Training Center, initially, then later as the Eastern Flying Training Command Headquarters, and the 'capper' military organization was the 75th Flying Training Wing. Although the official history states that advanced training started at the station in August 1941, this must have been ground instruction only, as no twin-engine trainers were yet available at that date.

While the initial assignments of some of the earliest AT-9s to Wright, Patterson, Chanute and Scott Fields for evaluation and training purposes predated the earliest arrivals at Albany by a short time, Albany was, in fact, the first major training station to receive substantial numbers of the brand-new trainers.

The first two AT-9s to arrive at Albany, direct from the factory, AC41-5746 and 41-5747, were flown in on Sunday, December 7, 1941 and, by October 22, 1942, had been followed by no fewer than 111 others. These were supplemented, commencing in September 1942, by seven AT-9As.

Seven AT-9s from the second major production batch shortly after arrival at Albany, GA. Most of these were assigned to the 556th School Squadron. Note the varying colors on the engine cowlings. Apparently only the initial aircraft in this batch were dispatched from the factory bearing their serial numbers on both the vertical fins and fuselage sides. (Norm Taylor)

The 146th AT-9 built, AC41-12084 (msn CW25-3407) pictured not long after arrival at Albany (later Turner Field) GA April 2, 1942. The aircraft suffered three accidents during its service career and went to Blytheville AAF, AR November 20, 1942 before going to surplus at Hat Box Field, OK September 20, 1944. Note the absence of any anti-glare paint in this early 1942 view. (Norm Taylor)

However, the build-up to that eventual total was slow and, by June 1942, the brand-new station, which was going through the triple turmoil of creating a new type of training curriculum, with a brand-new aircraft type, on a brand-new station, was both exciting and filled with endless shortfalls and frustrations at once. Each squadron-sized unit had its own Orderly Room, to handle the personal and administrative affairs of all of the men assigned and an Engineering Office to maintain the records and files connected with the actual aircraft assigned. Each unit had a Commanding Officer, Adjutant, Engineering Officer, Supply Officer, Armament Officer and Recreation Officer.

In the midst of this organized chaos, as part of the Lend-lease agreement with the British Commonwealth, British Cadets were added to the student flow as well.

By the end of 1942, the dedicated training aircraft on hand at Turner included 33 AT-9s and AT-9As, 80 assorted Cessna AT-17s, nine variants of the North American AT-6, seven Vultee BT-13As and several utility aircraft. The drop in the number of AT-9s was due to the transfer, in mid-May 1942, of more than half of the AT-9s to new twin-engine training stations being opened in Columbus, MS and Valdosta, GA. These were replaced, to the dismay of the cadre, by yet more AT-17s. Shortly thereafter, a raft of complaints filtered up through the chain of command that applauded the fact that the accident rate had diminished, but only because the AT-17s were "safer" and more docile than the muscular AT-9s, and lacked the performance to properly prepare their students for what lay before them.

The experience of the 94th School Squadron was typical of the training squadrons which made up the 75th Flying Training Wing. It had actually been organized at Maxwell Field, AL and its core cadre moved to Albany June 25, 1941, where they went through the process of locating their personnel, acquiring equipment and setting up shop. Their first aircraft, provided mainly to keep the cadre current, was a North American AT-6A, AC41-479, which they signed for on August 13, 1941. The unit was formally redesignated as the 94th Two-Engine Flying Training Squadron (TEFTS) on October 20, 1942, about the same time the other units were similarly re-branded. They subsequently received additional AT-6s, but these stayed only a short time before being transferred to other fields. They commenced receiving AT-9s in November 1941, the first one, AC41-5751 arriving November 8th.

The sheer number of training squadrons at Turner during the war is potentially misleading. For instance, the 95th School Squadron which, like the 94th, had originally been formed at Maxwell on March 1, 1941, and moved to Albany June 25, 1941, was redesignated as the 95th TEFTS on November 20, 1942 but was essentially disbanded June 1, 1943 when its aircraft and personnel were transferred to the neighboring 89th TEFTS as the system adjusted to the expansion of Training Command.

The 558th School Squadron commenced operations November 1, 1941, exclusively with 14 North American AT-6 and AT-6A aircraft but, on February 17, 1942, received its first AT-9. More AT-9s gradually arrived until, on May 7, 1942, the unit received its first AT-17, followed by five more the 18th of the same month. By May 20, 1942, the unit was truly cosmopolitan, with a total of 18 aircraft, six of them AT-9s and the remainder AT-17s. the last of the AT-9s were transferred out on the 27th. However, on August 17, all of the AT-17s were transferred out and replaced a week later by 14 AT-9s consolidated from other units on Turner! The cadre must have been dazed by this time but were probably even more so when, on November 16th, six of the AT-9s were transferred out and eight AT-17s arrived, making the unit mixed once again! The monthly flying training time for the unit illustrates the hectic schedule, as the units struggled to turn out graduates to meet wartime demands. In March 1942, the Squadron flew 4,010 hours, increased to 5,630 in June and a staggering 7,651 in September. While they experienced 10 accidents between December 29, 1941 and December 1942 (involving one

Training units at Turner Field were quick to discover a weakness in the AT-9 design: vision to the rear, essential in formation flight training. They engineered a 'fix,' consisting of small additional windows aft of the cockpit, as seen to the left of the officer examining the cockpit here. This may have led to the poorly defined designation AT-9C. This aircraft, built as AT-9A 42-56889, sporting Turner Field Code T568, arrived there September 24, 1942, moved on to Blytheville AAF, AR and went to surplus at Rome, NY in September 1944. Note that the anti-glare panels on the engine cowlings and nacelles runs almost all the way aft and that an earlier two-digit Field Code had previously been worn. (Tom Heitzman)

North American AT-6A, one BC-1A and seven AT-17s), only one involved an AT-9A, on the night of November 7/8, 1942 (42-56888).

Once again, the metamorphosis experienced by the 558th may be regarded as typical, throughout this study. The functions of the Squadron changed dramatically January 25, 1943 when 14 Officers and 60 cadets were placed on Special Duty with the unit and it commenced functioning as a complete unit from ground crew to Pilot instructor. But the biggest change came in December 1943, to the rejoicing of all, when no fewer than 54 North American B-25 *Mitchells* arrived and the remaining AT-9s, AT-10s (which had arrived during the year) and AT-17s were all transferred to other squadrons on February 1, 1944. Thus, between January 1, 1943 and February 1, 1944, the 558th had operated with an amazing array consisting of 59 AT-10s, 11 AT-9s, nine North American AT-24 *Mitchells*, two Cessna UC-78s, one North American AT-6 and one liaison aircraft. All of the AT-17s had gone away. In January 1944, the unit broke the single-squadron flying time record with 7,368:20 total hours of instruction flying – and they had set the previous record as well. Observant readers will, by now, have gained an inkling of the issues surrounding the colors and markings of assigned aircraft, and that even though an aircraft might carry the Field Numbers of a certain unit, it may in fact have not been assigned to the corresponding unit at the time of sighting due to the fluid nature of aircraft assignments. As valuable as the numbering system was, it must have been a nightmare for ground crews to keep the aircraft coded properly.

Some of the 'higher' numbered units did not migrate from other stations but, instead, were constituted and activated at Turner. The 728th School Squadron (SP) is a good example. It was activated at Turner May 11, 1942 but was redesignated as the 728th TEFTS October 23, 1942. The unit received its first three Cessna AT-17s November 12, 1942, supplementing its stalwart AT-9s but the last of the AT-9s departed for other stations November 16th and, to the dismay of the cadre, were replaced by 10 more AT-17s.

In view of Turner's premier role as a two-engine flying training station, it is probably not surprising that the very first fatal accidents involving AT-9s occurred with two aircraft stationed there. A 95th School Squadron aircraft, AC41-5757, crashed April 2, 1942, five miles south of Leary, Georgia killing Cadet E. W. Kaler, the Pilot in Command and an unidentified passenger. The aircraft had arrived at Turner on December 7, 1941. This was followed by the loss of 41-11961 of the 89th School Squadron on July 21st at the Leesburg Auxiliary Field while being flown by Cadet Thomas Moseley and another cadet, again, fatal to both. In both instances, the initial finding was that they both crashed as the result of the failure of the starboard (right) wings, midway between the wing root and engine nacelle while reportedly engaged in 'routine instrument flights.' Needless to say, these losses sent shock-waves through the AT-9 community at Turner and Moody, and Wright Field hastened to investigate, and resulted in the wing strengthening measures described in Chapter Two. These unfortunate losses resulted in a permanent 'fix,' however, and no subsequent losses were attributed to wing failures.

Only 47 of the 118 AT-9s and AT-9As assigned to Turner between December 7, 1941 and August 1944, when the last known example finally departed for storage, escaped any form of accident whatsoever. Of those a total of seven involved fatalities (four of which were in two accidents noted further on), including one British Commonwealth officer. The overwhelming majority of these were repairable, and usually involved some form of landing gear malfunction, taxiing accident or ground handling incident. There were several exceptions, however, worth noting.

The first occurred at 0810 hours, March 11, 1942, to a 94th School Squadron aircraft, AC41-5758, which had been accepted December 8th from the manufacturer at Turner main. With 315:55 hours on the aircraft, Cadet J. R. Schoenig, with Cadet D. P. Barnett serving as co-pilot. On advancing the throttles for take-off, and having reached about 50 mph, the right main landing gear retracted, resulting in a ground loop. The two Cadets immediately checked the position of the landing gear selector lever, and it was definitely in the 'Down' position. Interestingly, the pilot reported, upon being interviewed, when asked if he had ever been instructed to check the lever manually, or by putting his hand on it, he said "No, I don't think that I have ever been instructed to do that. I have always put my hand on it to check it, but I don't think that I have ever been instructed to do so." Upon examination of the lever, it was found that rivets in the block on the landing gear selector lever had sheared off, but it could not be determined how this had happened. This was the first of many accidents involving the main landing gear of the AT-9, usually the right main, that plagued the aircraft through the end of 1942. It was finally determined that the majority of these had taken place due to a combination of pilot error and materiel failure in the lever mechanism. The aircraft that Schoenig was flying had standard pre-war rudder stripes and painted engine cowlings (possibly red) but no discernible field number on the fuselage at the time of the accident.

Other accidents were a combination of pilot error and the brisk handling characteristics of the AT-9. On 1045 hours, September 17, 1942, Cadet John Olsen, PIC and Cadet Harold F. Lander, assigned to the 558th School Squadron, were performing a cross-country in AT-9 41-12161 from Turner to Jasper, Florida and then on the Tallahassee. Upon landing at Jasper, the aircraft was gliding on final at 105 mph with half-flaps when, over the final approach, the pilot cut the throttle and attempted to get the tail down. The aircraft floated nearly half the length of the field and, by the time it came to a stop, had overrun the runway. It went through a fence at the north end, a post of which impacted the tail, resulting in damage to the rudder, horizontal stabilizer and both props, all of which was repairable. The aircraft had 639:20 total time as of that date. Again, there were many similar accidents throughout Training Command.

During the research preparatory for this monograph, the author encountered frequent citations which, in varying tones, suggested that the AT-9 series could not fly with one engine out. While it is almost certainly true that, depending on loading, the aircraft could not sustain extended flight on a single engine, this was actually true of many two-engine aircraft of the era. In fact, this sort of incident occurred with some frequency, and the experience of Cadets John H. Heath and Phillip Gath of Class 42-I, 89th School Squadron, also on September 17, 1942, flying 41-11993 is typical. Flying from Jasper, Florida back to Turner, his port (left) engine failed about 10 miles south of the Municipal Airport at Valdosta, GA. Heath immediately trimmed the aircraft for single-engine operation, but as he could only maintain about 110 mph and was losing altitude steadily, he knew he couldn't make the Moody Army Air Field at Valdosta, so elected the Municipal Field, where he set down safely, only to realize that the field was under active construction – but rolled out too far and nosed over in a ditch. The aircraft was repairable. The reason for the engine failure was not determined.

Moffett Field, California (6)

Station Field Code: None known
Known Unit Markings: None known
AT-9 Operating Units: ★Headquarters, Western Flying Training Command
    A total of six AT-9s were, at least administratively, assigned to Moffett Field but, if any of them in fact actually reached the station, it was apparently for only a very brief period, and almost certainly in connection with the station being home to the HQS, WFTC.
    The first to arrive, direct from St. Louis, was AC41-5763, but it had been reassigned to Mather Field by December 18th. The second, 41-5764, was almost certainly diverted in transit as, even though administratively assigned to Moffett December 17, 1941 new, by December 24th, it was at Albany, GA. The final three, 41-5766 to 41-5768, also administratively assigned December 17th, were reassigned to Mather (on the same day) and Albany (by December 24th).
    This shuffle is representative of the turmoil that attended the immediate post-Pearl harbor period, when aircraft were being rushed hither and yon, communications facilities and instructions to ferry crews were extremely difficult, and aircraft assignment orders were, literally, being changed enroute.

Randolph Field, San Antonio, Texas (7)

Station Field Code: "G-" and "H-"
Known Unit Markings: G1, G3, G7, G8, G9, G11, H1, H3, H4, H6, H8, H-7, H9, H-10, H11, H-24, H-31, H-32, H-34, H-39
AT-9 Operating Units: ★44th Basic Flying Training Squadron ★47th Advanced Flying Training Squadron ★47th Basic Flying Training Squadron (by 3/7/1943) ★47th Twin-Engine Instructors Training Squadron ★2532nd Base Unit ★Randolph Central Instructors School (CIS)

The permanent 'home' of Air Corps flight training, beautiful Randolph Field, some 17 air miles northeast of San Antonio (but actually closer to the village of Converse, Texas) eventually saw the assignment of a total of 25 AT-9s and 26 AT-9As commencing December 19, 1941, although some of these were there for only brief periods. The aircraft assigned there were unusual in that the station used two separate Field Codes at the same time, and AT-9s stationed there witnessed an assortment of paint codes on their engine cowlings, with some painted only on the leading edges of the cowl, some segmented, some the entire cowl and some no paint at all. This curious mix may have been associated with the relative proximity of similar activities at Kelly Field, on the other side of San Antonio, where the same codes were in use.

A major component of the Central Flying Training Command, none of the AT-9 operating units at Randolph were the typical TEFTSs found elsewhere. Indeed, most were assigned to either the 47th Basic Flying Training Squadron or the gigantic Randolph CIS. This latter unit, as late as June 30, 1944, had an astonishing total of 175 aircraft, consisting of eight AT-9s, 47 assorted North American AT-6s, one Beech AT-7, 51 Beech AT-10s, 23 Beech AT-11s, 23 Cessna AT-17s, six Fairchild AT-21s, 13 Martin AT-23 *Marauders*, one Stinson L-1 and two TP-40Ns!

The 47th Training Squadron, which, as noted above, was redesignated to perform assorted specialized training functions during its existence at Randolph had, by around April 1943, been redesignated again as the 47th Twin-Engine Instructors Training Squadron – a virtually one-of-a-kind unit. The single-engine basic training aircraft the unit had operated heretofore were replaced with a mix of AT-9s, AT-10s and UC-78s. To no one's surprise, these types were completely unknown to both training

Randolph Field AT-9As wearing both "H" and "G" Field Codes, without hyphens, are visible in this mid-1943 view. The first AT-9As arrived April 20, 1943. The nearest aircraft, H9, has the name of a Lieutenant stenciled below the data block. The engine cowlings are believed to have been painted yellow. (USAAF)

A very nice echelon formation of six Randolph Field-based AT-9As. Note that by the time this image was taken, the Field Codes had introduced a hyphen between the code and the individual numbers, unlike earlier in the war. The aircraft all have different colors on their cowlings and in differing proportions! (via Alan Griffith)

AT-9s assigned to the "West Point of the Air," Randolph Field, TX, included those coded both "H" and "G", apparently sharing these codes with Kelly Field on the other side of San Antonio. Here, LT D. J. Kingsbury (left) and E. G. Harrington (right) of the Central Instructors School at Randolph pose with H3. This view shows the very well streamlined fuselage and the generous anti-glare panels which, on H3, appear to have painted on in gloss finish! (USAFHRA 24144AC)

cadre and ground crews alike and an inordinately extended period of time was required to locate and assimilate the required manuals, special tools and all-important flight manuals and operating instructions.

The 47th quickly recognized the considerable differences in these three types, and unusual for a training unit, enjoyed hand-picked field representatives dispatched to aid their transition by Curtiss-Wright, Beech and Cessna. Their additional-duty unit historian wryly noted that *"...the fly in the ointment was the retractable landing gear. Pilots were frequently obliged to "belly in" because of the failure of the wheels to come down,"* a malady he attributed to all three types. He lauded the AT-9 as being best able to stand up to the rigors of students and Texas weather but bashed the AT-10s and UC-78s as being the subjects of *"...much damage as the result of hail storms and high winds."*

AT-9 NIGHT FLYING RANDOLPH FLD - TEX

Of the 51 AT-9s assigned to Randolph, about half escaped any form of accident, which may at least in part be attributed to the experience level of their mainly high-time instructor students. Only two involved fatalities when AT-9As 42-56923 and 42-56966, both of the 47th BFTS, experienced a mid-air collision near the field on April 6, 1943 resulting in the death of 2LTs Don S. Graves and Albert A. Cullen. They apparently turned into each other in an uncoordinated formation flight.

Night photography of AT-9s is rare – and the photographer who took this shot must have been tucked in tight next to AT-9A 42-56875/H-39 of Randolph Field. After service at Randolph, this aircraft moved on to Blytheville, AR then Altus Field, OK, going to the RFC at Perrin Field October 20, 1944. (USAAF)

Mather Field, California (8)

Station Field Code: "T-"
Known Unit Markings: T-58, T-65, T-67, T-75, T-77A, T-87, T-92, T-92A, T-136
AT-9 Operating Units: ★335th School Squadron ★336th School Squadron (336th TEFTS by 1/1942)
★337th School Squadron ★338th School Squadron ★517th Twin-Engine Flying Training Squadron (?)

A legacy station, located 12 miles southeast of Sacramento, Mather Field had originally been established February 21, 1918 and was named for 2LT Carl S. Mather, who had been killed in a training flight at distant Ellington Field, TX, when his Curtiss JN-4D collided with another aircraft. The field closed in May 1923 but re-opened in April 1930 as a sub-post of the Presidio, San Francisco and was re-established as a separate post and activated May 13, 1941 as a training station.

Advanced training commenced at Mather June 7, 1941, but the first AT-9s did not arrive until December 12, 1941, followed by 99 others, making it one of the major *Jeep* operating stations. Indeed, early wartime photos of AT-9s – most of them taken by the legendary aviation historian William T. "Bill" Larkins – depicted AT-9s stationed at Mather

The AT-9s appear to have been distributed more-or-less evenly between the training squadrons noted above but the 517th TEFTS is questionable, as it had AT-6s and BT-13s only as late as August 1941 and was redesignated as a TEFT November 1, 1942, then being redesignated once again as a BFTS January 1, 1943. Thus, if it operated AT-9s, it was only for about a month.

The 336th School Squadron arrived on station July 30, 1941 and received its first aircraft in August, consisting of five North American AT-6s. By January 1942, the unit was redesignated as a Twin-Engine Flying Training Squadron but its aircraft strength certainly did not reflect this tasking, as it consisted of 16 AT-6As, five Vultee BT-13As and only three AT-9s. By the end of February, however, this had changed, and the unit had 19 AT-6As, three BT-13As and 11 AT-9s. By March, this ratio had changed yet again, and the unit had only AT-6As (15 of them) and 21 AT-9s. By April, there were 23 AT-9s (and only six AT-6As) but this was the last time AT-9s were mentioned. By November 1942, the unit, although still designated as a TEFTS, no longer had any twin-engine aircraft of any type, and knew of no plans to assign same!

Possibly taken enroute to its first assignment at Mather Field, CA, 41-11984 from the second major production batch arrived there March 5, 1942. It then moved to Higley Field/Williams Field, AZ August 1, 1942 and survived to go to RFC at Hat Box Field, OK September 30, 1944. (Authors Collection)

The 337th School Squadron had a similar but even more bizarre mix of equipment. Although organized at Randolph Field, TX March 1, 1941, it was transferred, at least on paper, to Mather July 27, 1941 and received its first aircraft (six AT-6As) on August 8, 1941. A study of the metamorphosis of the equipment of this unit between December 7, 1941 and January 1, 1943, is illuminating, and clearly establishes it as having been one of the most important AT-9 operators at Mather during this pivotal period:

DATE	AT-6A	BT-13A	AT-9	PT-17	PT-22
12/7/1941	12	7			
1/1/1942	8	5	2		
2/1/1942	19	3	6		
3/1/1942	20	3	12		
4/1/1942	20	3	22	1	
5/1/1942	20	3	23	5	
6/1/1942		3	18	5	29
71/1942		3	16	18	29
8/1/1942		3	37	10	18
9/1/1942		3	37	10	18
10/1/1942		3	37	10	18
11/1/1942			37	10	18
12/1/1942			37	10	18
1/1/1943			37	10	18

The 338th School Squadron's lineage was almost identical to the 337th, having been organized also at Randolph March 1, 1941. Its initial equipment also consisted of six AT-6As and, during calendar year 1942 operated as many as 12 AT-6As, six BT-13As, 18 AT-9s (sole equipment between June and October) and then joined by the first of at least 10 Cessna AT-17s in November 1942. The first North American B-25s arrived in the unit in March 1943 and, by the end of April 1943, the AT-9s were gone.

The accident experience of the AT-9 at Mather was remarkably good, compared to Albany during much the same period. Only 38 accidents have been identified, several of these involving the same aircraft. Only one known fatality has been identified, however, and once again, this involved a mid-air collision between two AT-9s, AC41-5857 and 41-5803 on February 19, 1942, west of the home station. 2LT Lloyd D. Collins died in 41-5857 but the fate of 2LT William G. Erck, Jr., in 41-5803 is not clear. Both aircraft were demolished.

The accident experience of the 338th School Squadron during 1942, involving nine AT-9s and one AT-17, appears to be fairly typical and they are tabulated below.

Date	Type	Serial Number	Pilot in Command	Description
2/2/1942	AT-9	41-5792	2LT Clyde I. Butts	Landing gear folded, total loss, no injuries
2/20/1942	AT-9	41-5764	2LT Joseph H. Carter	Landing gear folded in turn. No injuries. Repaired

3/16/1942	AT-9	41-11949	2LT Edwin Bowers	Ground loop, damaging left wing. No injuries. Repaired
4/28/1942	AT-9	41-11975	S/Sgt Dewey Forry	Wheels buckled on landing, no injuries. Repaired
7/22/1942	AT-9	41-5809	2LT Frederick L. Roth or LT J. E. Rapp	Landing made with gear retracted. No injuries. Repaired
7/28/1942	AT-9	41-12031	1LT Earl J. Younkers	Student pulled landing gear lever instead of flap lever at end of landing rollout. No injuries. Repaired
10/12/1942	AT-9	41-12027	LT S. E. Wall	Pilot started engine while mechanic was cleaning the engine and CPL J. Parker suffered leg injuries. No damage to aircraft.
10/20/1942	AT-17	42-20	LT T. N. Thompson	Student retracted landing gear on take-off. No injuries, Total loss.
11/19/1942	AT-9	41-5764	2LT W. M. Hoorer or 2LT Howard B. Grundman	Left main gear broke completely off after departing Municipal Airport and made a crash landing on arrival back at Mather. Repaired! No injuries
12/13/1942	AT-9	41-5809	1LT Randle M. Bennett	Pilot overshot runway and ran into a ditch. Repaired, no injuries

Although coded T-77A, AT-9 AC41-5838 had actually arrived at Mather Field February 5, 1942, well before T-58, pictured elsewhere, indicating the arbitrary assignment of these Field Codes. The significance of the "A" suffix used with some frequency at Mather can only be guessed at – possibly a second use of the same code – and it was the only station known to have used this convention. This well-traveled aircraft moved on to Victorville March 28, 1942, then in turn to Roswell, Williams and finally surplus at Arledge Field, TX February 7, 1945. (Authors Collection)

Published in a number of early war magazines and books, AT-9 41-12025. Coded T-58 at Mather Field, CA, was often credited as having been at Turner Field, AL. In fact, she arrived at Mather March 17, 1942, moved to Hamilton Field, CA May 17th and to Muroc April 20th – suggesting she may have been assigned there to a tactical P-38 OTU. She was surveyed April 25, 1944 due to wear-and-tear. (William T. Larkins)

This AT-9, coded T-92A, arrived at Mather Field March 18, 1942 but was reassigned to Victorville July 20th. It was lost to an accident July 1, 1943 at Williams Field, AZ. The aircraft is at the very end of its landing approach. (William T. Larkins)

The AT-9s service at Mather lasted from December 12, 1941 till June 1943, barely 18 months, but the majority of them departed for other stations between May and October 1942, mainly Higley (Williams) Field, AZ, Victorville, CA and a few to March and Luke Fields.

One airman of note who completed training at Mather, Lieutenant (later Brigadier General) James Stewart, of movie fame, had this to say about his association with the AT-9s there:

The highest Field Code number known for Mather Field, this AT-9, AC41-5850 had arrived on station February 8, 1942 – one of the first to get there. It moved on to Higley Field, AZ August 1, 1942 and was lost to an accident November 27, 1943. The Cadet on the wing, John R. Fontenrose of Berkeley, CA, was reportedly a navigator trainee at the time. (Wide World Photo A-15802 via eBay)

"I got to know the airplane pretty well at Mather Field, California, during the latter part of 1942. I instructed in the airplane for about four or five months. I remember that all of us had a rather unkind (and unjustified) appraisal of the airplane at the time, not so much because of its performance but because, in getting in and out of the airplane, it was almost impossible not to cut yourself or tear your clothing on the jagged points of metal that seemed to stick out everywhere We used to say that the airplane was constructed entirely of old flattened out Prince Albert tobacco cans!"

"I believe the concept behind the design of the airplane was very sound because, with the coming of the high-speed wing in fighter aircraft and light bomber aircraft of that period, a trainer with high-speed characteristics was very necessary, so the little aircraft was rather critical. Speed on final approach was 120 miles per hour, and, over the fence, was about 118, and that was about it. There was no flare and we landed tail high on the main gear."

"Everybody had a lot of respect for the little bird and I think the AT-9 was very valuable in the Air Corps training program at that time."

Ellington Field, Texas (9)

Station Field Code: None used

Known Unit Markings: 77, 212, 214, 219, 221, 620, 905, 909, 913, 921. Of these, the 69th School Squadron/69th TEFTS is known to have used large black numbers in the 900s on the fuselage (with no national insignia on the fuselage), and some of their aircraft had yellow engine cowls. The 70th TEFTS is known to have used large black fuselage numbers in the 200s, but farther forward on the fuselage and with the national insignia aft.

AT-9 Operating Units: ★HHS 68th TEFT Group ★55th Air Base Squadron ★59th School Squadron (59th TEFTS by 11/23/1942) ★69th School Squadron (69th TEFTS by 12/17/1942) ★70th Two-Engine Flying Training Squadron ★72nd School Squadron (72nd TEFTS by 11/22/1942) ★73rd School Squadron (73rd TEFTS by 12/23/1942) ★73rd AAFFTD (by 4/27/1943) ★76th School Squadron

Yet another legacy station which had figured prominently in the evolution of U.S. Army aviation during WW1, Ellington Field, in southeast Houston, Texas, the station was named for LT Eric L. Ellington, an Army pilot killed in 1913 in a crash at San Diego.

After WW1, the station went into caretaker status by 1923, but became a Texas National Guard base until 1927, when it once again reverted to prairie grass and, for the next 12 years, it was leased to local ranchers for use as open range grazing grounds.

As the world situation deteriorated in the late 1930s, Houston's Congressional leaders lobbied hard to once again reestablish Ellington Field as a dedicated pilot training station and, in 1940, construction commenced on a radically expanded, semi-permanent installation. The station was designated as one of the primary training facilities for, especially, bombardment pilots and crews.

As rapidly as the burgeoning Army system could accommodate the demand, beginning at five-week intervals, classes averaging 274 Cadets entered what was, at first, a 10-week course. The students moved from variants of the North American BC-1A and AT-6 to AT-9s, Beech AT-10s or AT-11s.

The first three AT-9s arrived at Ellington from Randolph Field on December 20, 1941 and were followed by 95 AT-9s and six AT-9As. These were followed starting January 3, 1942 by brand-new examples direct from St. Louis.

Ellington, together with Turner and Mather Fields, submitted the majority of the Unsatisfactory Reports (U/Rs) to Wright Field on the new type and, in the process, aided the inevitable process of ironing out teething issues. These were not long in coming.

The 72nd School Squadron submitted one on February 6, 1942 on AC41-5771, which had only been with the unit for 33 days (and which had already accumulated 125:15 total time), one of 15 AT-9s assigned to the unit by that time. They observed that the shaft for the Fuel Selector Valve had twisted off completely, and that they had discovered the same condition in three other of the 15 AT-9s in their care at the time, which were actively engaged in training Class 01-C. The 72nd School Squadron had been

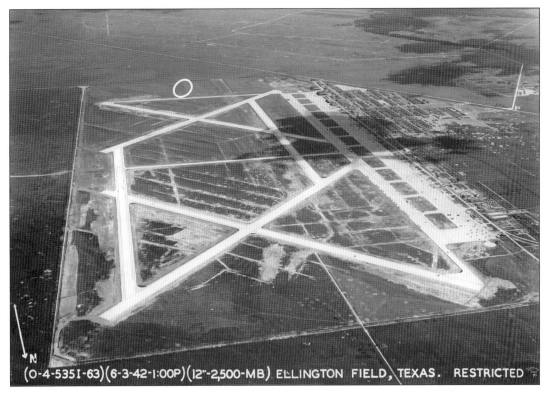

(O-4-5351-63)(6-3-42-1:00P)(12"-2,500-MB) ELLINGTON FIELD, TEXAS. RESTRICTED

One of the major AT-9 operating stations, this is how Ellington Field, TX looked to Cadets as of June 3, 1942, looking south. The unusual field layout must have been challenging for new trainees. (USAFHRA)

The obligatory "V" for "Victory" posed image reveals the cadets and staff of one of the Two-Engine Flying Training Squadrons at Ellington Field, TX as of December 2, 1942. The aircraft all bear Field Numbers in the 200s on all 13 aircraft, with no sign of anti-glare panels or cowling colors. (NMUSAF)

activated at Brooks Field, Texas on November 1, 1940 but had moved to Ellington April 21, 1941. It was later redesignated as the 72nd School Squadron (Special) and then to 72nd Two-Engine Flying Training Squadron.

Not to be outdone, the neighboring 73rd School Squadron submitted a U/R on July 23, 1942 which, once again, involved what they described as the Drive Assembly for the Fuel Control. They pointed out that there appeared to be a strong possibility of installing worn gears from the drive assembly housing of the engine selector valve control into the drive assembly of the tank selector valve control itself, resulting in a serious hazard. Wright Field replied that they had learned of this problem from other stations as well, and that corrective action had been initiated with the manufacturer. The 73rd had been organized December 5, 1940 at Randolph Field, but was transferred to Ellington May 2, 1941. It became the 73rd TEFTS and was inactivated on January 14, 1944.

As an early and, as it unfolded, major AT-9 operating station, Ellington based *Jeeps* suffered a slightly higher-than-average number of accidents. Of the 101 examples which were eventually stationed there,

Although of marginal quality, this flight-line view of an Ellington-based AT-9 with the low, two-digit Field Code 77, shows the ease of maintenance of the aircraft, the opened cowlings even providing a modicum of shade in the blistering Texas sun! (via Ted Young)

24686 A.C

This AT-9 arrived new at Ellington from the factory April 22, 1942 and, coded 219 in an unusual location far forward of the norm, also had gained yellow engine cowls by the time of the photo. It moved on to Williams Field, AZ then Altus Field, OK by August 20, 1944, but went to the RFC surplus center at Hat Box Field, OK September 22, 1944. (USAAF 24686A.C.)

only 36 escaped some form of accident experience. However, of those that did, an inordinate number involved taxiing accidents into other AT-9s or other types on the sprawling and crowded Ellington taxiways and apron.

The first known accident came on February 2, 1942, when a 72nd School Squadron aircraft, AC41-5770, which had arrived from Randolph on December 20th as one of the first three on station, suffered an unspecified landing accident at Ellington while being flown by 2LT David B. Crighton. It was repaired and actually enjoyed a lengthy service life at Ellington for the balance of its wartime existence, not departing until August 11, 1944 for storage and prep for surplusing at Rome, NY.

There were, however, six fatal accidents involving Ellington-based AT-9s and, of these, four were assigned to the 73rd School Squadron and one to the 72nd. One of these involved the loss of the starboard engine while on a night cross-country flight in the wilds of Texas when the two-man Cadet crew bailed out.

The hard-working ground crews at Ellington, as elsewhere, were far too often cited in official USAAF accident reports. The experience of Sergeant Joseph F. Nemeth of the 59th TEFTS on the cold, clear night of November 23, 1942, is typical example. SGT Nemeth had been repositioning AT-9 41-12010 for the following days training exertions, and was moving it on the ramp to a location where available lighting would facilitate his work, when the right main gear collapsed after taxiing only about 15 feet and executing a right turn. It was determined that, contrary to standing operating procedures, he had not been using the manually operated hydraulic pump, which was required when an AT-9 was being towed.

A considerable amount of night navigation and cross-country training was conducted on AT-9s at Ellington, and on the evening of May 19, 1942, around 1645 hours, Cadets John G. McLaughlin and Lawrence G. McLaughlin (not known if any relation) of the 72nd School Squadron were obliged to execute a forced landing about 15 miles southeast of Liberty, Texas, when they just ran out of fuel, having become totally lost – the second accident suffered by this aircraft. The aircraft was recovered and repaired, only to suffer two additional incidents, one on July 21, 1942 and the last, at Ellington, on November 16, 1942. It was once again repaired and reassigned to Blackland Army Air Field, near Waco, Texas (q.v.) December 14th. A great many AT-9s experienced more than one accident, even further marring the reporting on the aircraft – but the overwhelming majority were locally repairable.

The 73rd School Squadron suffered a devastating loss on the night of October 2, 1942, when AT-9 41-5789, flown by Aviation Students Theodore G. Sneider and Ernest B. Thomas, Jr. (who both, incidentally, held the official pay grade of Private First Class as A/S ratings) departed Ellington on a routine student night navigational flight to Yoakum, Navasota, and return. The next morning, a Mrs. Guy Botard had reported to Oacar W. Houchins of Sheridan, Texas, that she and her son had heard the engines of "...*a number of airplanes*" during the night, one of which was at about 9pm, and which had made an unusual amount of noise – as if in a power dive, followed by a loud noise like an explosion, which she estimated to have been from one to three miles from her home. Houchins reported all of this via telephone to Kelly Field in San Antonio, but it was not until the late afternoon of October 6th that the

wreckage of the aircraft was finally located, about five miles southwest of Sheridan. It had, in fact, been located by a CAP patrol from El Campo.

When crews arrived at the scene, there was little evidence as to what may have caused the obvious crash – aside from the fact that the aircraft had clearly come in at a rather steep angle, estimated at 45 to 60 degrees, and at a speed considerably higher than normal cruise. The port-side door was found three-quarters of a mile northwest of the wreck, and the pilot's body about 75 yards in line with the door. This appeared to indicate that the pilot had jumped immediately prior to the impact, but too low for safe use of his chute. The co-pilot had apparently stayed with the aircraft, as his body was found about 15 feet ahead of the main wreckage; however, the starboard door was never found.

Weather apparently played no part in the loss and the investigating board concluded that the Pilot in Command (Sneider) had become disoriented and lost, and that thunderstorms in the Yoakum area the night of the accident may have contributed to the disorientation.

The experience of AT-9 41-12092 of the 73rd TEFTS was apparently similar, but gives some indication of just how far afield the Cadets at Ellington ventured on their cross-country navigation flights. This aircraft had flown from Ellington to the Kansas City, MO Municipal Airport on January 7, 1943, and took off at 2340 hours (11:40pm) the next evening for Chicago on an instrument flight, crewed by 1LT Wayne S. Forsythe (PIC) and passenger 1LT Lewis E. Barrick, who was actually a Medical Corps officer. Their flight plan was to overfly Kirksville, MO and Burlington, IA enroute to Chicago and from there, on to the Naval Air Base, Port Columbus, Ohio and return. The Kirksville radio operator reported that he had attempted repeatedly to contact AR112092 at two-minute intervals and that the AT-9 should have overflown that city at 0036 hours.

According to witnesses on the ground, the aircraft in fact had crashed at about 0100 January 9th on a farm near West Point, Iowa, and, when the wreckage was located, the radio receiver dial was found to be set on the Burlington range, and the radio had been operating normally when the aircraft departed Kansas City. There was no indication of engine trouble found in the wreckage but the main fuel selector valve was found in the "Off" position; however, the Pitot Heat switch was in the "Off" position, which, it was surmised, may have accounted for an error in airspeed. The wreckage indicated that the aircraft was 'out of control' at the time of the crash, as if the pilot was attempting a forced landing, which seemed to be corroborated by witness statements. The investigating board concluded that the aircraft stalled and nosed in, due to the location of the engines and the fact that no corn stalks were broken down more than 10 feet from the point of impact. The aircraft had accumulated a total time of 852:20 by the time of the accident since new.

An accident on March 19, 1943 is of interest in that the Pilot in Command was recorded as Aviation Cadet Muriel W. Moore, one of the legendary WASPs, who had graduated from flight training at Randolph in Class 94-10. She suffered some form of take-off accident while assigned to the 73rd TEFT Squadron. The aircraft was repaired and there were no injuries, however.

At least one RAF Pilot Officer (P/O) was involved in an accident on September 16, 1943 at the Navasota Airport, north of Houston. Oddly, P/O Robert Cunliffe was assigned to the headquarters and Headquarters Squadron, 68th Twin-Engine Flying Training Group when he executed a successful forced landing – the final AT-9 accident suffered by an Ellington-based AT-9, AC41-5765, which just happened to have been the very first AT-9 assigned to the station.

The experiences on the AT-9 of Cadet Frank Luft, more recently of White City, Oregon, while in training at Ellington during the war are of interest, as he offered one of the few dissenting opinions regarding his training on the AT-9. While at Ellington, he flew the AT-9 as well as the North American AT-6 (for gunnery training) and the Beech AT-10. He reported that "...*the AT-9 was a relatively rare trainer, as most twin-engine schools flew the AT-10 or the Cessna AT-17. Actually, the AT-10 was the best of the three and, while the appearance of the AT-9 suggested speed, it did not perform near that expectation with the same Lycoming' as the AT-10. But it looked great!*" Frank went on to fly another Curtiss product, the C-46, for Air Transport Command and then, post-war with the NASA Ames Laboratory.

For the record, it should be noted that there were two other Two-Engine Flying Training Squadrons at Ellington during this period, the 71st and the 74th but, so far as can be determined, they operated only AT-10s and AT-17s and no AT-9s are known to have been assigned to either.

Victorville Army Air Force Station, Victorville, California (10)

Station Field Code: "V-"
Known Unit Markings: V-701 (41-11985), V-911 (41-11946)
AT-9 Operating Units: ★338th School Squadron ★513th School Squadron ★516th School Squadron (516th TEFTS 11/1/1942) ★517th School Squadron ★518th School Squadron ★519th School Squadron (519th TEFT by 11/1942)

As war clouds gathered in the late 1930s, and America slowly started preparing for the inevitable, local communities across the land began to actively seek Federal money to not only facilitate that expansion – but aid their own local prospects as well.

The good citizens of Victorville were no exception, and solicited for the Army to make use of the abundance of "...*wide open spaces, 360-days of sunshine per year and the High Mojave Desert dry conditions*" while extolling the virtues, perhaps with a tiny bit of exaggeration, of both Victorville itself as well as neighboring Adelanto. Like many other similar remote communities with land available for airfield development, the Army, possibly spurred somewhat by political suggestion, reach an agreement in 1941 and ground was broken on a 2,200-acre air field July 12, 1941.

The area available enabled construction of what was virtually an ideal training base, with a four-runway configuration and seven commodious hangars. Eventually, the base had a large number of buildings – more than 250 – and four auxiliary fields (Hawes No.1, Helendale No2, Mirage No.3 and Grey Butte No.4) and was designed to be as self-sufficient as possible.

The first of 50 AT-9s arrived direct from the factory between February and April 1942, followed by 41 on transfer from Mather (q.v.) between May 18th and 28th, 1942.

Actual training commenced almost immediately after the arrival of the first AT-9s, which were joined by substantial numbers of Cessna AT-17s and North American AT-6 variants. There were also some initial Beech AT-11s and Vultee BT-13s which equipped the 519th, 520th, 521st and 522nd Squadrons, but these were on the track for bombardier training. As it transpired, the majority of the two-engine graduates from Victorville went on to Douglas C-47 transport, or North American B-25 or Martin B-26 medium bomber units. The first class graduated April 24, 1942 by which time all of the training units at Victorville had been subordinated to the local 36th Flying Training Wing.

The evolution of the AT-9 operating squadrons was rapid, and the 516th School Squadron is a good example. It had been temporarily assigned to Moffett Field as of December 7, 1941, but had no aircraft as yet, only personnel, and made the tedious move to remote Victorville December 19th. By November 1, 1942, it had been redesignated as the 516th Two-Engine Flying Training Squadron. Initial operating equipment consisted of eight AT-6As, but these were joined by five AT-9s at the end of March 1942. Two more arrived in the first half of April and, by May 26, 1942, all of the AT-6s had been reassigned, leaving only 12 AT-9s. Then, in mid-summer, seven more AT-9s were assigned and, by August 3, 1942, the unit *Remote, barren Victorville* was busily operating 20 AT-9s. The unit lost all of its AT-9s in mid-November 1942 when the two-en-*Advanced Flying School,* gine flying training mission was transferred to La Junta AAF, Colorado, Roswell AAF, New Mexico and *California, as it appeared* Douglas and Williams (Higley) AAFs, Arizona, and a mass migration of all Victorville AT-9s headed *January 20, 1942, about* southeast to those new, arid stations. Oddly, one AT-9, AC41-5764 remained at Victorville as late as Feb-*a month before the first* ruary 1943, but then it was reassigned to Mather on April 20, 1943, the last AT-9 to depart Victorville. *AT-9s arrived. (USAFHRA)*

RESTRICTED
C023-108-J-9MFX1-20-42-1:52-PX12-1500) ADV. FLYING SCHOOL, VICTORVILLE,CALIF.

The experience of the 519th and the other AT-9 units at Victorville was similar. It had, however, been activated at Mather August 1, 1941, but then was administratively reassigned to Moffett Field November 7, 1941 and finally on to Victorville January 2, 1942, later being redesignated as the 519th Two-Engine Flying Training Squadron. According to unit records, it was transferred to Marfa AAF, Texas by January 14, 1943, but by then was equipped entirely with Cessna AT-17s. This was probably only a transfer of the nameplate.

While AT-9s were working at Victorville, there were 50 assorted accidents experienced, the first of which involved 41-11967 on April 6, 1942, and which had arrived on station February 27th, 1942. While being flown by Cadet Walter T. Stewart of the 518th School Squadron, he lost both engines about 10 miles west of Victorville and the aircraft was completely demolished. The fate of the pilot isn't clear.

While the vast majority of the accidents suffered by AT-9s assigned to Victorville involved assorted landing accidents of one sort or another, it is interesting to note that, even though this was one of the initial 10 operating stations for the type, not a single fatal accident was experienced on the type. Indeed, only 12 were surveyed as total losses and, of these, two moved on to Class 26 duties as instructional airframes.

One accident became a matter of considerable interest to Wright Field, however, and this was the accident experienced by 41-11961 on March 9, 1942 five miles south of Victorville on Highway 395 while being flown by 2LT Knox Parker of the 519th School Squadron. Parker apparently lost control of the aircraft while 'under the hood' and took to his parachute successfully. He claimed that the right wing had failed during his attempt to recover, echoing the reports of about this same time that Wright Field had received from Turner Field in Alabama. It turned out that the wreckage of the aircraft could not substantiate his claim.

The final accident involving an AT-9 at Victorville occurred on the very eve of the departure of the type from the station. AT-9 41-12079, which had arrived May 3, 1942 new, experienced a landing accident on Runway 160 November 19, 1942, while being handled by Cadet John A. Sipher, who was assigned to the 519th. The aircraft was repaired and moved on to Douglas AAF, AZ December 11th, so the damage must not have been too severe.

One of the instructors at Victorville during the roughly 10 months that AT-9s operated there was LT Jack Kaltenbach. He described some of his experiences training cadets on AT-9s there in the June 1953 issue of *Flying* magazine, and they are quoted here with his permission. "*A Cadet and I had departed Victorville late in 1942 and, routinely, started climbing towards 5,000 feet – just another routine transition flight. The AT-9, a relatively new and highly respected twin engine advanced trainer at the time, was a 'hot' airplane. We brought it in for a landing at 115 mph and, with power off, it stalled out around 75 mph. We were under orders not to teach students full flap, power-off landings, because the glide angle bordered on the perpendicular. The gear of several AT-9s had been knocked off attempting these unusual landings.*"

"*We climbed towards the mountains, and as we reached 5,000 feet, I decided to have the Cadet perform a simulated single engine landing. I had given each of my five students a sheet containing the complete procedure for setting up single engine operation, and the method for starting up the dead engine after the practice was completed. I knew all the procedures to perfection, having logged a thousand hours of instructor time at that point. There was no need for me to follow any check list, for I knew them all backwards and forwards; or so I thought.*"

Photos of AT-9s stationed at Victorville, CA are rare. Here, 41-11965, coded V-701, assigned to the 517th School Squadron, cruises over the mountains nearby. The aircraft arrived at Victorville February 27, 1942 and suffered two accidents there, the last on June 27, 1942, and went to Class 26 as an Instructional Airframe as a result June 31st, ending her brief operational existence. (via Ken Crist)

This AT-9, 41-11946, coded V-911 at Victorville, moved on to Mather Field not long afterwards, then in turn to Roswell, Williams, and Douglas AAFs, before going to the surplus center at Arledge Field, TX February 9, 1945. (via Ken Crist)

"I turned off the switch on the port engine and watched the Cadet cut off the mixture control, ease the throttle back and bring the prop into high pitch. He looked down, saw that we were too far from Victorville to make it back safely, for the AT-9 wasn't capable of holding altitude on one engine, and made a wide, descending turn towards the closest of the Auxiliary Fields which lay within range. He was doing a flawless job."

"We had orders not to land on this Auxiliary Field, as the runways there were too short for the AT-9. However, in this simulated emergency, the student used fine judgment. In time of distress, it's a case of any old port in a storm, and this Auxiliary Field was the best place for a landing within range. He rolled out on final approach to the short runway below and eased the throttle back. 'I could make it from here with full flaps,' he yelled as we glided down. The normal procedure at that point would have been to start the dead engine and climb back to altitude, with the simulated single engine landing completed. We were at an altitude of 400 feet and had gone far enough on the practice maneuver. However, riding with five different students every day, repeating the same instructions five times gets monotonous. One of the rewards is to see a student grasp the knowledge you're throwing his way. This student was doing a mighty fine job, and I was curious to see if he could follow through. I'd let him take it on down to within 50 feet of the ground, to check his technique and also to break the monotony. Then we'd climb back to 5,000."

"'Go ahead, try it,' I signalled."

"He let down full flaps, eased the power off and we dropped like a rock. By lowering the nose, he kept the speed up to 115 mph and did a neat job of bringing it down to within 50 feet of the runway. 'OK,' I called, 'Get going, I'll take care of the dead engine.'"

"He shoved the prop pitch forward, eased on full throttle and milked up the flaps. I automatically went through the procedure to start the dead engine. I eased the mixture control and prop pitch forward and advanced the throttle. I was watching the approaching desert terrain ahead, and I hurried through the operation. He moved both throttles forward as the runway flashed past about 40 feet below. I settled back and glanced at the airspeed indicator, expecting my student to start climbing."

"With both throttles full forward, the indicator hovered at 120 mph, then slowly edged down toward stalling speed. Cactus and trees were racing toward us and we were rapidly losing precious altitude."

"'I've got it!' I yelled. I grabbed the throttles and shoved forward, bending them over the throttle stops. But there was no fresh surge of power. The port engine was dead."

"Flying on one engine 40 feet off the ground, with the airspeed dropping toward the stalling point, I fought to keep the plane airborne. I had to lose more precious altitude to keep from stalling as we started over the rough desert terrain. Twenty-five feet below the wings, cactus and boulders swished by. My stomach was an icy knot as I zig-zagged through the Joshua trees, careful not to bank too much. I angled for the dry river bed a short distance ahead, trying to figure out what was wrong with the port engine. I was too busy to check visually for the cause, and my student sat motionless, pale as a ghost."

"I could either struggle to keep the plane flying, on the vague chance that the engine would come back to life, or I could set it down in a crash landing. If I could keep flying, there was a dim possibility that it would start; a speck of dirt in a gas line, a loose wire – any number of malfunctions might clear up if I kept going."

"On the other hand, I had witnessed planes that had crashed in the desert and the sight hadn't been pleasant. If the AT-9 were to smash into rocks, giant cactus or boulders, we'd be finished."

"It wasn't particularly warm in the cockpit, but perspiration was pouring off me as I decided to continue the fight to keep the plane airborne"

"I nursed the plane along, just off the desert and eased it down the course of the dry river bed. Any hope I might have had of setting it down, wheels up, on a smooth, dry river bed, evaporated when I saw the jumble of boulders, debris, and rocks below. My student had reached a point where he couldn't sit still any longer."

"'Let's crash land!'" he yelled. At the same time, he reached up and flipped off the engine switches. The plane sagged momentarily from the loss of power. I've never moved so fast in my life. My hand shot up and I had all switches back on in a split second."

"As the switches clicked back 'on,' the dead engine surged to life. With both engines at full power, I held it level, picking up speed. We were level with the jagged banks of the river bed. When I reached 120 mph, I started climbing."

"I leveled off at 3,000 feet, leaned back, exhausted, and let the student fly the plane. It was quiet in the cockpit as we returned to Victorville; neither of us felt like talking. When we landed, I turned to the Cadet and broke the silence."

"'Let my mistake be a lesson to you,' I said. 'Always use a check list and never hurry when you are flying an airplane.' I didn't have to explain; he was well aware of the mistake I'd made."

"When I had told him to climb back up to altitude after coming in over the edge of the Auxiliary Field, I had gone through the procedure of starting a dead engine. Hurrying through the operation, which I had performed a hundred times in the past, I had neglected to turn 'on' the magneto switch. With that switch in the 'off' position, the engine couldn't possibly start. When a crash landing had seemed imminent, he had reached up and flipped 'off' the main and right magneto switches. In the tenseness of the moment, he hadn't noticed that the left switch was already in the 'off' position. A split-second later, I had instinctively turned 'on' all three switches, and the dead engine had roared back to life."

Lieutenant Kaltenbach, recalling this sobering event, wondered just how many of the AT-9 accidents experienced during 1942-43 may have been attributable not to any failing of the aircraft, but to repetitious drills such as this, not performed by the numbers by instructor pilots lulled into a sense of complacency.

Williams Army Air Field (Higley Air Base No.7), Arizona (11)

Station Field Code: "Y-"
Known Unit Markings: Y-109, Y-187, Y-255, Y-261, Y-275, Y-451, Y-465, Y-466, Y-467, Y-468
AT-9 Operating Units: ★331st School Squadron ★333rd School Squadron (333rd TEFT by 11/28/1942) ★334th School Squadron ★337th Two-Engine Flying Training Squadron ★531st Two-Engine Flying Training Squadron ★533rd Two-Engine Flying Training Squadron ★535th Two-Engine Flying Training Squadron ★536th School Squadron ★538th School Squadron ★553rd Two-Engine Flying Training Squadron ★944th Single-Engine Gunnery Training Squadron ★3010th Base Unit

As the listing of operating unit suggests, this remote training station was a major player in the AT-9 story, and due at least in part to the succession of names associated with the base during its evolution, has been the source of some confusion amongst historians.

The Air Corps broke ground on what was initially cited as Higley Air Base No.7, some eight miles east of Chandler, Arizona and 12 miles southeast of Mesa, June 19, 1941 and construction was rapid, the base being officially activated as a two-engine advanced flying school September 25, 1941, even though the advance group of officers and enlisted staff did not start arriving until October.

By January 19, 1942, the spanking new base was being alternatively referred to during the preceding four-month period as Mesa Air Base, Mesa Military Airport and Higley Field, while some local newspapers simply referred to it as "...the Air Training Base near Higley," but was officially named Williams Field on this date in honor of Lieutenant Charles L. Williams, who lost his life July 6, 1927 near Fort DeRussy, Territory of Hawaii. Although almost to a man, the field was remembered in later years as "Willie Field," and with only very slight affection in most cases. Williams was assigned to the Western Flying Training Command.

The first AT-9s to arrive at Higley (as all of the initial assignments were noted on the Individual Aircraft Record Cards) were aircraft flown in starting May 1, 1942 from Mather, Victorville, Roswell, and La Junta and by November 1942 a total of 130 had arrived on station. These were joined in June and July 1943 by 64 AT-9As most of which had previously served at Roswell, Stockton, La Junta and Kirtland.

Two-engine training commenced on Cessna AT-17s on February 24, 1942 and, as the AT-9s started arriving, these supplemented the *Bobcats*. These stalwarts were augmented by a curious mix of other quasi-operational types, such as significant numbers of Lockheed P-322 *Lightnings*,[1] Boeing B-17s, early North American A-36 and P-51 *Mustangs*, and even some weary Curtiss RP-36A and RP-36C *Hawks*. By the time the station closed at the end of the war, more than 9,024 pilots had been graduated at Williams (1,094 in 1942, 3,686 in 1943 and 4,244 in 1944) and this included two-engine students from more than 20 Allied nations as well. This included two complete classes of Chinese Nationalist Air Force Cadets.

The protracted exposure of the AT-9 fleet to the extreme desert heat and dryness experienced at Williams soon manifested itself in some unexpected serviceability issues – the heat routinely climbed to 120 degrees out on the ramps. The 538th School Squadron, which had 16 AT-9s by May 4, 1942, submitted an Unsatisfactory Report to Wright Field on that date. They reported that 41-11943, which was a relatively new aircraft, had suffered chaffing of the rod that supported the blind flying hood at the point where it extended through the top of the windscreen support, apparently due to the extreme heat drying out the support and nearby starter cable, which then shorted out – and which, in turn, caused the hood to burn, the rod and cable to literally melt while also damaging other wiring running through the windscreen channel. For some reason, the staff at the 538th seemed to believe that the blind flying hood and support had been a post-manufacturing modification, but in fact it had been a standard item of Curtiss-Wright equipment when built – but only installed when needed.

As noted earlier in this account, Williams hosted a most unusual AT-9 in late December 1942 when 41-5745, the very first aircraft, arrived to perform tests at the nearby Ajo Gunnery Range with its nose-mounted .30 caliber machine gun. Still there, or possibly returned, by April 28, 1943, 41-5745 was reported in need of modification to the gun installation, as some form of unspecified malfunctioning was occurring.

Aerial view of desolate, remote Williams Field, Higley, AZ as it appeared April 27, 1942, by which time AT-9s had been operating there for several months. It was a major AT-9 and AT-9A operating station. (USAFHRA)

---

1   According to an unattributed article in *Flying* magazine during the war, students advancing to the RP-322s were required to successfully complete 10 hours in AT-9s before climbing aboard the *Lightnings*. "*The common wisdom was that if a pilot could master the AT-9s, he would have no trouble with the P-38.*"

RESTRICTED

(03-212-G-W.C.TC.X4-27-42-3.54PX(2-2500)   WILLIAMS FIELD, HIGLEY, ARIZONA

The extremely high temperatures at Williams led to yet another unexpected problem. By July 1943, the heat was causing problems with the R-680-9 engines, causing detonation when extremely hot. Wright Field authorized Williams operators to use 91 octane fuels as long as the extremely high temperatures persisted, and the problem was resolved.

Besides Cadet programs for USAAF and foreign students, Williams also operated a two-week transition course for Regular Army and Reserve Officers who were either completing flight training or transitioning from other types. This course started with eight hours on North American AT-6s, followed by two on AT-9s and completed with 20 on the 'hot' Lockheed RP-322s. By July 20, 1942, an associated special course was ordered by Flying Training Command to answer the need for trained P-38 pilots. Williams was instructed to track single-engine graduates with five to 10 hours transition on two-engine trainers (including AT-9s) for direct assignment to tactical P-38s units. The rational was simple, although not entirely popular with the single-engine pursuit graduates: they had already received pursuit tactics training, while the regular track two-engine Cadets had not. This program did not last long, however.

By January 11, 1943, Williams became the site of a new two-engine fighter course, which included 23 hours of transition in RP-322s. The graduates then moved on to P-38 units, which might be best described as Operational Training Units, in Fourth Air Force and then right into line units. By November 1943 the RP-322 course, which included substantial time in AT-9s and BT-13As, was reduced to just 10 hours. By November 1943, the BT-13s were replaced by AT-6s and the curriculum included 66 hours in the *Texans*, four in AT-9s and then 10 in RP-322s.

The Fall 2002, Vol.25, No.3 issue of the USAFM "Friends Journal," in an article on Williams by Lou Thole, recorded that the AT-9 at Williams had "...*gained the reputation of being too difficult for low-time students to fly; however, by late 1943, there were 167 assigned to the field. By March 1944, there were only 18.*" He also reported that the docile AT-17s had actually been replaced by AT-9s, and by the end of 1943, all of the AT-17s were gone.

One of the graduates of the latter program was none other than Royal D. Frey, destined by 1975 to become the Director of the United States Air Force Museum. A member of Class 43-E, he transferred from the Basic Flying School at Pecos, Texas in early 1943 and was transferred to Williams. There, he spent a grueling 70 hours flogging around the Arizona barrens, followed by six hours of dual gunnery in assorted AT-6s, followed by 10 hours in AT-9s. He famously recalled that, "...*if you can fly the AT-9 without getting killed, you can fly anything!*". He did survive and then checked out on RP-322s, his dream come true. He graduated May 20, 1943 and was sent to an OTU at Muroc AAB, CA.

Another Williams alumni was John M. Larsen, Jr, who completed primary at Dos Palos, CA on Ryan PT-22s followed by Basic at Merced, CA on Vultee BT-13As. Then he was off to Williams where "...*pilots were*

prepared to fly the wonderful P-38 – if they could survive the rigorous training. First, we flew the twin-engine AT-9s, which was dubbed 'The Curtiss Rock' due to its extremely steep gliding angle. The first time I saw one land, I thought it was crashing. You learned to get close to the runway, level off, then 'zip,' you were on the ground!"

Given the high number of AT-9s assigned to Williams, and the urgency of the training programs, it is perhaps not surprising that, of the 130 AT-9s assigned from start to finish, only 36 escaped unscathed by some form of accident. Of the 64 AT-9As, the experience was somewhat better, with 39 being accident-free during their tenure there. However, of the total of 194 aircraft, there were only nine documented fatalities, and four of these were in two aircraft of that total.

The first known accident came early when AT-9 41-5872 of the 536th School Squadron made a very hard landing at one of the Auxiliary Fields 13 miles south of Casa Grande, AZ on April 3, 1942 while being flown by Cadet Burt J. Cardwell and was a total wreck, although Cardwell apparently survived, crediting the aircraft in saving his life.

At least one British Commonwealth pilot, P/O Leslie W. Harker, was involved in an AT-9 accident, on August 20, 1943, when AT-9A 42-57044 of the 533rd TEFT Squadron collided with AT-9 41-11041 on take-off. It was repaired, however, and moved on to Douglas AAF. The unfortunate P/O Harker, was, however, involved in an earlier AT-9 accident April 21, 1943, while assigned to the same squadron – but it was a "bad landing" and was repaired before moving on to Douglas AAF. At least three Chinese Nationalist Air Force students were also involved in AT-9 accidents while training at Williams, as was WASP Isabel E. Tynon (Class 3-70, Gardner) when AT-9A 42-56972 was involved in a landing accident at the main field. It was assigned to the 3010th Base Unit at the time. A number of WASPs are known to have flown AT-9s at Williams, as well as Vultee BT-13s on engineering, administrative and ferrying duties.

The last reported accident involving an AT-9 at Williams was on July 17, 1944 when AT-9A 42-56911, by then assigned to the 3010th Base Unit, was damaged by ground handler Arthur E. Hahn on the ramp. She was repaired and was sold surplus after the war.

But no fewer than three Williams-based AT-9s ended their days in Mexico. AT-9 41-12118 of the 533rd TEFT Squadron crashed January 14, 1943, while being flown on a routine navigation training flight by Cadet Lloyd T. Daniels and Charles W. Fletcher 1.5 miles south of Sonita (also given as Sonoita), Mexico, but was recovered, after rather enormous exertions, and repaired. AT-9A 42-57127 apparently became lost, exhausted all fuel and crashed near El Espia, Mexico while being flown by Cadets John H. McLaughlin and Donald J. Kliment, also of the 533rd TEFT Squadron, on October 30, 1943, and the remains were apparently not recovered – followed, a day later, on October 31st by 42-57121, which went down 45 miles southeast of Columbus, NM and 41.5 miles north of Eleepia, Chihuahua. This aircraft was judged a complete wreck and was also apparently left in the remote region where it went down and, so far as is known, the remains of these latter two may still be there – "exports" of a non-traditional nature!

Lubbock Army Air Force Station, Lubbock, Texas (12)

Station Field Code: None used
Known Unit Markings: 413, 510, 512, 513, 514, 515, 516, 518, 517, 519, 520, 521, 620, 701, 702, 703, 708, 728
AT-9 Operating Units: ★71st Two-Engine Flying Training Group ★71st Two-Engine Flying Training Squadron ★436th School Squadron ★494th School Squadron ★495th School Squadron (495th TEFT Squadron by 11/12/1943) ★496th School Squadron (496th TEFT Squadron by 111/8/1942) ★497th School Squadron (497th TEFT Squadron 11/11/1942) ★498th School Squadron (498th TEFT Squadron by 3/9/1944) ★499th School Squadron

As part of the vast Air Corps expansion effort, what was originally termed the Air Corps Advanced Flying School, Lubbock, Texas, construction commenced in August 1941 on the vast plains about 10 miles west of what was then a very remote ranching community in far west Texas.

Designed from the start for training large numbers of Cadets, the layout of the field, consisting of three 6,500-foot asphalt runways, arranged in a triangular (N/S, NE/SW, E/W) pattern, the station also enjoyed five Auxiliary Fields, known as West Lubbock, South Lubbock, North Lubbock, Opdyke Field and Abernathy Field.

The formal name of the school was changed to a more precise Lubbock Army Flying School before the first class of Cadets reported – and they started their studies even before the field was completed, which wasn't for two more years, not being declared finished until mid-1944.

By early 1942, the resident school was named the Army Air Corps Advanced Flying School and actual flight training started on February 8, 1942 – although the formal dedication of the base did not occur until June 21st. The first class, Cadet Class 42-0, reported for duty February 25, 1942 and graduated – initially – as single-engine pilots April 29, 1942. A total of 326 pilots successfully graduated in this and the two following classes.

Shortly thereafter, however, the function of the stationed changed almost exclusively to the training of two-engine pilots, although the first class, as noted above, the second, and about half of the third all trained on single-engine aircraft, mainly North American AT-6As.

The fourth class to matriculate, however, Cadet Class 42-H, reported on June 3, 1942 and all members of that and subsequent classes trained on two-engine aircraft. These consisted of large numbers of Cessna AT-17A, AT-17B, UC-78 (which, at Lubbock, were coded, for example, as 044, 046, 048, 049,

This aerial view of Lubbock Army Air Field, dated August 4, 1942, looking southwest was taken well after the first AT-9s had arrived. The hot, dry, wide-open-spaces proved nearly ideal for advanced two-engine training. (USAFHRA)

(O-2-399B-BF)(8-4-42-15:25)(12-3500) AAF, AFS, LUBBOCK, TEXAS.   RESTRICTED

132, 139, and 933) and Curtiss-Wright AT-9s. A measure of the intensity of this effort may be gleaned from the fact that, between June 1942 and the end of the year, 1,237 two-engine pilots were graduated.

Cadet Edgar A. Walsh was a member of Class 42-H and successfully graduated September 6, 1942. He recalled that the AT-9 was "...*a great airplane and fun to fly. You recovered from your first power-off, gear down, full-flaps landing! Not to worry, if you looked through the slotted window just above the regular windshield, the runway was waiting for you, one way or the other! You had to maintain air speed: 110 to 120.*"

Cadet Bill Haase was in the following class, 42-I, during the second half of 1942. He remembers that "...*it was great fun flying dog fights. On power-off landings, you viewed the air strip through the upper window!*"

The experience of the 496th School Squadron is typical. The nucleus of this unit, formed at Brooks Field near San Antonio, departed there at 0800 on January 22, 1942, bound cross-country – a real trek in those days – for Lubbock. The strength of the unit at the time was one solitary officer and 50 enlisted ranks. Fifteen of the EM, who had been living off-base in San Antonio, used their own transportation, while the other 36 bounced along in two-and-a-half-ton Army trucks. The rather curious convoy straggled into Goodfellow Field, San Angelo at 1700 and stayed the night. The next morning, once again at 0800, they set out for Lubbock, and arrived at 1700 on the 23rd.

The 496th was surprised to find that they were one of eight school squadrons organizing at Lubbock and, soon after arriving, received two AT-6As. This was gradually increased into the summer, when they were replaced by AT-17s and AT-9s, a total of 16 being on hand, predominantly AT-9s. Eventually, the 496th was equipped entirely with AT-9s.

The 497th School Squadron was also organized at Brooks Field August 1st, 1941, and moved to Lubbock January 25th, where it also initially received AT-6As. In March, the unit received its first AT-9s and, by July 1942, had only AT-9s. Starting February 6, 1943, to the dismay of the training cadre, the AT-9s started to be replaced by AT-17s but this was short-lived, as the unit was redesignated as the Headquarters and Headquarters Squadron (HHS), 72nd Two-Engine Flying Training Group on April 7, 1943.

The first of 72 brand-new AT-9s started arriving at Lubbock direct from St. Louis March 23, 1942, the last of these flying in by June 19th. They were joined by six others from other stations, for a total of 78 from July 1942 through January 1943.

The accident experience of the AT-9 as a series at Lubbock proved to be unusually high, and is probably a reflection of the intensity of the training cycle there. A total of 63 accidents were suffered, some by the same aircraft as many as three times and, of these, nine fatalities occurred – four of these aboard two aircraft that experienced a mid-air collision.

The first loss took place on April 15, 1942, when 41-12063 of the 499th School Squadron, which had arrived on station on March 27th, made a very poor landing at the CAA Intermediate Field at Clarendon, TX, while being flown by 2LT Raymond A. Gilbert. The main gear collapsed and the aircraft was engulfed in flames, although the crew escaped. It was a total loss.

Unlike some training stations, Lubbock continued using AT-9s well into 1944. The last known accident involving a Lubbock-based AT-9 was on March 9, 1944 when 41-12238 – which had been involved in two previous accidents on July 27, 1942 and November 12, 1942 – collided with another aircraft while taxiing at Lubbock. It was being handled at the time by Edward H. Dance (rank unknown, but believed to have been a ground crewman) and was assigned to the 498th TEFT squadron at the time. A truly resilient aircraft, it was once again repaired and reassigned to Altus, OK September 30, 1944.

William R. Maxson was one of the long-suffering instructors at Lubbock during the war, having also performed that duty at Altus and Enid, Oklahoma. His experiences, recounted in the Vol.20, No.1, Spring 1997 issue of the NMUSAF "Friends Journal," paint a vivid picture of the trials and tribulations they faced.

"Early at Lubbock, we had not yet gotten any twin-engine aircraft, so we were instructing in the venerable AT-6A. The AT-9s finally arrived and the AT-6s departed for other bases. On a training flight with a student, I had him in the left seat and we were shooting landings at the auxiliary field. My policy with students was to let them learn by their own mistakes (within reason), so I rarely had to grab the controls from them."

"On this day, the student made a nice approach, but at the last minute I realized that he had not flared for the touchdown. The plane hit hard on the left wheel as I was grabbing the yoke and applying full throttle. We became airborne again, but the left landing gear was bent so badly that it would not lock down and would not retract."

"The locking indicator on the AT-9 was a pin that protruded up through the nacelle. When the wheels were down and locked, the pin was 'up.' When the wheels were up, the pin disappeared. In this case, I had no pin on the left nacelle, indicating that, although the gear was down, it was not locked. The right nacelle pin showed that the right gear was properly locked in the 'down' position."

"I flew back to the field and reported my trouble. The tower said to buzz them so they could look at the gear. I was happy to comply, of course. They said they couldn't tell whether the gear was locked but suggested that I fly around and use up the fuel. So I flew around, diving and pulling up hard in an effort to lock the gear down, to no avail."

"The tower then said to come in and land on the grass so I wouldn't mess up the runway for the afternoon training flights. I came in with full flaps and landed (amongst the fire trucks and ambulance) on the grass with all of the weight of the plane on the right wheel, then gently let down the left side as flying speed diminished."

"To my amazement, instead of ground-looping with a collapsed gear, the plane came to a halt straight ahead with the left gear still down. As I climbed down and started to go under the wing to look at the wheel, the Crew Chief said, 'Don't go under there, Sir, the gear is not locked!'"

A similar accident actually did impact AT-9 41-12238 of the 496th School Squadron on November 12, 1942. While being flown by 2LT's Richard S. Cornell, Jr. and Richard M. Horridge, the right gear yoke had broken in two places, and that gear, not surprisingly, gave way upon landing. The subsequent investigation, however, cleared the AT-9 as a type, as it was found that the co-pilot had unlocked the tail wheel too soon after landing, apparently without the knowledge of the Pilot in Command.

On yet another AT-9 flight, Maxson reported that "...I learned to trust my instruments on a night formation flight out of Lubbock. I was leading six ships again, and we were heading from Lubbock to Amarillo over mesa that I knew was flat as a table. It was a clear night, and I was flying VFR."

"I was looking out the side window of the AT-9 and noticed lights on the ground as though they were on the side of a hill. Very strange. There are no hills here. I checked my instrument panel then and saw that my turn-and-bank indicator was cocked way off level, indicating that I had my entire formation in a hairy

This trio of AT-9s in echelon was taken by Sgt. Herbert R. McCrory of the Lubbock AAF Photographic Section and he received an award for the image, which was published a number of times prior to August 19, 1943. The aircraft bear Field Codes in the 600s, and have their individual numbers wrapped around their extreme noses. (Sgt Herbert R. McCrory via David W. Ostrowski)

This young Cadet, unfortunately unidentified, was a member of Class 44-D at Lubbock, and stands with Field Number 701. The Lubbock AT-9s with Field Numbers in the 700s wore these on both sides of the noses. Note the cover over the wheel to avoid oil and fuel contamination. (via NMUSAF)

bank to the left! I corrected our attitude and proceeded on to Amarillo and return, carefully watching my instruments. I don't believe the rest of the flight ever knew anything was out of the ordinary.!"

Allen S. White of Alexandria, Virginia, who had been a student at Lubbock in Class 43-B, had arrived there in December 1942. He recalled that "...my first flight was in the AT-9, which I enjoyed, including the 'elevator landings.' However, during the second flight, practicing on an auxiliary field, shooting landings, the right landing gear strut broke while taxiing. As a result, all AT-9s were grounded. Cracks were found in a number of the struts. It was disappointing to finish my stay at Lubbock flying AT-17s."

Like other major AT-9 operating stations, the units at Lubbock filed their fair share of U/Rs as well, in addition to the temporary grounding noted by Cadet White above. As early as April 22, 1942, the Sub-Depot Engineer at Lubbock, Captain Robert P. Baldwin, reported that 41-12101, which had arrived new from St. Louis only 18 days earlier, along with five other AT-9s, had experienced serious leaks in the

Cadets and Cadre of Class 44-D at Lubbock AAF posing with AT-9 Field Code 708. These aircraft are believed to have been assigned to the 71ˢᵗ Two-Engine Flying Training Group and were amongst the last pilots trained on AT-9s there. (via NMUSAF)

hydraulic time lag Check Valve Assembly, and the aircraft had flown barely 8:50 since arriving. Curtiss-Wright immediately dispatched a Tech Rep, and the problem was quickly resolved.

Similarly, the 494th School Squadron reported on April 27th that they found that the gear in the elevator mechanism on 41-12059 had not been lubricated at all and had flown 78:10 since arriving new from the factory, and rather politely suggested that perhaps someone at the factory had overlooked this rather fundamental task.

The 496th School Squadron submitted yet another U/R on May 11, 1942, pointing out the difficulties with the port-side pilot's door assembly hinges – which had, as noted earlier, been reported by other stations as well. The aircraft in question, 41-12061, had already amassed a respectable 205:05 flight time.

Two Cadets of the 496th also tested the durability of AT-9 41-12210 on November 18, 1942. At about 2300 hours that night, Cadets Richard A. Randolph (PIC) and Marshall E. Ramsey III, departed on what they thought would be a routine night transition training flight. They first became aware that something was amiss at Littlefield, Texas, their first check point, about 30 miles from Lubbock, when the fuel gage indicated that excessive consumption had occurred between Lubbock and Littlefield. However, the amount of fuel expended between Littlefield and Amarillo was apparently normal.

The fuel gauge registered between 50 and 55 gallons at Amarillo. But about 15 minutes out of Amarillo, excess consumption once again became apparent. The crew contacted the Lubbock tower through a relay from AT-9 41-12215, and

they gained permission to make an emergency landing. A turn was made to try landing at the Plainview Airport, but the crew overshot the field.

After going around a second time in an effort to land, the engines stopped suddenly. The aircraft was then dead-sticked in about four miles east of Plainview.

After bouncing, hard, four times, and knocking down not less than 75 yards of fencing and two railroad switches, the aircraft finally stopped. She was a total loss, but the two relieved Cadets did not get a scratch.

No doubt popular on the flight line, members of the Woman's Army Corps (WAC) served in some numbers at Lubbock AAF during the war. Although this young lady is posing with an AT-17 or UC-78, they shared the duties up and down the line, and almost certainly also serviced AT-9s. The colored cowling of the AT-17 reveals that such markings were used at Lubbock, but for some reason, not on AT-9s. (USAFHRA)

Columbus Air Force Station, Columbus, Mississippi (13)

Station Field Code: "CO-"
Known Unit Markings: CO51, CO53, CO54, CO56, CO57, CO61, CO65, CO66, CO67, CO69, CO71, CO253, CO259, CO262, CO263, CO265, CO266, CO267, CO270, CO273, CO275, CO276, CO280, CO281, CO290, CO330 CO912
AT-9 Operating Units: ★HHS 28th Training Group ★423rd School Squadron (423rd TEFT Squadron by 1/25/1943) ★427th School Squadron (427th TEFT Squadron by 10/28/1942)

As part of the huge Army Air Corps expansion program, the War Department approved the establishment of an Army Air Station for the Columbus, MS area on June 26, 1941, following months of intense lobbying by local citizens.

On August 12th, 1941, Columbus leased a tract of land to the United States Government for $1 per year and construction commenced September 12th. On January 13, 1942, the first 100 Air Corps troops arrived and set to work building the new station.

Surprisingly, the good citizens of Columbus had not suggested a name for the new facility so, on January 22, 1942, the War Department announced that it would be named Kaye Field, in honor of Captain Sam Kaye, a World War One ace who hailed from Columbus. That name went into effect on February 24th, with accompanying signs, letter-head stationary, and APO mailing address.

However, the new name quickly became a bone of contention and potential confusion, since another nearby and recently established air base, Key Field in Meridian, MS, had a very similar sounding name. To the consternation of all concerned, the War Department arbitrarily rescinded its earlier directive and abruptly changed the name from Kaye Field to simply the Columbus Army Flying School. The new base was, initially, assigned to the parent Army Air Forces Southeast Training Center, with an AAF Pilot School (Advanced Two-Engine) activated.

The new school received its first aircraft in early 1942, consisting of nine Beech AT-10s and 21 of the survivors of the 33 Cessna AT-8s built. The first students moved to the school in mid-curriculum from Barksdale Field, Louisiana, consisting of 25 Cadets. They hit the ground running, however, starting intensive training on February 9th and graduated March 6th.

Thirty brand-new AT-9 arrived from St. Louis between May 3, 1942 and September 18, 1942, and these were augmented by 12 more "used" aircraft from Turner (Albany), GA, Valdosta and Maxwell. By March 1943, a total of 50 'straight' AT-9s had been assigned and had been joined, starting in January 1943 by the first of 27 AT-9As.

Thus, with this mix of AT-10s, AT-8s and AT-9s (joined by B-25s later) Columbus averaged a very respectable 195 two-engine graduates per month. A total of 7,766 cadets reported to the school and, of these, 7,412 graduated. The main base, with its rather unusual "V" configuration, was augmented by no fewer than eight Auxiliary Fields, most of which the students came to know well, including Columbus Auxiliary, River, Caledonia, Waterworks, Columbus Municipal Airport (the original site), Vaughn, Stinson and Starkville.

The 77 AT-9s assigned to Columbus during the war suffered a rather stunning total of 53 accidents of varying degrees of severity, of which five resulted in fatalities. The first was on May 27, 1942 when 2LT Charles A. Melody of the 427th School Squadron ran 41-5753, a former Turner Field aircraft, off the end of the primary and into a ditch. It was repaired, but was wrecked again July 16th, also in a landing accident, only to be repaired again at Brookley Field, AL, and returned to Columbus. Yet it survived, and was reassigned again to Ellington Field, TX June 7, 1943, which perhaps gives a better appreciation for the otherwise stark accident statistics.

Columbus also submitted its share of U/Rs on its resident AT-9s and, like several other stations, reported on the horizontal stabilizers and elevators, starting with 41-12140 of the 423rd TEFT Squadron on January 25, 1943. They reported cracks on the undersides of the skin, immediately behind the beam assembly, resulting in replacement of the entire assembly. In defense of the aircraft, however, by January 1943, it had amassed 851 hours at the hands of aggressively trained Cadets, and the resulting stress, according to Wright Fields response, was not unexpected.

An accident on June 29, 1942, in which Cadets Forrest J. Johnson and R. F. Gordon of the 427th School Squadron died, highlighted the ill-advised practice of conducting formation training with dissimilar types. AT-9 41-12259, coded CO266, flown by Johnson and Gordon, joined another AT-9 (coded CO330), one other AT-9 (code not known) and an AT-8 (AC41-19, coded CO218) at about 2,000 feet on the right wing, forming an echelon to the right. The pilot of CO330 wanted to get his original formation in position again, and signaled CO266 to form a "V". The AT-9, which was in the No.3 position, apparently did not see the signal, which the leader repeated more vigorously – but still was not acknowledged by the crew of CO266. As a result, the AT-9, which was in the No.2 position, crossed to the left of the lead ship and the AT-9 that was in the No.3 position moved up on the right wing of the

lead. Later, the leader gave the signal for echelon to the right. The AT-8 duly crossed under to take the No.3 position, and the formation then made a 180 degree turn to the left and gave the signal to reform in a "V" once again. Immediately, the AT-9 crossed under into the No.3 position, the AT-8 moved forward and up and then CO266, apparently realizing that the AT-8 should have moved, came back into the No.2 position and collided with the AT-8. The starboard prop of the AT-8 hit the fuselage of the AT-9 and, effectively, severed its rear fuselage. The remains of CO266 went straight into the ground. The crew of the AT-8 bailed out and survived.

Some of the accidents were due to simply poor handling. AT-9 41-5762 suffered damage November 4, 1942 when Cadets Edward L. Merrigan and R. O. Fricks of the 423rd School Squadron taxied the aircraft too fast in high grass and ran the aircraft into a depression, folding the main gear back into the cowling.

One Columbus Cadet named Frisbee recalled that "…*going from single-engine to two-engine aircraft with retractable gear, constant speed props, and more complicated systems was the most difficult transition of the entire flying training program. After wallowing around for a few hours in the Cessna AT-8, we moved up to that little hump-backed, all-metal Curtiss AT-9, which was a joy to fly. It had hydraulically operated gear and flaps, a business-like pedestal, and a panel of switches overhead. For the first time, it seemed that we were getting close to the real thing.*"

"*The AT-9 was designed with flying characteristics similar to light bombers of the time. It stalled at 85 to 90 clean; about 80 with gear and flaps down. Final approach speed was 100 mph – pretty hot for a 1940s trainer – and it was solid, light on the controls, and very responsive.*"

"*Our first instructor checked us out in the AT-8. He had one memorable peculiarity. He insisted that we taxi using only the throttle to make turns – no brakes. He was a pro at it, but most of us cadets pirouetted all the way from the ramp to the end of the runway.*"

"*When it came time to check out in the AT-9, the instructor flew once with each Cadet and then called the four of us together. 'I don't like that AT-9,' he said. 'It's a dangerous airplane. Brennan, you check Frisbee out, then Frisbee, you check Brennan out.'*"

"*A few days later, not having flown with our instructor in the meantime, night flying came up on the schedule. He told Brennan to fly the AT-9 to the sod Auxiliary Field where we would shoot night landings, then instructed Brennan and me to check each other out again.*"

"*The next day, we had a new instructor. Instructor A disappeared. I guess his one claim to fame was taxiing without brakes.*"

"*Our new instructor was older, right out of Central Casting, and a fighter pilot at heart. He loved the AT-9 and taught us to get maximum performance out of it without killing ourselves. Formation flights usually ended with him leading a rat race through towering cumulous clouds. You knew that other AT-9s were doing the same thing – and that there'd be no traffic lights at the corners.*"

Although very busy, this photo of the Columbus Army Air Field ramp on May 16, 1943 is rich with detail. At least 22 AT-9s and 10 AT-10s are on the hard-standing, as well as one solitary North American AT-6, CO15. AT-9's CO253 and CO280 at the lower right have a flag attached to their pitot tubes on the port wing, which is usually a device used to indicate an armed and loaded aircraft. In the nearer, lower left foreground are at least two AT-9 nose-cones on field work stands, and these appear to be in the process of being modified to accommodate guns. (NARA RG342FH B24204)

Another CAAF veteran, Dave Hanst, related that he flew AT-9s in advanced school in 1943. He recalled that *"…it was a great flying aircraft; landed pretty fast, and terrific for formation flying. The wings were so short you could spit over the end from the cockpit!"*

Moody Army Air Field, Valdosta, Georgia (14)

Station Field Code: "MO-"
Known Unit Markings: MO227, MO228, MO231, MO243
AT-9 Operating Units: ★31st Two-Engine Flying Training Group ★457th School Squadron ★461st School Squadron (Sp) (416st TEFT Squadron 10/23/1942) ★462nd School Squadron (462nd TEFT Squadron by 4/30/1943) ★464th School Squadron (464th TEFT Squadron 10/1942) ★466th School Squadron (466th TEFT Squadron 10/1942) ★467th School Squadron (Sp) (467th TEFT Squadron 10/23/1942)

Not to be outclassed by the citizens of Albany elsewhere in the state, the leading residents of Valdosta and surrounding Lowndes County, in the far south of Georgia, similarly appealed to Air Corps officials at Maxwell Field to engage their very willing community in the vast expansion scheme.

Impressed with the offers being extended, Air Corps engineers identified a good site some 11.5 miles north-northeast of Valdosta, near the quiet village of Bemis, part of the so-called Lakeland Flatwoods Project, amounting to some 9,300 acres which, significantly, was rated as unsuited to cultivation. To the surprise of the Air Corps planners, it was learned that the land in question was in fact owned by the U.S. Department of Agriculture, which had been doing experiments there with forest grazing. In May 1941, the USDA transferred the land to the Air Corps and construction commenced July 28th for what was envisioned as a dedicated two-engine advanced training base. It was designed to accommodate some 4,100 officers and enlisted troops and eventually consisted of 160 buildings, including 72 barracks, four 5,000-foot runways (two asphalt and two concrete) and a spur from the Georgia and Florida Railroad.

Originally cited on most aircraft assignments as simply Valdosta Army Airfield, after it was formally opened September 15, 1941 (although it had been activated on orders June 26th), it was designated as Moody Army Air Field December 6, 1941 in honor of Major George P. Moody who, ironically, had lost his life testing the very first Beech AT-10 at Wichita on May 5, 1941. Like Turner Field in Albany, Moody, too, was a major element of the huge Southeast Training Center.

Moody, like nearly every other major AT-9 operating station, enjoyed the use of five Auxiliary Airfields, and these were Moody Auxiliary No.1 (sometimes called Rockford Field) at Quitman, GA; Moody Auxiliary No.2 (Lake Park Field) near Valdosta; Moody Auxiliary No.3 (Bemiss Field); Moody Auxiliary No.4 (New River Field) at Nashville, GA; and Moody Auxiliary No.5 (Valdosta Regional Airport).

On January 8, 1943, the War Department constituted and activated the 29th Flying Training Wing (Advanced Two-Engine) at Moody and assigned it to the renamed AAF Eastern Flying Training Command.

The first of 61 AT-9s arrived from Turner Field starting on April 30, 1942, this number including 33 'used' aircraft (besides former Turner aircraft, others arrived from George Field and as far away as Ellington Field) and the balance were 'new' aircraft direct from the factory. These were followed by four 'brand new' AT-9As in September and October 1942 and 25 'used' aircraft from George Field, all on June 1, 1943, for a total of 90 AT-9s assigned.

To establish the cadre at Moody, units which had actually been formed at Turner Field were moved from that station to Valdosta – a very common exercise during the war, and all too familiar to veterans who, from ground level and boots-on-the-ground, often failed to comprehend the seemingly bizarre march and counter-march orders. These included the 461st School Squadron (Sp) which had been formed at Turner August 11, 1941, and moved to Moody January 26, 1942; the 462nd and 464th School Squadrons, both activated at Turner August 1, 1941 and moved to Moody February 2, 1942; and the 466th School Squadron, formed at Turner in December 1941 and moved to Moody in February 1942.

From available records, it appears that the units identified as operating AT-9s at Moody also mixed considerable numbers of AT-10s in amongst these in the same units, and the Beech type eventually outnumbered the AT-9s considerably. Between July and September 1944, the majority of the surviving AT-9s started departing to assorted stations, with some going to RFC surplus sites direct. Both these and the remaining AT-10s were then replaced with North American TB-25s.

Of the 90 AT-9s which saw wartime service at Moody, 47 experienced some form of accident, including five fatalities. Several of these involved Cadets from the British Commonwealth and the Nationalist Chinese Air Force. The last of these was on October 22, 1943, when Cadet Girard O. Keverkian of the 462nd TEFT Squadron executed a successful wheels-up landing near Cochran Field, Macon, GA, when he ran out of fuel. The aircraft was recovered, however, repaired, and flown to Patterson Field, OH for surplus action. The majority of the accidents experienced by Moody-based AT-9s involved take-off or landing accidents, with mid-air collisions the next most numerous. A total of 16 Moody AT-9s were surveyed as total losses; the remainder were all repairable.

Cadet Jim Davis was one of 30 cadets in Class 43-J that trained there on AT-9s, and recalled that the students were repeatedly told that they were training for assignment to P-38s. He recalled that *...that didn't happen. I remember a gunsight restricted forward visibility* [which seems to suggest that his class flew at least a few of the armed AT-9s, auth.] *and a few were lost flying into the ground during gunnery, and we were supposed to have been the last class in AT-9s at Moody. A quick snap of the yoke could generate a high-speed stall. The instructor told us if we had to bail out that we had to open the doors at the same time. With one open, the other door could not be opened at high speed."* This is the only such claim located by this writer, and is not reflected in the Pilots Manual for the aircraft.

Rosecrans Army Air Base, St. Joseph, Missouri (15)

Station Field Code: None known
Known Unit Markings: None known
AT-9 Operating Units: ★Air Transport Command 1st Operational Training Unit (Prov.) ★50th Ferry Squadron (50th Transition Training Squadron) ★51st Ferry Squadron (51st Transition Training Squadron)

Two brand-new AT-9As, 42-56854 and 42-56853 arrived at Rosecrans field on May 8, 1942. Since at the time ATC, which was the major tenant unit at Rosecrans, had responsibility for the delivery of huge numbers of new aircraft from manufacturers to the ever-expanding Army Air Forces both domestically and overseas, there was a demand for a modest local transition and familiarity training capability.

It isn't clear from surviving records what unit actually held Property Book accountability for these two aircraft – it may have been the 406th Base Headquarters and Air Base Squadron – but the units listed above apparently enjoyed the use of the two aircraft.

One of these, AT-9A 56853, while being flown by F/O Dale G. Baumgartner, pilot, and 2LT Ernest W. Vanina, Jr., both assigned to the Air Transport Command OTU (51st TTS) at the time, was obliged to perform an emergency landing back at Rosecrans at about 1030 hours December 11, 1942 while on a local navigational training flight. Apparently, the congealed oil in the prop hubs rendered the prop controls non-functional, and this was blamed on the pilot not having warmed up the engine sufficiently in the cold Missouri winter. As the field was in the process of grading some areas and had not completed snow removal, the damage was sufficient to declare the aircraft Class 26 (Instructional Airframe) by December 28, 1942.

The other AT-9A remained at Rosecrans, presumably to continue such transition training, until transferred to Altus, OK.

The ramp at Moody Army Air Field, Valdosta, GA sometime after June 1, 1943, showing not fewer than 26 AT-9As on the line, with the Crew Chief of each proudly at Parade Rest in the fore. Note that, like their cousins at Turner AAF in Albany, each had the crest of the AAFSEATC on the fuselage side just aft of the cockpit. The Moody anti-glare panels on the noses extend down over the nose of each to a point, and the engine cowls were believed painted light yellow. (NMUSAF)

Maxwell Army Air Field, Montgomery, Alabama (16)

Station Field Code: "M-"
Known Unit markings: M550, M551, M556, M557, M560
AT-9 Operating Units: 82nd School Squadron (Sp) (82nd TEFT Squadron by 2/15/1943)

One of the legacy Air Corps fields, and the original center of the Eastern Flying Training Command (Wing 4), it is not surprising that Maxwell received a sufficient number of AT-9s and AT-9As to essentially equip most of one Two-Engine Training Squadron.

Of the 14 AT-9s and six AT-9As eventually assigned, only two AT-9s and three AT-9As were 'new' aircraft, the remainder all being reassigned to Maxwell from other stations, notably Turner, Moody, Columbus, and Kelly. The first three arrived May 18, 1942 from Turner, while others dribbled in during July, August, September, and December 1942.

It is of interest to note that, of the AT-9As assigned to Maxwell, two were consistently cited in station and accident reports as type AT-9B – the significance of which, as noted earlier, has eluded determined investigation.

Being very much a Regular Army and by-the-book station, it is not surprising that the staff at Maxwell eventually ended up submitting more Unsatisfactory Reports (U/Rs) to Wright Field, per capita, than any other operating station! The first of these, dated October 23, 1942, concerned 41-12243, which had experienced cracks in the main wheel forks – a discrepancy noted elsewhere. The aircraft had a total time of 459:10 since new and the engineers at Maxwell reported they had replaced the fork once already, and that it developed cracks again after only 39:43 hours of flying.

Another U/R, dated November 2, 1942 involved all AT-9s at the station at the time. The Sub-Depot Engineering staff had found that the electrical system in the port (left) wheel wells of all of their aircraft were being exposed to excessive heat and smoke from the engine exhaust, and this had resulted in "numerous" electrical failures. Oddly, Maxwell is the only known station to have reported this problem, and Wright Field suggested local fabrication of a small access door and vents cut in the nacelle to route the fumes away from the electrical systems. It is not clear if the Sub-Depot actually made such a non-standard installation in the aircraft there or not but, if so, it must have been the subject of curiosity when the aircraft that survived moved on to other stations.

The U/R cited above may have been associated with the first known accident at Maxwell, which occurred on September 4, 1942, when 41-12226, while being flown by P/O Peter Sherriff (possibly a British Commonwealth student), assigned to the 82nd School Squadron at the time. He suffered an unspecified taxiing accident at Deatsville, AL, however, the aircraft was not badly damaged and was repaired – later passing back to Turner April 20, 1943, from whence it had arrived July 6, 1942.

The final incident at Maxwell occurred on February 15, 1943, when 41-5821 suffered damage during a bad landing. It was repaired and departed for Turner April 20, 1943 when, apparently, all surviving AT-9s at Maxwell were transferred out.

Photos of AT-9s assigned to the legacy Maxwell Field, AL are rare, thus this view of AT-9 41-12165, bearing AAFSEATC crest rather far aft of the cockpit, and Field Code M550, even though marginal, holds information value. The aircraft was assigned to Maxwell from Albany May 18, 1942 and then moved on to Turner April 20, 1943. It was lost to an accident June 1, 1944 at Luxora Auxiliary Field, AR and surveyed. (USAAF)

Kelly Field, San Antonio, Texas (17)

Station Field Code: "H-" [apparently shared with Randolph Field]
Known Unit markings: H-7, H-10, H-24, H-31, H-32, H-34
AT-9 Operating Units: ★61st School Squadron (61st TEFT squadron by 12/11/1942) ★62nd School Squadron (62nd TEFT Squadron by 12/29/1942) ★391st School Squadron ★667th School Squadron (SP) (667th BFTS by 10/28/1942 and 667 TEFTS by 11Feb43)

Yet another of the legacy Air Corps stations, Kelly Field had been the site of what was probably the very first USAAC course for multi-engine crews when, in September 1936, a course entitled Advanced 2E Pilot School opened – not formally closing, as such, until March 1943. However, it is not clear whether the duties of this organization became wrapped into the units listed above or not. It is known that, the curriculum included a course entitled Latin American Advanced 2E by 1942 and yet another labeled 2E Transition, which lasted from June 16, 1941 until February 11, 1943. It is possible that some AT-9s may have been assigned do these entities at some point.

A total of 11 AT-9s and 50 AT-9As were assigned to Kelly Field. However, in this instance, the AT-9As – all but three direct from the factory – arrived ahead of the older AT-9s between August 10, 1942 and December 12, 1942. One solitary AT-9 had been assigned 'new' to Kelly March 9, 1942, and wasn't joined by the other 10 'used' aircraft, mainly from Ellington, until April 20, 1943

All AT-9 operating units at Kelly were apparently organized differently than those assigned to other, conventional ATC stations. The 667th School Squadron (SP) is an example. This unit wasn't even organized at Kelly until May 15, 1942 and, by October 28, 1942, had been redesignated as the 667th Basic Flying Training Squadron – then back to 667th Two-Engine Flying Training Squadron February 11, 1943! The very first aircraft assigned to the unit were AT-9As 42-56861 and 42-56862, which arrived August 14, 1942 – indicating that, at least initially, the unit was a skeleton unit for planning purposes. Additional AT-9As followed, but these were joined by North American AT-6As, BC-1s and Beech AT-10s during 1942. On February 19, 1943, the unit was transferred, lock-stock-and-barrel, to Altus AAF, OK (q.v.).

By November 1, 1942, Kelly was station to no fewer than 10 Two-Engine Flying Training Squadrons – the 60th, 61st, 62nd, 63rd, 64th, 389th, 390th, 391st, 1028th and 1048th – but, of these, only those shown above have been positively identified as having operated AT-9s.

The AT-9s assigned to Kelly had perhaps the lowest accident rate of any major station. Of the 61 AT-9s and AT-9As assigned, only 13 accidents occurred and, of these, one was a mid-air collision involving

Kelly Field, TX, one of the Air Corps legacy stations, was home to at least 11 AT-9s and 59 AT-9As between August 1942 and June 1943 and thus many of these had arrived by the time of this August 7, 1942 aerial view, looking northwest. For Instructors and students, it was a far superior existence to some of the quickly established wartime stations. (USAFHRA)

(O-2444-467G-BF)(8-7-42-16:30)(12-3500)   AAF, AFS, KELLY FIELD, TEXAS. RESTRICTED

One of the more colorfully marked AT-9s, this aircraft, pictured at Kelly Field September 9, 1942, is probably AC41-5804, Field Code 131. The cowls were bright red, with a central blue line edged in white – possibly to reflect the colors of the Lone Star State. (via Dana Bell)

two aircraft, and both pilots in these aircraft were killed – one of them, P/O Claude V. Barry (flying AT-9A 42-57007), apparently, a British Commonwealth trainee.

Many of the accidents at Kelly were trivial. The experience of AT-9A 42-56996 of the 391st School Squadron on December 11, 1942, is perhaps typical.

The aircraft was being handled by Crew Chief SGT Frank A. Baldauskas, aided by PVT Gilbert Jandegian, and they had just completed a pre-flight inspection of the aircraft. SGT Baldauskas had started to taxi the aircraft to its ramp position at Kelly, and had made a right turn of about 30 degrees and a left turn of 180 degrees. He then tried to make another left turn, wending his way between other parked AT-9s when his left main gear collapsed. PVT Jandegian, riding as passenger in the right seat, had been using the hydraulic hand pump to keep the pressure up. Apparently, he inadvertently hit the landing gear selector handle, knocking it into the 'up' position. Apparently, when the aircraft dropped onto its port wing when the wheel folded up, it severely damaged the spar, and the aircraft was declared a total write-off!

Roswell Army Air Field, Roswell, New Mexico (18)

Station Field Code: "W-"
Known Unit Markings: W8
AT-9 Operating Units: ★548th School Squadron (548th TEFT Squadron by 11/18/1942) ★556th School Squadron

Yet another wartime expansion station, Roswell Army Air Field was activated September 20, 1941 on land acquired from a local rancher named David Chesser.

Roswell was actually a dedicated bombardier training station, and although it had one AT-9 equipped unit, the other three Two-Engine Flying Training Squadron resident there – the 549th, 550th and 551st – were all equipped with Beech AT-11s, which of course were designed specifically to train bombardiers. Three additional TEFTS were activated there in 1943 and, besides the AT-9s and AT-11s, the ramps were occupied with numbers of the ubiquitous Cessna AT-17 as well as Vultee BT-13A and BT-15 single-engine trainers.

The 548th was the first School Squadron to be established at the brand-new station and, shortly after activation, the hastily assembled cadre – none of whom knew each other – hustled to prepare for the first class of cadets. The eventual total of seven concrete runways (two parallel North/South, two parallel Northeast/Southwest, two parallel Northwest/Southeast and one East/West), weren't even completed as yet – so the unit initially used the rather inadequate Roswell Municipal Airport runway.

The Roswell Airport had just one building, which just happened to be a small hangar as well. This was immediately requisitioned by the USAAC and converted into a small Sub-Depot. Tents were used to accommodate the Engineering Section and Supply Rooms for the squadron.

The Air Corps personnel who were selected to perform day-to-day services at the Municipal Airport were transported each morning and evening to-and-from the slowly expanding Army Air Field by means of trucks. Mess for the men at the Airport was handled by bringing prepared food from the base in large metal containers.

Finally, the first aircraft were assigned to the Squadron, which consisted of a mix of North American AT-6As, Cessna AT-17s and AT-9s. The area surrounding the runway was rather rough, so the few level spots were used as *ad hoc* parking areas. Supplies heading for Roswell were, initially, sparse and in fact for a time the unit had to resort to local cannibalization to keep more than two of each type airworthy.

In spite of all of this, the first class of Cadets were graduated and commissioned on July 27, 1942.

Since the 548th and the other units which followed were initially operating at about 50% of authorized strength, a much-needed influx of new recruits was eagerly awaited, and these finally started dribbling in during the second half of 1942.

The second unit to organize at Roswell was, oddly, the 556th School Squadron but, by January 1, 1942, it was very understrength and unable to contribute much to the training effort, with a mix of AT-6As and AT-9s totaling eight by the last day of February. One more joined the unit in March and, by the end of April 1942, it had 12 AT-9s.

By the middle of May 1942, the unit had 10 AT-9s and two AT-6As but then, on the 20th, the AT-6As were finally transferred to another unit and, to the dismay of all, were replaced by six Cessna AT-17s, with the 10 AT-9s leaving by the end of the month. By the end of May, the unit was all AT-17, with 17 on hand.

The shortcomings of the AT-17 in the extremely hot and dry conditions at Roswell resulted in the complete withdrawal of the type to more temperate climes, and by January 31, 1943, they had been replaced by 10 Beech AT-10s (which manifested the exact same challenges), nine North American AT-24 *Mitchells* and three Vultee BT-13As. However, the durability and reliability of the AT-9 was loudly proclaimed to the Wing Commander and, between February and May 1943, five of the type were once again introduced in the squadron – the only known instance in Air Training Command that has been identified of the re-introduction of the type to a unit which had transitioned out of it.

What makes this all the more compelling is the fact that a total of only 12 AT-9s (all but one transferred around June 25, 1942 from Victorville, CA) and 25 brand-new AT-9As were stationed at Roswell – although at least four of them were identified as AT-9Bs.

An anomaly exists in the use of AT-9s at Roswell, however. The unit records for both the 548th and 556th School Squadron clearly denote the numbers of AT-9s that were with each unit as early as January 1942 and prior to June 1942. Yet, according to Individual Aircraft Record Cards, the very first AT-9 did

Remote Roswell Army Air Field in New Mexico as it appeared July 24, 1942, with three groups of AT-17s (2) and AT-9s (1), the first AT-9s having just arrived the month before. The station wasn't to become a household word until much later, following the post-war UFO phenomenon. (USAFHRA)

RESTRICTED

(016-339-0-WCDC) (7-24-42--11:35) (12-1500) ROSWELL ARMY FLYING SCHOOL, ROSWELL, N.M.

548TH. SCHOOL SQUADRON

1942

not arrive at Roswell until June 20, 1942! The AT-9As (and AT-9Bs) did not start arriving until September 1942, with the last one arriving in November 1942. It must be assumed, therefore, that the at least 12 AT-9s that were operating with these two units prior to June 1942 must have been Temporary Duty from one of the California stations, either Victorville or Mather.

The AT-9 safety record at Roswell was good, with only six accidents amongst the 37 known aircraft assigned. None were fatal.

The last AT-9s departed Roswell for other assignments starting in June 1943 and, by the end of July, all were gone. The majority went to Williams Army Air Field and Yuma.

Although only one 'complete' AT-9 survives today as part of the collection of the National Museum of the USAF at Wright-Patterson AFB, OH, the fuselage of another (42-56882) – a Roswell-based example – was recovered from its crash site in the Gila national Forest in 1991 and is now in the collection of the Pima Air and Space Museum in Tucson, AZ.

George Army Air Field, Lawrenceville, Illinois (19)

Station Field Code: "G-" and "GE-"
Known Unit Markings: G7
AT-9 Operating Units: ★Training Squadron 5 ★Training Squadron 6 ★Training Squadron 8 ★708th School Squadron ★709th Two-Engine Flying Training Squadron ★710th School Squadron (Sp) (710th TEFT Squadron 10/20/1942) ★711th School Squadron (Sp) (711th TEFT Squadron 9/9/1942)

A late-starter as part of the Air Corps expansion, George Army Air Field (not to be confused with the much more recent George Air Force Base in California) was not authorized until April 1942, with actual construction commencing in June.

Initially known simply as the Lawrence Army Flying School, it was formally dedicated as George Army Air Field in honor of General Harold H. George, who had lost his life in an accident in Australia in April 1942.

The rather distinctive field layout – from the air, appearing to be two large "V's" superimposed over one another, was made up of four main 5,200 foot concrete and asphalt runways, each one making up one of the legs of each "V".

Like most of the Air Training Command stations, George had four Auxiliary Fields, numbered simply No.1 (Presbyterian Field at Mount Carmel, IL), No.2 (Emison Field, Vincennes, IL), No.3 (St. Thomas, IN) and No.4 (Palestine, IL), all of which subsequently became well-known to AT-9 drivers.

The resident Advanced Flying School itself opened shop on August 10, 1942 as an element of the Eastern Flying Training Command and the capper organization at the station eventually was designated as the 30th Two-Engine Flying Training Group.

The first equipment delivered to the station was a large number of Beech AT-10s. These were followed, starting November 17, 1942, by 22 AT-9s (nearly all from Turner Field, GA) and were preceded (by five days) by the first of 32 factory-new AT-9As (at least two of which were identified as type AT-9B).

Apparently, after the activation and arrival of the conventionally numbered School Squadrons, the station organized at least three *ad hoc*, locally designated squadrons to consolidate training by type. These account for the non-standard Training Squadrons 5, 6 and 8 shown above, but each is known to have operated at least one AT-9. The use of these non-standard designations persisted, at least locally, however, as late as March 4, 1943.

The 708th School Squadron was activated at George Field April 10, 1942 (it had been at Moody AAF, GA). It shared a mix of North American AT-6s, AT-10s and AT-9s initially, but as other units were formed, all but the AT-6s were transferred out.

Like the 708th, the 710th School Squadron (Sp) had been activated at Moody Field, GA two days earlier, April 8, 1942, but moved to George the same day as the 708th. The 711th School Squadron (Sp) followed an identical path but arrived at George Field a day earlier on September 29th. It was equipped entirely, initially, with AT-10s.

George Field suffered a disastrous flood in May 1943, which undoubtedly not only curtailed operations but water-logged many of the wooden AT-10s that could not be evacuated. Some of the AT-9s were partially submerged, but were far easier to recover.

Although the George Field AT-9 fleet suffered 25 accidents, none were fatal, and a surprising number involved ground collisions and take-off accidents. One was lost when the port (left) propeller sheared off in flight, the only known instance of such an accident involving an AT-9.

One incident involving AT-9A 42-56933 is noteworthy. Delivered new to George November 12, 1942, it was reported missing "*...somewhere in the Continental United States*" as of December 15, 1943

Often, AT-9s that suffered accidents that resulted in damage that was considered uneconomical to repair were reclassified to what was called Class 26 (Instructional Airframe). Only one AT-9A was so designated at George Field, IL, 42-56932, which had been assigned on November 7, 1942 and suffered an accident on March 18, 1943. It went to Class 26 April 20, 1943, and this is almost certainly that aircraft. (USAAF)

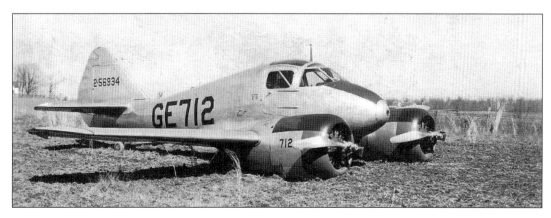

Photos of George Field AT-9s wearing the code "GE" are very rare, and GE712, serial number 42-56934, came to grief on March 3, 1943 near Lamar, Indiana, while being flown by Aviation Cadet Jay H. Chananie. Like so many forced-landings, the rugged AT-9s were quickly repairable. (via John Voss)

and, apparently, has never been accounted for since. It was administratively transferred to Valdosta, GA March 28, 1943 so as to maintain a paper-trail should its remains be located, but to this day the fate of the aircraft remains unknown. However, a completely separate accident report for the same aircraft shows it having been crashed at Moody on April 2, 1943 and declared a total loss as a result! This appears to have somehow involved an administrative SNAFU!

Cadet Joe Wolos was a student at George but, at 6 foot one, was too tall for the fighter assignment he coveted, and thus ended up at George. He reported that his training there included not only AT-9s and AT-10s, but AT-11s as well – and that it was "cold and cloudy" most of the time. He recalled one AT-9 accident while waiting for takeoff. The AT-9 ahead of him had commenced his take-off roll, accelerated, and then shot straight up, for about 30 feet, then executed a perfect wing-over to the left. It went straight in and, he said, killed both cadets aboard. However, no known accident at George matches this account.

Another Cadet at George Field, Cecil J. Ross, flew AT-9s in March and April 1943 and described the aircraft as "...a very nice plane, and much better than the AT-10s. They alternated the AT-9s and AT-10s by classes."

Stockton Field, Stockton, California (20)

Station Field Code: "K-"
Known Unit Markings: K-40, K-44, K-52, K-55
AT-9 Operating Units: ★374th Two-Engine Flying Training Squadron

An element of the Western Flying Training Command (initially known as the West Coast Training Center, headquartered at Santa Ana), Stockton Field was essentially created out of the Stockton Municipal Airport when, on August 15, 1940, the Army entered into a lease arrangement with the city of Stockton to construct and operate an Air Corps Advanced Flying School there.

The 'caretaker' unit responsible for Stockton Field was the 68th Air Base Group (Special) which, itself, was subordinate to the Flying School. The first Air Corps troops reportedly arrived on a wet December 5, 1940 on trucks. They set about erecting a tent city and then construction of the semi-permanent facilities commenced in earnest, to supplement the solitary adobe hangar which dominated the formerly civil airfield.

By December 10, 1940, a Headquarters had been established and, by January 2, 1941, the first of 90 Cadets and 25 Second Lieutenants had arrived. Initially, the station provided both Basic and Advanced training, and the station hosted an exceptionally cosmopolitan array of aircraft, including Boeing-Stearman PT-13s, PT-17s, Vultee BT-13s, BT-13As and BT-15s, North American AT-6Cs, Cessna AT-17Gs and

Stockton Field, California as it appeared June 30, 1942. It would be five more months before the first AT-9As arrived. The hard-standing and runways were to the left of this image. (USAFHRA)

98

UC-78s, Beech AT-11s, Avro (Federal) AT-20s, Stinson L-1s, North American O-47As, Northrop A-17As and starting November 5, 1941, the first AT-9s were flown in from Barksdale Field, LA. These aircraft must have been on Temporary Duty (TDY) assignment to Stockton, as there are no entries on any Individual Aircraft Record Cards substantiating this assignment. The first of 35 AT-9As did not start arriving until November 5, 1942.

Stockton was actually the first of the three major training fields in California, the others having been Victorville and Mather (q.v.). Like the other training fields, Stockton enjoyed the use of not fewer than five Auxiliary Fields to aid instruction, A1 (Kingsbury), A3 (Tracy New Jerusalem), A4 (Modesto), A5 (Tracy) and A6 (Franklin).

The Stockton Field Advanced Flying School was formally dedicated January 11, 1941 and, within five weeks the 68th Air Base Group (Special) had been joined by the 80th and 81st School Squadrons. So far as can be determined, however, neither of these operated AT-9s. The first class of Cadets (90) and Commissioned students (25 2LTs) graduated on March 14, 1941. By the end of the year and with the entry into the war, Stockton had outgrown the original runway layout, and three 800 by 4,600-foot runways were eventually completed as well as 60 more buildings.

The Stockton school eventually graduated an average of 200 Cadets every eight weeks or so and, of the 36 pilots who flew on the famous Tokyo Raid led by Colonel Jimmy Doolittle in 1942, 11 had actually graduated at Stockton, and thus trained at least in part on AT-9s.

The 374th TEFT Squadron submitted an interesting Unsatisfactory Report (U/R) to Wright Field on February 21, 1943 involving the Type M-2 generators installed on, oddly, only the port (left) side engines of the 28 AT-9As assigned, which by then averaged about 230 hours total time each since arriving brand-new. These had been observed to be overheating and burning out in excessive numbers – a fault not noted at any other AT-9 operating station! 1LT E. M. Douthett, the Engineering Officer for the Squadron, recommended a local 'fix' for this condition, involving the installation of a fuse in the left nacelle junction box. Probably to his surprise, Wright Field concurred in his recommendation and authorized him to retrofit all of his AT-9As in this manner, thus making them unique in the USAAF. He also noted, as a rather oblique compliment to the aircraft, that "...*no other U/Rs have been submitted on the AT-9s*" by his unit or station.

Of the at least 35 AT-9s assigned to Stockton, only seven experienced accidents – all but one involving take-off, landing or taxi accidents, and only one aircraft (42-56958) was a total loss, all the others being repaired and, starting June 1, 1943, being passed on to other stations – mainly Williams Field in Arizona. The single lost aircraft, AT-9A 42-56958, flown by 2LT Ralph A. Bush of the 374th TEFT Squadron, had somehow damaged his undercarriage on take-off and considered a forced landing at the

AT-9As served at Stockton, CA only briefly – less than a year – and most moved on to training stations in Arizona. Rarely illustrated, these three bear Field Codes K-52, K-44 and K-40. The middle aircraft, 42-56943, arrived new around November 10, 1942. Oddly, the Individual Aircraft history Card for this aircraft is missing, although it is known to have been at Douglas AAF, AZ by March 1944. (USAAF via Peter M. Bowers)

A lineup of three of the principle types found at Stockton AAF in late 1942. Nearest is AT-9A 42-56955, which arrived new November 13, 1942, next to a rare Cessna AT-17G and an AT-6C. The Stockton AT-9As were devoid of even anti-glare paint, although K-55 does appear to have had her nose cone painted yellow or orange. The aircraft moved on to Williams AAF, AZ June 1, 1943 and was surplused February 15, 1945 (USAAF via Peter M. Bowers)

Modesto Auxiliary Field but were advised to take to their parachutes instead. Stockton thus enjoyed the best safety record on AT-9s of any of the 25 major operating stations.

Two of the accidents that it did suffer, however, are probably typical of those experienced elsewhere in the USAAF training establishment, and attest to the fact that, all-too-often, pilot error contributed to the 'hot' reputation of the aircraft.

On January 14, 1943, 2LT Owen V. Kiggins, accompanied by 1LT Thurlo T. Gerlach of the 374th were getting ready to ferry AT-9A 42-56989 from Stockton to Victorville. Prior to take-off, the PIC, 2LT Kiggins, told passenger 1LT Gerlach, who was a non-rated Squadron Engineering Officer, to take care of raising the wheels. Gerlach claimed that, after the take-off begun, the pilot nodded his head, at which time he dutifully pressed the hydraulic power button to raise the gear. Then the PIC said "OK" and Gerlach raised the wheels. Before raising the gear, Gerlach did not look to see if the aircraft was actually off the ground, but acted on what he thought was the PIC's signal only. The pilot, on the other hand, claimed that he neither nodded his head nor said "OK!"

The Accident Investigation Board was not amused. They stated bluntly that Lieutenant Gerlach "... *might have erroneously interpreted one signal, but not two*" and that pilot Kiggins had actually given the "wheels up" signal – whatever it was – too soon, and was thus charged with "*100% poor judgement.*" The aircraft, despite what was described as a "*spectacular cleaving of the runway with thousands of sparks thrown off*" was repaired and transferred to Williams Field June 1, 1943. It is probably safe to bet that it never flew quite right again after this experience.

2LTs Vernon M. Gray and C. E. Good were thoroughly embarrassed on April 1, 1943, after having been asked to demonstrate the flying qualities of the AT-9A (in this case, 42-56926) to an upper class of Aviation Cadets in Class 43-F then in training at Chico Basic Army Flying School in far northern California. PIC Gray made his final approach to Chico wheels-up, flaps down – and all the while the Chico tower thought the pilot was demonstrating and was going to make a high-speed, low pass after retracting his flaps. Gray, on the other hand, claimed that the indicators on the instrument panel showed the wheels "down and locked," and fully intended to land – which he did, to the enormous gratification of Class 43-F. This aircraft, too, after somehow being repaired, was sent off to Williams Field, AZ for further adventures.

Blytheville Army Air Field, Blytheville, Arkansas (21)

Station Field Code: "BL-"
Known Unit Markings: BL101, BL102, BL103, BL107, BL109, BL111, BL114, BL118, BL125 BL128, BL157, 208M
AT-9 Operating Units: ★Cadet Detachment, HHS Blytheville AAF ★HHS 25th Two-Engine Flying Training Group ★HHS 26th Two-Engine Flying Training Group ★698th Two-Engine Flying Training Squadron ★699th Two-Engine Flying Training Squadron ★700th Two-Engine Flying Training Squadron ★701st Two-Engine Flying Training Squadron ★702nd Two-Engine Flying Training Squadron ★703rd Two-Engine Flying Training Squadron ★708th Two-Engine Flying Training Squadron ★2111st Base Unit

Part of the USAAF's huge 70,000 Pilot Training Program, Blytheville Army Air Field wasn't activated for flight operations until June 10, 1942, and its initial caretaker unit was the 326th Base Headquarters

Although a bit fuzzy, BL101 (41-12274) was the first AT-9 assigned to Blytheville AAF, arriving from Moody AAF via Tyndal AAF, FL November 3, 1942. It survived to go to the RFC October 27, 1944, and was probably another of the armed AT-9s. (Carharts via Northern Ky Photos)

and Air Base Squadron. One of the western-most units of the Southeast Training Command, the 25th Two-Engine Flying Training Group was activated June 25th with, initially, four subordinate units – the 700th, 701st, 702nd and 703rd TEFTS's.

The station was located three miles northwest of Blytheville and, at peak activity, had three Auxiliary Fields in support: Cooter, located 19 miles northeast of the base; Manila, 13.5 miles west and 1.3 miles northeast of the town of the same name; and Steele, 12.3 miles north and 2.5 miles west-northwest of Steele, MO.

The station was one of the major operating stations for Beech AT-10s, Cessna AT-17s and AT-9s and, between November 20, 1942 and the end of the war, a total of 68 AT-9s and 80 AT-9As were assigned there.

The station was very much an 'expansion' facility. The 700th School Squadron (Sp) had actually been activated at Columbus, MS May 16, 1942 but was moved to Blytheville October 23, 1942 and redesignated as the 700th TEFT Squadron. Initially, it had Vultee BT-13s and BT-13As, which were shortly exchanged for North American AT-6s and Beech AT-10s. Then, starting in January 1943, every single AT-9 and AT-9A then at Blytheville was assigned to the squadron. Significantly, this unit's official history attests to the little-known conversion of at least 19 AT-9s to carry a single .30 caliber machine gun in the nose. It stated that "...a group of the airplanes had been equipped with .30 caliber machine guns to give gunnery practice to Cadets." Indeed, on September 11, 1943, 14 AT-9s so equipped flew in formation to Eglin Field, Florida, for the express purpose of gunnery practice, firing somewhere in excess of 20,000 rounds in the process. A second such mission was dispatched to Columbus, MS along with their own organic armorers, and 18 AT-9s fired more than 30,000 rounds there over a 10-day period. The 700th TEFT Squadron was, so far as can be determined, the solitary ATC unit so equipped and tasked, and the unit was disbanded April 30, 1944, its gun equipped AT-9s being subsequently dispersed.

The 701st School Squadron (Sp) was also activated at Columbus, MS but was transferred to Blytheville July 24, 1942, where it was redesignated as the 701st TEFT Squadron October 29, 1942. Although primarily equipped with AT-10s and AT-17s, it is believed that a few AT-9s were assigned intermittently, and at least two AT-9A were with the unit as of January 13, 1944.

The 702nd School Squadron also originated at Columbus, MS, where it was activated May 16, 1942, but moved to Blytheville July 25th. It, too, was redesignated as the 702nd TEFT Squadron October 20,

Blytheville AAF, Arkansas, was a major AT-9 station. This AT-9A, BL128 is one of the rarely illustrated armed aircraft, the muzzle of the .30 caliber machine gun visible just above the passing light aperture on top of the nose cone. With red engine cows and anti-glare panels extending the length of the nacelles, plus the SEATC emblem aft of the cockpit, the aircraft has no ant-glare panel over the nose!. (NMUSAF)

A very well-traveled aircraft indeed, 41-12122, coded BL157, had served in turn at Turner, Moody and George AAF's before moving to Blytheville AAF, AR very late on July 13, 1944. It was surplused to the Aeronautical University of Chicago, where it was used in a rather desultory manner as a training aid. The unusually small size and placement of the serial number on the vertical fin is of interest. (NMUSAF)

1942, and was disbanded April 26, 1944. Although surviving unit records do not speak of equipment assigned, it is believed the unit used a mix of AT-10s, AT-17s and AT-9s in about equal numbers and AT-9As were definitely assigned to the unit as of December 21, 1943. The experience of the 703rd School Squadron (Sp) was similar, but it was activated at Blytheville August 13, 1942 and redesignated as the 703rd TEFT Squadron October 23, 1942. It, too, is believed to have used a mix of AT-10s, AT-17s and AT-9s, and definitely had AT-9As on strength as late as February 10, 1944.

Blytheville's AT-9 fleet suffered perhaps the highest accident rate of any operating station. Of the known total of 148 AT-9s and AT-9As assigned, only 40 remained completely unscathed! As elsewhere, however, the vast majority of the incidents experienced involved landing, take-off or taxiing accident and the majority of these were assigned to the large 700th TEFT Squadron at the time of their accident experience. However, since there was an unusually high number of night formation flight training sorties from Blytheville, apparently in response to an ATC request, at least 11 aircraft were involved in such events – all but one of which were lost. A total of nine Cadets were killed as the result of accidents involving AT-9s based at Blytheville, four of them aboard two of the AT-9s which had collided, however.

The first AT-9 accident at Blytheville was on November 25, 1942 when Cadet Ralph W. Howard of the 698th TEFT Squadron experienced a landing accident in AT-9A 42-56872 (although the Accident Report had garbled the serial number, giving it as "42-36672" which was a Piper L-4A that never served at Blytheville). A surprising number of 'straight' AT-9s which suffered accidents while stationed at Blytheville were, perhaps erroneously, cited on the official report documents as type AT-9A.

Some of the accidents experienced by AT-9s based at Blytheville occurred far-afield, and AT-9A 42-57131 (BL125) of the 700th TEFT Squadron is a good example. This aircraft was on a long-range navigation training flight to Rochester and Albany, NY when it stalled and crashed on take-off at Albany. Similarly, AT-9 41-5824 (BL113), was on a cross-country flight from Blytheville via Knoxville, TN to Hickory, NC on September 24, 1943 when, upon landing, the port main folded, resulting in a ground-loop to the left, although the pilot, 2LT Charles Lindsay, admitted it had been an "exceptionally" hard landing. The aircraft was assigned to the HHS 26th TEFT Group at the time. AT-9 41-12161 of the 700th TEFT Squadron had an exciting time on February 22, 1944 while taking part in formation flight training with Cadet Willis C. Holder at the controls. While trailing the lead aircraft, cadet Holder noticed a slight oil leak on top of the port cowling, and immediately brought this to the attention of the Instructor, 2LT Edward C. Pinckert, followed shortly by an explosion. Lieutenant Pinckert immediately assumed control of the aircraft and trimmed it for single-engine operation, but they could not hold altitude, true to the AT-9's reputation. However, they managed to make a complete turn to the north to try and make home field, but it didn't appear that would be possible. The crew could see Millington Naval Air Station, however, to the southeast, and they informed the lead aircraft that they were going to try for it. By then, their altitude was only about 1,000 feet and, after turning towards the NAS, they kept sinking. The lead aircraft flew on ahead and guided 41-12161 to the NAS and obtained clearance for them to make an emergency landing. At about 200 feet, they were within gliding distance of the southwest runway and, after lining up, put the gear down. Lieutenant Pinckert then greased it onto the runway, and at the same time instilling confidence in the much-maligned AT-9 in the mind of Cadet Holder!

The final accident suffered by an AT-9 at Blytheville occurred on June 19, 1944 at the Manila Auxiliary Field while being flown by Raymond C. O'Neil. Ironically, it, too, was a landing accident, and the aircraft was assigned to the 2111th Base Unit at the time, suggesting that it was most likely a purely administrative flight. It was sufficiently damaged to be surveyed as a total loss June 20th. Apparently, by around April 1944, the primary TEFTSs had been essentially stood-down, and most, if not all, of the surviving AT-9s at Blytheville were reassigned to the 2111th Base Unit. At least one AT-9A, 42-57015, was assigned to the HHS, 26th TEFT Group by May 10, 1943.

Bob Abresch was initially assigned to fly as a Cadet on Beech AT-10s at Blytheville but recalled that *"...they took all of the AT-10s away and brought in AT-9s. We were told at the time that we were the only base with AT-9s and were training to go into P-38s. They lied, and they all ended up as co-pilots in Boeing B-17s. The AT-9 was a great aircraft and I did aerobatics in them."*

Blackland Army Flying School, Waco No.2, Waco, Texas (22)

Station Field Code: None used
Known Unit Markings: 220, 224, 230, 313, 318, 320, 328, 599
AT-9 Operating Units: ★33rd Flying Training Wing (Advanced Two-Engine) ★73rd Two-Engine Flying Training Group ★871st Two-Engine Flying Training Squadron ★873rd Two-Engine Flying Training Squadron

Often confused by some historians as the base just to the northeast of Waco, Texas (Waco No.1) Blackland AFS (Waco No.2) was actually located about 6.5 miles northwest of Waco. An element of the Central Flying Training Command, the base was not activated for two-engine flying training until December 15, 1942, so was a relative late-comer to ATC. Prior to that, it had been designated as of July 2, 1942 as a dedicated glider training station. Most of the initial cadre were moved there, overland, from the former AAF Gulf Coast Training Center based at Ellington Field

Besides the three units known to have operated AT-9s at Blackland, there were five other TEFTs (the 868th, 869th, 870th, 872nd, and 874th) and one Single Engine Flying Training Squadron (the 875th) at Blackland by November 1, 1942.

A total 26 AT-9s and 34 AT-9As (all but one of them factory-fresh) were stationed at Blackland between December 12, 1942 and January 14, 1943. Most of the AT-9s were formerly at Ellington Field near Houston, although six flew in from Lubbock. The base also operated much larger numbers of

Often overlooked in the Training Command scheme of things, Blackland AAF was the "other" Army field near Waco, Texas, and at least 26 AT-9s and 34 AT-9As served there between December 1942 and mid-1943. This August 4, 1942 view is looking almost due east, with Waco off to the lower right some distance. (USAFHRA)

103

AT-9 41-12172, a former Ellington AAF machine, Field Code 224 and two AT-9As formate over Texas out of Blackland AAF after December 14, 1942. The BAAF AT-9 fleet were unique in all having the lower sides of the rear fuselage painted black. Note that all three have antiglare panes extending the entire length of the engine cowls and nacelles, but only the AT-9As have the area in front of the windscreen painted. (AAHS)

Beech AT-10s (with Unit Markings in the '100s'), Cessna AT-17s and UC-78s (with Unit Markings in the '400s') and, eventually, North American TB-25s.

Although an overwhelming majority of Cadets at Blackland were USAAF Cadets, the station hosted three Peruvian Air Corps 1st Lieutenants for a 10-week two-engine course starting October 19, 1944 – but it is doubtful if they flew AT-9s, as they were being prepared for the Lend-Lease delivery of a batch of Cessna AT-17Bs. Twelve Cuban Army Air Force pilots also trained at Blackland but they, too, probably only trained on AT-10s and AT-17s.

The accident experience of the AT-9s at Blackland was good, with only 11 incidents having been recorded, although there were two fatalities – one was when AT-9A 42-57006 and AT-9 41-12099 experienced a mid-air collision (in a flight of six aircraft) about 25 miles northwest of Waco on January 24, 1943 (the latter landed successfully and was repaired) and the other February 2, 1943 about 4.5 miles southwest of the main base when Ralph L. Lightsey, Jr. collided with the ground while apparently hot-dogging.

There was one perplexing mass transfer of at least 23 of the 26 AT-9s on or about January 31, 1943 when they were transferred, at least on paper, to Winnsboro, Texas. There was no known AAF or ATC activity at Winnsboro during the war, and the reason for this transfer is a mystery. All had returned to Blackland by February 28, 1943.

The AT-9's sojourn at Blackland lasted until as late as November 20, 1944, when most of the survivors were flown out to Altus, OK.

This Blackland AAF, TX AT-9A, 42-57149, Field Number 599, shows the rear fuselage undersides black paint that was unique to aircraft stationed there. Only two training squadrons operated AT-9s at BAAF. (NMUSAF)

104

Douglas Army Air Field, Douglas, Arizona (23)

Station Field Code: "A-"
Known Unit Markings: A-25, A-420
AT-9 Operating Units: ★HHS 37th Two-Engine Flying Training Group ★986th Two-Engine Flying Training Squadron ★987th Two-Engine Flying Training Squadron ★988th Two-Engine Flying Training Squadron ★1109th Two-Engine Flying Training Squadron ★1112th Two-Engine Flying Training Squadron ★1113th Two-Engine Flying Training Squadron ★3014th Base Unit

Construction commenced on the former Douglas Municipal Airport in June 1942, destined to be renamed, simply, as Douglas Army Air Field, using some 2,000 acres of former ranch land. The field was located 8.5 miles north-northwest of Douglas

By the time construction concluded, the new training station boasted six operational runways, all over 7,000 feet in length, 16 taxiways, a large parking ramp and seven generous hangars as well as an eventual total of some 418 buildings.

The vast expanses of the arid, good weather region were nearly perfect for advanced, two-engine training – aside from the ever-present heat and scarcity of water. DAAF, like most of the training stations, had five Auxiliary Air Fields. These were McNeal Field (Auxiliary No.1); Forrest Field (Auxiliary No.2); Webb Coutland (Elfrida) Field (Auxiliary No.3); Auxiliary No.4 (the name of which had not been noted) and Hereford Army Air Field (Auxiliary No.5).

DAAF was formally activated May 28, 1942 as an element of the AAF Western Flying Training Command, and the major operating unit was the 83rd Flying Training Wing (Advanced Two-Engine).

Initially, DAAF was home to a substantial number of North American BT-14s, which were flown in from Randolph Field, TX, quantities of assorted North American AT-6s, large numbers of Cessna AT-17s and UC-78s, and of course AT-9s.

Although at least 44 AT-9s and 73 AT-9As were nominally assigned to Douglas, commencing as early as December 12, 1942, the vast majority formerly assigned at Williams and Yuma, it is not clear how many of these were actually engaged in two-engine training there. Only 15 of the AT-9As were factory-fresh, new aircraft; all the rest were 'used' aircraft. By March 14, 1944, a total of 138 AT-9s (75 AT-9s and 63 AT-9As) were all assigned to the massive 987th TEFT Squadron and, at the same time, all AT-17s and UC-78s at the station were assigned to the 986th TEFT Squadron. Operations were apparently in decline, due to the curtailment of demand for multi-engine pilots as the war situation improved – but also because DAAF had been experiencing an acute shortage of AT-9 struts, tires and tubes – while the AT-17/UC-78 fleet, similarly, was experiencing a shortage of type-specific tools.

A peek in the Curtiss-Wright St. Louis hangar reveals one of the first of the C-76 transports, with an excellent opportunity to compare the scale of AT-9A 42-57068 under her port wing. This aircraft was flown directly to Douglas Army Air Field January 13, 1943 and spent its entire service lifer there, being surplused February 3, 1945. Note the complete absence of any insignia, including anti-glare paneling and the improved-tread tires. (Curtiss via Mark Nankivil)

In fact, the official DAAF history went so far as to proclaim that the training establishment there was "...*apparently at the extreme end of the supply chain, exacerbated by the fact that the station had grown so rapidly that supply procedures and trained personnel were simply not prepared for delivery of the requested spares in any event. Thus, a definite supply "problem" was created and soon, certain grounded aircraft were being stripped to supply others so that they might continue operation. Another important problem that the supply system had to contend with was that, somehow, the 986th TEFT Squadron had been assigned several different types of aircraft, instead of the one type – AT-17s – used by most of the other line squadron in existence at the base at the time.*"

The complaints of the 986th appear to have been justified. This single unit had on strength examples of the Vultee BT-13A and BT-15, Cessna UC-78Bs and UC-78Cs, AT-17s, AT-17A and AT-17Bs and, of course, AT-9s and AT-9As! The BT-13s and BT-15s appear to have suffered more than the twins, but it ranged the gamut: starters, tires, wheels, canopy sections, spark plugs, instruments, throttle cables, struts, tail wheels and, last but not least, replacement engines.

By the end of December 1942, after DAAF came on line for training, the field was operating a total of 124 AT-17Bs and an assortment of 106 UC-78s and AT-17Cs, plus 84 AT-9s and AT-9As, plus 41 BT-13As and 26 BT-15s. The sheer numbers of *Bobcats* dictated the numbers of flying hours during the month, leading with a very-respectable 8,500 hours, followed by the AT-9 fleet with a modest 1,600 hours.

Only one Unsatisfactory Report (U/R) was submitted to Wright Field by any DAAF unit, and that originated with the 986th TEFT Squadron on March 18, 1943. Once again, and echoing the experience at other stations, it involved cracks and failed spot-welds on the horizontal stabilizer. Given that all of the AT-9s at DAAF were very "used" aircraft, perhaps this was, in retrospect, not too surprising. The aircraft in question was AT-9A 42-57081 which had amassed 215:55 since arrival at the station.

The AT-9 accident experience at DAAF was dismal. Every single AT-9 experienced some form of mishap, of which at least five were fatal. Of these, at least 16 were experienced by the 987th TEFT Squadron, followed by the 3014th Base Unit with 14, the 986th TEFT Squadron with nine, the 1112th TEFT squadron with only one and the 1113th TEFT Squadron with three. The majority involved taxi, take-off and landing accidents but were punctuated with the almost inevitable mid-air collisions as well. The AT-9As fared somewhat better with a total of 23 incidents, with two of them involving fatalities – again, due to a mid-air collision. Of the total of 23 incidents, 10 were while with the 3014th BU, six with the 986th TEFT Squadron, two with the 987th and one while with the 1109th TEFT Squadron.

As with Williams Field, also in fairly close proximity to Mexico, DAAF contributed one AT-9A to the list of known *Jeeps* to end their days in the remote reaches of the Republic to the south. AT-9A 42-57069, which had arrived new from St. Louis February 16, 1943 crashed less than a month later about 145 miles south of DAAF near Nacon, Chico, Sonora, Mexico on April 20, 1943. The pilot, P/O David M. Kerr, reportedly an RAF two-engine student, along with passenger 2LT Frank B. Neal, had become completely lost on a navigation training flight and exhausted his fuel. Over extremely rugged and deso-

An excellent color study of AT-9A 42-57038, which arrived new at Douglas AAF, AZ January 7, 1943 and was coded A-420. Moving on to Yuma by August 25, she was involved in a collision with AT-6C 41-32872 there and sent to Class 26 in November 1943. Colour photo see page 171. (NARA RG342-FH via Stan Piet)

late terrain, with no suitable landing area anywhere in sight, they had taken to their parachutes, apparently successfully. The aircraft crashed and burned.

The Cadet experiences at Douglas were similar to other two-engine training bases. Cadet Phillip G. Day of Class 44-C arrived there in early January 1944. He recalled the AT-17s and UC-78s with disdain, referring to them as "...*conventional geared (main wheels retractable), twin engine nothing. It taxied poorly, but it flew practically by itself. I called it 'nothing' back then, but really it was an excellent plane for its intended use and I did enjoy flying it,*" a rather oblique observation on the pleasant handling qualities of the aircraft. He often flew from the Hereford Auxiliary Field about 40 miles west of DAAF. He spoke highly of the AT-9, however, citing it as having been "...*far more realistic and more like a combat aircraft for training.*"

The Individual Flight Record of 2LT Donald J. Armand, assigned as an Instructor to the HHS of the 37th TEFT Group as of April 1944 provides a snap-shot of what might be regarded as a typical monthly flight experience at DAAF as of that time. During the month, he flew a total of 31:20 in AT-9s, 8:50 in AT-9As, 36:30 in UC-78Bs, 9:00 in AT-17Bs and 3:45 in AT-17Cs.

He recalled his unit starting to receive AT-9s in February 1944, in an article in the Spring 1997 issue of the NMUSAF "Friends Journal." "*Although it was about the same size as the AT-17s, it was a whole lot more airplane to fly.*"

"*My first flight in an AT-9 was on February 12th, and I immediately knew I wanted to get into an AT-9 squadron. I managed to sandwich in flights in AT-9s between my regular student flying, and by the time I had built up around 20 hours in them, I was moved into that type for my next class, which started around March 19th.*"

"*My first class in the AT-9 consisted of five students, and except for one of them, they were all a year or two older than I, since I had just turned 20 on January 20th. They were a good group, and had no more than the usual problems in dealing with advanced training. I remember one thing, though. They were really impressed with the AT-9.*"

"*As my time built up in the plane, I liked it more-and-more. It demanded my full attention, but as long as I stayed ahead of it, it was a joy to fly.*"

Robert Dawson, who was an NCO Crew Chief on AT-9As at Douglas during the war on 42-56913 recalled that the aircraft was widely regarded as "...*a fine aircraft, and my aircraft never gave me any problems. All of the AT-9s in our squadron had large numbers painted in red to indicate they were instrument training ships,*" a factoid that came as a surprise to this writer.

A number of WASPs were assigned to DAAF, including Marge Martin (*nee* Neyman), and they flew an assortment of utility, administrative and engineering flights on BT-14s, UC-78s, AT-17s, B-25s and AT-9s. Marge recalled the AT-9 as "...*a terrible airplane to fly! It was a 'hot ship,' and would ground loop, and was hard to get slowed down and back on the ground!*"

La Junta Army Air Field, La Junta, Colorado (24)

Station Field Code: "J-"
Known Unit Markings: J-76, J-82
AT-9 Operating Units: ★1010th Two-Engine Flying Training Squadron
Assigned as a facility of the West Coast AAF Training Center/AAF Western Flying Training Command, this expansion training field was active between August 4, 1942 and June 30, 1945. Located 4.2 miles north-northeast of La Junta, the base had four Auxiliary Fields: Rocky Ford (Auxiliary No.1, 13.4 miles NW of La Junta AAF); Las Animas (Auxiliary No.2, 19 miles NE); La Junta No.2 (1.5 miles WSW) and Arlington (Auxiliary No.4, 28 miles NNE).

La Junta AAF did not receive its first AT-9s until mid-November 1942, when the first of 27 started arriving – all from Victorville, California. These were followed December 19th by 15 new AT-9As.

The AT-9 experience at La Junta was relatively short-lived, however and, by November 1943, all had been transferred out, the majority going to Williams AAF, AZ, Yuma AAF, AZ or Lowry AAF, CO.

The single known AT-9 operating unit had arrived at La Junta from Minter Field, CA as the 1010th School Squadron (Sp) sometime after August 12, 1942, with a transfer staff of two officers and 75 enlisted ranks. By November 27th, it had been redesignated as the 1010th Two-Engine Flying Training Squadron.

The safety record of the AT-9 at La Junta, where they joined numerous North American AT-6s of various subtypes, the ubiquitous AT-17s and UC-78s, as well as a couple of exotic North American P-64s, was better-than-average. Only seven accidents were record amongst the 42 AT-9s which eventually reached the station, the first on March 3, 1943 – and perhaps to no one's surprise, it was a landing accident. Every single one of these was repaired and returned to service, with the last recorded accident occurring to a Class 43-E student, cadet Charles R. Waddell at the Rocky Ford Auxiliary on April 28,

An interesting overhead view of the La Junta Army Air Field, Colorado, as of November 13, 1942, two days before the first AT-9s arrived. (USAFHRA)

Two AT-9s and an AT-17 on the ramp at La Junta AAF, CO in December 1942. The AT-9s appear to have had the leading edges of their cowlings painted different colors, but show no evidence of anti-glare paneling. Since there was only one AT-9 operating unit at La Junta, this suggests that different cowl colors were used for sections within one unit there. (Sgt. Meyers, Base Photo Office via USAFHRA)

1943 – a wheel-up emergency landing when both engines failed simultaneously. In correspondence dated November 27, 1942, the station Engineering Officer did not mince words: he blamed a number of technical difficulties being experienced on the AT-9s received from Victorville on very poor maintenance of the aircraft there just prior to their transfer – unfortunately an all too common occurrence throughout the AAF!

La Junta AAF AT-9s are rarely illustrated wearing their Field Codes. Here are J-82 (AT-9A 42-57088 which arrived new on January 13, 1943) and J-76. Note AT-17 J-2 in the background. J-82 was transferred to Williams AAF, AZ by June and survived to go to the RFC January 11, 1945. (Sgt. Meyers, Base Photo Office via USAFHRA)

Marfa Army Air Field, Marfa, Texas (25)

Station Field Code: "N-"
Known Unit Markings: None known
AT-9 Operating Units: ★932nd Two-Engine Flying Training Squadron [unconfirmed]

For anyone who has ever been to Marfa, Texas – in more recent years a delightful artists' colony – there will certainly be agreement on one central observation: you have to work pretty hard to get there. It is about as remote as one can get in the huge state of Texas.

A station of the Western Flying Training Command, Marfa witnessed large numbers of Cessna AT-17s and UC-78s (at least 49 by January 1943; by the end of 1943 there were 364!), and, later, North American TB-25s. It was also host to a modest Nationalist Chinese Training Detachment from late 1944, and graduates of the Advanced Flying Training School there included some famous personalities, including Robert Serling and Mario Lanza.

Inexplicably, between January 21 and February 9, 1943, Ferry Command crews flew in a total of 18 AT-9As to Marfa direct from the factory, via intermediate stops. However, by June 1, 1943, every single one of them had been transferred out, mainly to Yuma AAF, AZ, but others went back to Ferry Command stations for further reassignment.

Station histories of Marfa confirm that six AT-9s arrived in January, followed by more in February, but do not cite the unit of assignment. Concurrently, the 932nd TEFTS relocated to Marfa AAF January 15, 1943 (see accompanying photo of their Orderly Room sign). This unit had been activated at Albuquerque, NM July 16, 1942, moved to Carlsbad AAF, NM in August and then to Marfa. The unit history of this squadron makes no mention of the aircraft they were to train on, so it may be that they were intended to use AT-9s, as their sign proudly illustrates, but "the powers that be" settled on standardization at the station on AT-17/UC-78s instead. Thus, if any of the AT-9s that actually reached Marfa got the Field Code prefix "N," it was probably only very briefly.

The Orderly Room sign for the 932nd TEFTS certainly suggests that the Marfa AAF, TX-based two-engine training squadron had some relationship with the AT-9! However, if so, it was apparently either truncated or short-lived. (via Ken Crist)

ASSIGNMENTS
OF AT-9 AIRCRAFT TO TACTICAL UNITS

Many readers will be surprised to see the above chapter heading, and perhaps to learn that not only were a small number of AT-9s assigned to tactical combat and support units, but that they in fact served with some of those units for a considerable period.

It will come as no surprise, however, that nearly all of these assignments were to Lockheed P-38 *Lightning* two-engine fighter units, and that all were stationed at strategic points along the West Coast of the United States. The decision to assign AT-9s to these units in particular, is in a way a virtual vindication of the design purpose of the aircraft, which apparently, Air Corps planners regarded as the best aircraft to perform necessary transition functions for those units. It is significant that no Beech AT-10s or Cessna AT-17/UC-78s were assigned to these units for this purpose.

The AAF was assigning a very high priority to bringing these new interceptors on line to defend against potential Japanese air raids against war related industrial and military targets along the lengthy coastline, several of which had in fact occurred with submarine-launched aircraft. Thus, a high priority had been assigned to getting new production P-38s to these units as rapidly as possible and to convert as many available single-engine pursuit pilots as possible to the new aircraft.

It seems clear that, since these aircraft were assigned in the coastal defense zone to tactical units, that at least some of them were camouflaged and, according to one veteran, some even wore the distinctive unit insignia of the P-38 unit to which assigned, although, unfortunately, no photographic evidence has surfaced to support this latter report.

The units of assignment have been listed in numeric order, based on the Squadron and Group of assignment.

7th Tow Target Squadron, 4th Ground Air Support Command

While stationed at March Field, California, this unit, although not exactly a "tactical unit" in the conventional sense, was for reasons that are not clear, assigned AT-9 41-5775 on July 10, 1942, having arrived from the little-known Army component of North Island, CA Naval Air Station.

Exactly what a Tow Target Squadron was expected to do with an AT-9 isn't clear, as so far as is known, no dedicated target towing mechanism was ever designed or engineered for the type. It may

have served as a relatively high-speed tracking target for the vital anti-aircraft batteries and search-light units spotted around major California cities, industrial and military facilities.

The aircraft suffered an accident on August 3, 1942 while practicing touch-and-go landings and take-offs as part of transition training, under the control of two Reserve Officers on Extended Active Duty, 2LT Russell S. Wilson (PIC) and 1LT Dorsey E. Pohlenz. It isn't clear exactly what happened. The aircraft had touched down and the tail came up, as though preparing to take off again, when the aircraft abruptly nosed over The official Accident Report described it as a 'ground loop,' but extant, low-quality photos of the aircraft clearly show it on its back. Remarkably, Wilson suffered no injuries whatsoever, while

Pohlenz received slight cuts and bruises in exiting the aircraft inverted. The aircraft had amassed 414:05 total time since delivery to the Air Corps December 23, 1941. It was surveyed as a complete write-off July 15, 1942.

So far as can be determined, this was the solitary AT-9 operated by a Tow Target Squadron, and, at the time, the 7th was also operating North American BC-1s, AT-6As, Culver PQ-8s and Stinson L-1As.

83rd Fighter Squadron, 78th Fighter Group

Two AT-9s, 41-11957 and 41-12025 were assigned to this unit on May 17, 1942, while it was assigned to Hamilton Field, both having arrived from Mather AAF. 41-12025 was transferred to Oakland AAB shortly thereafter, on June 12, but returned to Hamilton September 20th. It then moved to Oakland on October 8th but once again returned to Hamilton November 16th. It then moved to Muroc Air Base with the unit on November 11th, probably providing not only a training platform for transition, but a convenient unit 'hack' as well.

The other aircraft, 41-11957 was transferred briefly to San Bruno on June 10, 1942 and then on to Oakland June 19th, but returned to Hamilton July 3rd. It went to Mather again on August 21s, but again returned to Hamilton on September 1st – these movements probably reflecting the organizational reassignments that were taking place throughout California as newly formed units were moved about to adjust to crowded conditions and conflicting priorities at this point in the war. The aircraft suffered a landing accident at Hamilton on September 14, 1942, while being flown by Marlon J. Leikness. It was repaired, however, and transferred to McChord Field, Washington November 18th to yet another P-38 unit (q.v.).

The 83rd had been constituted originally as the 83rd Pursuit Squadron (Interceptor) on January 13, 1942 and activated February 9th at Baer Field, Indiana. It had been redesignated as the 83rd Fighter Squadron May 15, 1942 after having moved to Muroc AB, CA April 30th, just before getting the AT-9s. It moved to Mills Field, CA May 10th, then Hamilton on June 23rd before movement overseas to England around December 1, 1942.

97th Fighter Squadron (TE), 82nd Fighter Group

This unit received two AT-9s, 41-12024 on May 21, and 41-12038 on May 26, 1942 (both from Mather Field), while the squadron was stationed at March Field, CA. Of these, 41-12038 suffered an accident August 8, 1942 on arrival at Long Beach Municipal Airport at 0930 while being flown by S/Sgt Harry R. Morris, Jr., a rare Army NCO Pilot, and co-pilot S/Sgt Jack R. Kingrey, who were described on the Accident Report as "Specialized Trainees". They were on a training flight from their home station at March.

The aircraft had been accepted from the manufacturer March 16, 1942 and had, as of the date of the accident, amassed 562:25 total time. As had happened so often with AT-9s, the PIC had inadvertently released the landing gear lever after the aircraft had landed and had taxied about 200 yards, apparently having mistaken the landing gear lever for the tail-wheel lock release. Both pilots had already had more than 25 hours on the aircraft, so the error was surprising.

41-12038 was sent to Santa Ana, CA, and then Glendale, probably for repair to the modest damage, and then on to other assignments. The other aircraft, 41-12024, was apparently only with the squadron a brief time, or possibly transferred with it when it moved to Glendale on May 26, 1942.

332nd Fighter Squadron Training Detachment
329th Fighter Group, IV Fighter Command, Fourth Air Force

The 332nd Fighter Squadron was constituted June 24, 1942 and activated July 10th at Hamilton Field, CA. It apparently received AT-9 41-12024 from Mines Field, CA around November 10, 1942 and moved it to Santa Ana December 8th, where its Training Detachment was located. Then, on January 31, 1943 it moved to Glendale and on to Muroc AB February 28, 1943.

The AT-9 was performing a transition training flight with instructor 1LT R. M. Spradlin checking out 2LT Joseph C. Solko on the aircraft at Santa Ana on December 21, 1942 when, while preparing to take-off, Lieutenant Solko mistook the landing gear lever for the tail wheel lock – an all-too-familiar mistake. The aircraft may have been wearing Mission Symbol U-5 at the time, but this isn't clear. Five 332nd Lieutenants had been scheduled to be checked out in the aircraft that day at Santa Ana. The aircraft was repaired and survived the war, eventually going to the surplus center at Hat Box Field, Muskogee, OK.

A very well-traveled AT-9. 41-11978 is pictured here, camouflaged, with the 338th Fighter Squadron at Mc-Chord Field, WA on August 10, 1942. Delivered new to Mather Field, CA March 3, 1942, she moved with the P-38 unit on numerous occasions in Washington and Oregon before going to Luke Field October 23, 1942, then on to routine twin-training duties at Williams and Douglas AAF, AZ by June 1, 1943. She was surveyed due to fair wear-and-tear July 15, 1944. (Peter M. Bowers)

This unit had been constituted as the 97th Pursuit Squadron (Interceptor) January 13, 1942 and also activated on February 9, 1942 at Harding Field, LA. It was redesignated as the 97th Fighter Squadron May 15, 1942 after having moved to Muroc AB, CA April 17th. It moved, at least on paper, to Long Beach between May 22nd and September 16, 1942, preparatory to overseas deployment to Northern Ireland and then Algeria starting in October 1942.

337th Fighter Squadron, 329th Fighter Group
IV Fighter Command, Fourth Air Force

Constituted on August 29, 1942 and activated September 11th, this unit was essentially an Operational Training Unit. Initially stationed at Glendale, CA, it moved, probably for training, to Muroc AB, CA by March 12, 1943.

The unit was assigned at least one AT-9, 41-5852, which had arrived, as noted below, from McChord Field, WA on October 13, 1942. It was at Glendale by November 11th, then went to Van Nuys on the 16th, then to Muroc AB December 21st, and back to Glendale January 31, 1943. This aircraft gained the dubious distinction of being the solitary AT-9 known to have crashed with four persons aboard – the type's design limit – while on take-off on an administrative flight from Glendale to Muroc. An unnamed Lieutenant had flown the aircraft from Muroc just prior to the flight to pick up the other three on board and return them to Muroc, where the Squadron was temporarily based for training.

The aircraft took off after an "*...unusually short run,*" considering it had four on board, swerved sharply to the left and, according to several witnesses, "mushed" at about 50 feet – barely missing the control tower – then the empennage of the aircraft struck a high-tension wire pole, severing it completely and doubling it back over the center section of the fuselage, and the remains crashed into a street in Glendale, hurtling end-over-end. Surprisingly, there was no fire.

The actual cause of the crash was difficult to determine. Three of the four on board were killed, including pilot Captain Robert H. Kacy, co-pilot S/Sgt Merle F. Robison, and passenger PFC George E. Herman. The fourth person on board, also a passenger in the rear, T/Sgt Joseph Corell, was seriously injured. The Accident Investigation Board concluded that the aircraft may have been about to ground-loop, and was headed towards the control tower at the time and the pilot, seeing the obstruction ahead, forced the aircraft into flight too early, not being able to achieve flying speed. There was also a possibility that the starboard (right) cabin door may have blown open just after the aircraft left the ground, or shortly thereafter, which may have caused the aircraft to swerve.

The accident was actually the result of a series of errors, and the result of hasty, last-minute decisions. S/Sgt Robison, an NCO pilot, was supposed to fly the aircraft back to Muroc and had commented to the very fortunate survivor, T/Sgt Corell, that he felt there was "*...something wrong with the aircraft,*" and that he "*was jittery*" and that the flight down from Muroc, with him as co-pilot to the unknown Lieutenant, "*...was some trip.*" He also volunteered the information that, although he had been listed as co-pilot on the flight from Muroc, he had himself not as yet flown an AT-9 as PIC, and that the return flight would have been his first time. Corell recalled that, when he boarded the aircraft for the return flight to Muroc, he had climbed into the co-pilot's seat on the right and that Robison had assumed the Pilot's seat when, suddenly, a Lieutenant Brooks and Captain Kacy came running out to the aircraft shouting that they would have to make room for another man, which was Captain Kacy. Corell moved to the snug back seat with PFC Herman, and Robison asked who would fly. Kacy indicated that he would, and quickly started both engines. According to Corell, at that point, both Kacy and Robison complained that the aircraft "...*was not acting right*," as the tail kept jerking around. They then had to wait a while as a civilian airliner was on approach. As they finally started their take-off roll, Corell said that "...*after about 25 feet, the plane jerked left – the whole thing.*" The pilot then pulled up, there was a sudden explosion, and the last thing Corell remembered was Captain Kacy saying "*Oh oh.*" He also said he felt good about Kacy flying the aircraft, as he had been flying the aircraft quite a bit during transition training.

One witness, who saw the aircraft arrive earlier, stated that he had observed the aircraft arriving, and noticed that the starboard door had flown open while the aircraft was on final approach.

The 337th may have operated one other AT-9, 41-12025, which arrived at Glendale from Hamilton November 11, 1942 and followed almost exactly the same movements as 41-5852. It survived the war to go to the surplus center at Hat Box Field, OK.

338th Fighter Squadron, 55th Fighter Group

Not constituted until September 10, 1942 and activated on the 12th at Paine Field, Everett, Washington, this P-38 unit conducted intensive training in the Pacific Northwest, moving back-and-forth to Olympia, WA, McChord Field, Tacoma, WA and Portland, OR – with occasional detachments to remote Port Angeles, WA, covering the vital Strait of Juan de Fuqua, until finally deployed to England in mid-September 1943.

During its Operational Training in Washington and Oregon, the 338th enjoyed the services of four AT-9s. Aircraft 41-11978 had actually arrived at McChord from Portland on June 12, 1942, ahead of the squadron, which had been expected earlier. This aircraft, along with 41-11957, had the distinction of having been the most northerly assigned AT-9s, as they both moved to Port Angeles, WA January 31, 1943 with a small detachment of P-38s and, it is alleged, made several 'international' flights to Royal Canadian Air Force stations in nearby British Columbia, Canada, while there. The truth is, they were almost certainly used as light transports to move personnel and light equipment from the parent unit at McChord. 41-5852 arrived at McChord on July 20, 1942 from Olympia, whilst 41-5797, having arrived at Olympia on July 30, 1942, moved on to Paine Field August 18th, then to McChord August 24th and back to Paine Field September 30th. It then moved south to California to yet another P-38 unit, the 337th Fighter Squadron (q.v.). Finally 41-11957, which arrived from Hamilton Field, CA, on November 8, 1942.

It appears that all four of these AT-9s were camouflaged while operating in the PNW. One of them, 41-11957, which had apparently been "making the rounds" of P-38 OTU units, suffered an accident at McChord at 1350 hours on July 21, 1943 while Corporal Roland H. Quartemont, the Crew Chief, was running up its engines during a routine pre-flight check. Once again, the poorly positioned gear lever was the culprit. Corporal Quartemont stated that, while pressing the time lag handle, the landing gear selector lever "...*jumped from down position to 'up' position' and the gear abruptly collapsed.*" The aircraft was repaired and survived the war, last being stationed at Altus AAF, OK, and in fact may be the subject of our un-serialed color side view.

371st Fighter Squadron, 360th Fighter Group
IV Fighter Command, Fourth Air Force

Constituted December 20, 1942 and activated January 15, 1943 at March Field, CA, this unit moved, effectively the same day, to Glendale and then on to Muroc April 14, 1943. For all intents and purposes, it was an Operational Training Unit (OTU).

One AT-9, 41-12038 was delivered to the unit while at Glendale February 28, 1942 and then moved, with the unit, to Muroc by April 20, 1943. It suffered an accident there on May 13, 1943, while being flown by 1LT John A. Stege, PIC, and 1LT J. C. Lentz, while they were taxiing out to take off for a cross-country training flight to March Field. Stege, in true fighter pilot fashion, was reportedly taxiing too fast – about 30 mph – while enjoying a brisk tail wind as well, and promptly ground-looped. This aircraft was one of the few assigned to a tactical unit that was not camouflaged, but it did have red chevrons running aft diagonally from inboard of the engine nacelles to the trailing edges of the upper wings. The damage to the aircraft was apparently more severe than existing images of the wreck suggest, as it was surveyed in September.

OTHER AT-9
ASSIGNMENTS

In previous Chapters, virtually all assignments of AT-9s direct to stations and training as new-build units were described in more-or-less chronological order of assignment.

But as with many other Air Corps and AAF types, as the initial wartime emergency and urgency waned, AT-9s found their way into some nearly bizarre circumstances.

In this chapter, we resort to a simple alphabetic order to these myriad assignments, for the sake of simplicity and reference. Some of these assignments involved truly remarkable numbers of aircraft, especially as the war situation improved and the demands on the far-flung Air Training Command installations and units dropped precipitously. The AAF recognized that the AT-9s remained valuable training assets, but decided to consolidate many of them at several specific stations, while others were apparently released from dedicated training duties to perform what amounted to, it at least appears, liaison and communications duties.

A few of the assignments found on the Individual Aircraft Record Cards have defied explanation while other assignments, which inexplicably were *not* noted on IAHCs but which were found in official AAF documents, have also remained a mystery.

Aeronautical University, Chicago, Illinois

Station Field Code: N/A
Known Unit Markings: N/A
AT-9 Operating Units: N/A
One AT-9 (apparently 41-12122, formerly at Blytheville, AR as BL157) and one AT-9A (42-56954), formerly at Kelly Field, were acquired via different means by this trade school. The AT-9A was actually bailed to the University direct from Kelly Field as a Class 26 (Instructional Airframe) January 21, 1943 – the earliest known bailment to a civilian institution. The aircraft had suffered an accident at Kelly January 3, 1943 and was apparently judged non-economically repairable for continued flight operations.

AT-9 41-12122 after being passed to the Aeronautical University of Chicago in rather poor condition after the war, with a North American O-47A in the background. Formerly BL157 at Blytheville AAF, note the presence of color on the leading edge of the engine cowls and complete absence of anti-glare paneling. Now examine the following image. (NMUSAF)

Here is AT-9 41-12122, ex-BL157 at Chicago Midway Airport as photographed by Robert L. Taylor of the AAA shortly after the war. Compare this with the previous image. The engine cowls now have no color on the leading edge, there is evidence of anti-glare paneling on top of the cowl and nacelles and in front of the windscreen, and some sort of writing on the fuselage just under the windscreen! Clearly the students at the Aeronautical University had been busy! (Robert L. Taylor, AAA)

Photographed at Chicago Airport in 1946, AT-9 41-12064 was last assigned to Randolph Field, TX, but the coding on the fuselage, 208M, is strongly suggestive of some association with Altus AAF, OK. It is believed to have been passed to the Aeronautical University along with perhaps two others, but the paper trail is silent on ownership. (Art Krieger via David W. Ostrowski)

The AT-9 was acquired as war-surplus under a priority system giving educational institutions first-pick sometime after going to the Reconstruction Finance Corporation October 4, 1944.

Also known as the Curtiss-Wright Aeronautical University, the downtown building at 1338-1342 South Michigan Avenue was apparently supplemented by a hangar and small structures at Midway Airport, where the AT-9s, a North American O-47, at least one Cessna AT-17 and possibly several other aircraft were used to give students at the University hands-on experience in structures, repair and servicing. The facilities at Midway apparently survived as late as 1950, when they – and presumably the aircraft – were destroyed in a hangar fire.

Air Transport Command

Station Field Code: None known
Known Unit Markings: None known
AT-9 Operating Units: Possibly ★526th AAF base Unit

At least three AT-9As, 42-57126, 42-57128 and 42-57129, which had originally been assigned to Marfa, TX (42-57126 February 6, 1943) and Blytheville, AR (the other two, February 5, 1943), were transferred to Nashville, TN June 1, 1943 for ATC. The trio were actually picked up on the Property Book of ATC at Washington, DC but stationed at Nashville.

Since the only known organization at Nashville structured to operate and service aircraft was the 526th AAF Base Unit, it is likely that they were maintained by that organization for support of Ferry Command activities.

All three had moved on to Altus AAF, OK sometime between October 1943 and February 1944 where they returned to training activities.

Ajo Gunnery Range, Ajo, Arizona

Station Field Code: "X-" and "Y-"
Known Unit Markings: None known
AT-9 Operating Units: ★944th Single-Engine Gunnery Training squadron

The Ajo Gunnery Range was established August 22, 1941 on about 1,426 acres at the remote village of Ajo, AZ and, initially, was designated as a sub-post of Luke Army Air Field as a sub-set of the larger Gila Bend Gunnery Range in Maricopa County. The principle garrisoned unit, initially, was the 543rd School Squadron which was in actuality, a tow-target unit providing targets for aerial gunnery.

In June 1943, however, the Ajo Range was transferred to Williams Army Air Field and was upgraded with three runways and a sizeable parking apron. By then, it was operated by the 472nd (Reduced) Army Air Force Base Unit and was an element of the AAF West Coast Training Center.

Besides the very first AT-9, 41-5745, which was dispatched on special assignment from Wright Field to Ajo to test the installation of the .30 caliber machine gun in its nose, a single Beech AT-10 was apparently similarly modified and tested at Ajo at around the same time. The AT-10 did not fare well, as it was found very difficult to keep the gun on target due to the flex in the wooden structure supporting the mounting.

AT-9s from Williams operated into Ajo with some frequency, and apparently at least four, 41-5778, 41-5880, 41-11978 and 41-12026 were assigned to the 944th Single-Engine Gunnery Training Squadron, which was detached there from Williams for a short time between July and September 1943, although one can only wonder what use was made of the aircraft with such a unit. These may have been amongst the aircraft converted under TI-1395 to carry .30 caliber guns.

Naval Air Station Alameda, Alameda, California

Station Field Code: N/A
Known Unit Markings: N/A
AT-9 Operating Units: Unknown

This entry constitutes one of the enduring mysteries of the wartime use – or perhaps intended use – of the AT-9 series.

No fewer than 44 AT-9s and three AT-9As, all but one of which had originally been identified for delivery new from the manufacturer to Albany, GA, suddenly had their initial posting changed to Alameda between September 26 and November 1942. Then, just as suddenly, the same aircraft were once again assigned, according to their IAHCs, to Albany or, in two instances, Blytheville, AR.

It appears that only one of these 47 aircraft actually made the trip to California, and that was AT-9 41-11959 which had previously served at Victorville, where it suffered a serious accident on July 15, 1942 and then, for some reason by way of the Las Vegas AAF, NV, was assigned to the Post Schools at Alameda as a Class 26 instructional airframe.

So far as can be ascertained, other than the Post Schools noted above, the Army Air Corps did not have a significant presence at Alameda at this point in the war, other than some use as a loading point (Port of Embarkation, or POE) for some aircraft being shipped with urgency to Australia.

It has been speculated that, since the Lockheed P-38 series was, by this juncture, being introduced in some numbers to Fifth Air Force units in and around Australia, that the AT-9s were in fact intended for shipment there to aid local single-engine Army fighter pilots transition out of P-39s and P-40s into P-38s. While this would be consistent with AAF procedures then being engaged in P-38 units in California, Oregon and Washington state at about the same time, it may well have been decided that using valuable deck space on ships bound for distant Australia might be better served by dispatching more combatant types, rather than two-engine trainers.

Altus Army Air Field, Altus, Oklahoma

Station Field Code: None used
Known Unit Markings: 25, 26M, 33, 39, 137, 176M, 184M, 195-A
AT-9 Operating Units: ★HHS 66th Two-Engine Flying Training Group ★453rd Base Headquarters and Air Base Squadron ★667th Two-Engine Flying Training Squadron ★1097th Two-Engine Flying Training Squadron ★1100th Two-Engine Flying Training Squadron ★2508th Base Unit

Established initially as the AAF Advanced Flying School, Altus, OK, and not renamed as Altus Army Air Field until April 8, 1943 and finally the AAF Pilot School (Advanced TE) August 6, 1943, the station had initially been assigned as an element of the AAF Gulf Coast Training Center on June 26, 1942, but passed to the AAF Central Flying Training Command July 31, 1943.

The field was – and still is – located 3.5 miles east-northeast of Altus, a small town of about 8,600 souls. It eventually boasted four runways, each of 6,000 feet by 150 feet and, during the war, two large hangars. It eventually had four Auxiliary Fields: Auxiliary No.1 (Blair Field, 10 miles NNW); Auxiliary 2A (Victory Field, 10 miles West); Auxiliary No.3 (Olustee Field, 13.3 miles SW) and Auxiliary No.4 (Headrick Field, 9 miles ESE). It is known that there was also an Auxiliary Field at Hobart, OK, as well, but for some reason the number has not survived.

Work on construction of the field in remote, far southwestern Oklahoma, started on June 3, 1942, amidst difficulty in locating firms which could manage to undertake the task at so isolated a destination. Above average rainfall hampered the efforts of the construction crews during the late summer and into the fall of 1942, although the construction substantially improved the fortunes of the ranchers and farmers surrounding the new station – and the unusual rainfall helped bring in record alfalfa, cotton, and wheat crops, as well as an experimental peanut crop.

But it wasn't until January 10, 1943, that the first training aircraft landed at the freshly completed station, in this instance a formation of Beech AT-10s direct from Wichita, Kansas. They were followed, four days later, by the first Curtiss-Wright AT-9s, and training commenced in earnest two days later. The AT-10s and AT-9s were eventually joined by substantial numbers of Cessna AT-17s and UC-78s.

Although there was no way of knowing it at the time, Altus was destined to become one of the major AT-9 operating stations, but with the nearly unique distinction of acquiring only used and, in some instances, *very* used aircraft. Between January 14, 1943 and the end of the war, a total of 135 AT-9s and 64 AT-9As reached the base from every point on the compass

The four Two-Engine Flying Training Squadrons that eventually operated at Altus (1097th through 1100th) had originally been formed at Kelly Field, TX by November 1942, but of these, only the 1097th and 1100th, plus the 667th, are known to have operated AT-9s in a dedicated training role.

From the commencement of training, the 667th TEFT Squadron was the first to stand-up with AT-9s, although this had started while the unit was still at Kelly Field, TX in August 1942 – the unit having been activated there May 15, 1942 as the 667th School Squadron (Sp). It was redesignated as the 667th TEFT Squadron October 28, 1942. The very first aircraft assigned were two AT-9As (42-56861 and 862). The unit transferred to Altus February 19, 1943, accounting for the "zero" aircraft on strength entry for January 1943. Their experience with the aircraft assigned between August 1942 and February 1943 is fairly representative of a TEFT and the gradual standardization which most experienced. The following

A sunny day, May 4, 1944 at Altus AAF, OK, showing AT-9A 42-56953 bearing the bright red empennage (with yellow serial numbers) and peculiar Field Code style unique to Altus. The entire engine cowling also appears to have been painted red. This well-traveled aircraft had started at Kelly AAF, TX, then migrated to Pampa and George AAF, IL before arriving at Altus sometime after July 6, 1943. It survived to go to the RFC April 30, 1945. (USAFHRA)

chart tracks that experience. The numbers clearly reflect not only the turbulence experienced in terms of the breadth of aircraft types on strength, but also the sheer size of the organization during this period.[1]

Aircraft Assigned to the 667th Two-Engine Flying Training Squadron, between August 1942 – April 1944

Month and Year	Aircraft Type	Number on Hand	Aircraft Received from Factories	Aircraft at Depots	Aircraft on Survey
August 1942	AT-6A	7	0	1	0
	AT-9	2	2	0	0
	AT-10	6	6	2	0
	BC-1A	8	0	2	0
September 1942	AT-6A	2	0	0	0
	AT-9	3	2	1	0
	AT-10	15	12	0	1
	BC-1A	7	0	0	1
October 1942	AT-9	3	0	0	0
	AT-10	20	4	3	0
November 1942	AT-9	4	2	1	0
	AT-10	9	0	2	1
December 1942	AT-9	0	0	0	0
	AT-10	1	0	1	0
January 1943	0	0	0	0	0
February 1943	AT-9	8	0	2	0
	AT-9A	4	0	0	0
March 1943	AT-9	8	0	2	0
	AT-9A	4	0	0	0
April 1943	AT-9	17	0	4	0
	AT-9A	7	0	1	0
May 1943	AT-9	17	0	5	0
	AT-9A	7	0	0	0
June 1943	AT-9	17	0	4	0
	AT-9A	7	0	0	0
July 1943	AT-9	16	0	4	1
	AT-9A	7	0	3	0
August 1943	AT-9	27	0	4	0
	AT-9A	8	0	2	0
September 1943	AT-9	29	0	6	0
	AT-9A	9	0	2	0
October 1943	AT-9	11	0	1	0
	AT-9A	10	0	3	0
	AT-10	3	0	0	0
November 1943	AT-9	11	0	4	0
	AT-9A	10	0	1	0
	AT-10	4	0	0	0
December 1943	AT-9	30	0	1	0
	AT-9A	11	0	2	0
January 1944	AT-9	33	0	0	0
	AT-9A	19	0	0	0
	AT-17	2	0	0	0
	AT-17B	5	0	0	0
	UC-78B	56	0	0	0
	UC-78C	4	0	0	0

---

1   In studying this chart, a brief look at the total numbers of two-engine training aircraft in the Central Flying Training Command as of June 30, 1944 might be helpful. Scattered throughout the Command were 363 Beech AT-10s, an astonishing 642 Beech AT-11s, 244 Cessna AT-17s and 205 Curtiss-Wright AT-9s. Of these, a combined 197 were at Altus but, by August 1944, this had dropped to 140.

	AT-9	46	0	0	0
	AT-9A	25	0	0	0
	AT-17	2	0	0	0
February 1944	AT-17B	5	0	0	0
	UC-78	1	0	0	0
	UC-78B	50	0	0	0
	UC-78C	6	0	0	0
March 1944	AT-9	69	0	0	0
	AT-9A	41	0	0	0
April 1944	AT-9	67	0	0	0
	AT-9A	41	0	0	0

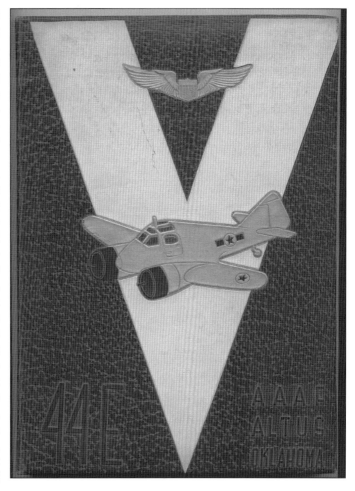

AT-9 caricatures graced the front covers of a surprising number of so-called Class Books, including that for Class 44-E, one of the final AT-9 classes, at Altus AAF. (Class 44-E via Ted Young)

The 667th was an extremely aggressive operator of the AT-9. Of the 94 accidents suffered by AT-9s at Altus during their tenure there, 42 of them were amongst aircraft assigned to this squadron (30 on AT-9s and 12 on AT-9As) while the AT-17s suffered only one and 11 more on the UC-78Bs which, to no one's surprise, were not flown as much. The above chart ends in April 1944 for the pure and simple reason that the unit was stood down and its aircraft and personnel assimilated into the 2508th Base Unit and HHS, 66th Two-Engine Flying Training Group on April 30th.

HHS 66th Flying Training Group became a hybrid unit. Usually, a Headquarters and Headquarters Squadron was simply that: they usually comprised only the Commander of the Group, his staff, and perhaps a small flying detachment. By the end of April 1944, however, the Squadron had become much larger than its TO&E authorized and was actively assuming many of the actual training functions of the defunct 667th, which had been one of its subordinate units. It had been transferring out the AT-17s and UC-78s which had previously been on strength and assimilating AT-9s in their place. By June, the Squadron had 68 AT-9s, 37 AT-9As and 18 UC-78Bs. With these, they managed to train "on the line" 207 Cadets, who had been attached to the unit. Presaging things to come, while the instructors found the aircraft refreshing after the AT-17s and UC-78Bs, the greatest trouble with the AT-9s was directly attributable to their landing gear. The unit suffered 11 AT-9 accidents, and every one of them was attributed to the main gear; however, again in fairness, a number of these had taken place because the gear had not been locked-down when landing. S/Sgt Leo B. Robinson of the Squadron, an electrical specialist, was credited with designing and perfecting a device that lit a green light when the gear on AT-9s were down-and-locked. It was a very simple device to install and it was thought might have prevented untold numbers of AT-9 accidents had it been conceived years earlier. Thus, the aircraft of HHS 66th TEFT Group were the sole AT-9s so modified. The Commander rewarded Robinson by sending him TDY to Wright Field to demonstrate his device. Unfortunately, it came too late for the AT-9 as a type. Robinson got back to Altus to learn that his unit had been disbanded effective April 30, 1944 and, like the 667th TEFT Squadron, all personnel and equipment were transferred to the 2508th Base Unit.

The following chart provides a useful snapshot of the overall aircraft assignment picture for Altus that were actually engaged in training activities during the peak period of January 30, 1943 through February 29, 1944.

Aircraft Assigned to Altus AAF between January 30, 1942 – February 9, 1944

Date	AT-9 and AT-9A	L-3C	AT-10	RB-18	AT-17	BC-1A	UC-78	Total
1/30/43	15		6		15	3		39
2/28/43	25		1		67	3		96
3/31/43	25				81	3	18	127
4/30/43	25				35	3	93	156

5/31/43	25				36	3	94	158
6/30/43	25	1			18	3	106	153
7/31/43	24	1			25	3	129	182
8/31/43	33				35	3	139	210
9/30/43	39				22	3	106	170
10/31/43	42				2	3	31	78
11/30/43	43		12		6	3	118	182
12/31/43	43			1	12		144	200
1/31/44	51	1		1	12		180	245
2/29/44	72	1			12		178	263

The Altus AAF maintenance folks designed a blind-flying installation unique to AT-9As and, according to their own history, AT-9Bs stationed there, placed in use around October 15, 1943. This has never been illustrated previously. (USAFHRA)

Altus maintainers also designed and fabricated special wheel covers for the considerable numbers of AT-9s and AT-17s assigned, to protect them from the intense heat and engine liquids. (USAFHRA)

While illuminating in terms of following the ebb-and-flow of the several trainer types, these numbers are only part of the story. Clearly, during this 13-month period, the AT-9 fleet expanded significantly, while the largely worn-out AT-17s were gradually replaced by UC-78s. However, what was actually happening was that after February 1944, at least 100 more AT-9s and AT-9As arrived, and most went to operable storage and, as the three AT-9 operating units experienced losses or accidents, these were replaced by the best and lowest-time AT-9s that were in operable storage.

The period between March 1 and May 1st, 1944 saw enormous changes in the training tempo and organizational structure of the formerly hectic station. The previously heavily tasked Headquarters of the supporting 393rd Sub-Depot was inactivated as a functioning organization during the first week of March. The Base Supply Division, which had been mainly concerned during March and April with requisitions and stocking of parts for the burgeoning AT-9 fleet at Altus, which had arrived in a flood specifically to replace the AT-17s and UC-78s, witnessed an almost complete clear out of parts for the Cessna types. One can only imagine the daily trauma this must have generated in the stock rooms.

The hard-working Base Maintenance Division, where all types were serviced had, by the second week of March 1944, achieved a very commendable in-commission rate of 96%. As the AT-9s started arriving on practically an hourly basis, the condition of many of the aircraft, added to a momentary surge in the accident rate of the type due to lack of experience on type, put a strain on the Division and the in-commission rate dropped to 82%. Beginning with Class 44-E on March 15, 1944, all flying instruction at Altus was given exclusively on AT-9s, and intensive use of these continued through May 1944.

On April 30, 1944, at one minute to midnight, the base was stunned to learn that the Headquarters and Headquarters Squadron of the parent 66th Two-Engine Training Group was inactivated and all its personnel and equipment were transferred to the now mammoth 2508th AAF Base Unit. Altus suddenly had only one massive unit.

On May 31, 1944, a committee of officers from Headquarters, CFTC, ATC and Air Service Command met at Oklahoma City and then at Altus to consider the advisability of continuing instruction on AT-9s. After the conference, and the physical examination of a number of the aircraft, the committee concurred in grounding all AT-9s for student training purposes – a momentous decision under any circumstances. The decision was based on a number of reasons, a growing shortage of spare parts being one of the main reasons – but the chief culprit was the main landing gear which, after nearly four years of very hard daily use, were failing in ever increasing numbers.

During the month of May alone, 24 aircraft accidents had occurred at Altus. After the grounding order, the total dropped to 10 in June. Undoubtedly, the reduction in accidents was due in part to the change in aircraft types used for student training. However, during June there was also an extensive awareness program launched at the base to achieve greater safety consciousness – and more efficient maintenance, so it wasn't all about the AT-9 as a type

As a result of the committee's decision mentioned above, 199 AT-9s and AT-9As were formally grounded effective May 31, 1944. This action followed a month during which the AT-9s had clocked an amazing 24,232 flying hours – and with the grounding, necessitated their replacement with corresponding numbers of other similar types as soon as possible – and ironically, these consisted almost entirely of Cessna AT-17s and UC-78s – the very types that the AT-9 had replaced not long before as unsuitable! The official Altus station history had this to say about the committee's decision. "*The AT-17 and UC-78s were considered to be types affording the poorest training possibilities, and it was noted that, at Lubbock*

This AT-9 migrated to Altus April 20, 1943 and had previously served at Ellington and Blackland in Texas. Coded simply '25" (repeated in small numerals on either side of the nose cone) is was apparently assigned to Class 44-E and wore orange engine cowls and ant-glare on the inner-sides of the cowlings and part of the nose. (Class 44-E via Ted Young)

121

Humor was often associated with the AT-9, and this image, appearing in the Class 44-E commemorative book, pretty much says it all. (Class 44-E via Ted Young)

Night flight training in the AT-9 invariably involved a very high "pucker factor," and this is expressed vividly in this caricature from the Class 44-E book – as well as a subtle reminder of the short AT-9 wingspan! (Class 44-E via Ted Young)

AAF, replacement of these types with even the Beech AT-10 was effected, while awaiting incoming North American TB-25s"

As AT-17s and UC-78s once again started returning to the station, by July a significant number of AT-9s – which by then had nearly all received the two and three-digit numbers suffixed with the letter "M" noted above – were being used by the 453rd Base Unit (which had been activated at Kelly Field, TX October 17, 1942 but moved to Altus December 5, 1942) and the now over-strength 2508th Base Unit. The significance of the "M" suffix is unknown, but may have indicated a second-line, maintenance status.

Although the accident experience of the AT-9 at Altus was central to the fate of the aircraft while stationed there, a closer look at some of these may be instructive.

The first AT-9 to experience an incident was AT-9 41-5831 which had arrived on station from Ellington Field, TX January 15, 1943. While assigned to the huge 667th TEFT Squadron, the aircraft was simply being pushed into a parking area by Crew Chief Corporal J. Sonnen on February 25, 1943 when the left main gear inexplicable collapsed. However, this same aircraft suffered two more accidents before being surveyed on July 18th. In the first of these, Cadet William C. Bumm was obliged to make a forced landing on June 3rd at Altus when he exhausted his fuel, which couldn't have done the aircraft much good. She was repaired yet again, but was lost to a fatal accident about six miles south of the base while being flown by 2LT Robert A. McConnell (and Cadet co-pilot T. J. Abts) who "collided with ground." The aircraft had cleared the field just after midnight at 0105 and, after formatting, became the lead aircraft of a three-aircraft formation, all AT-9s. Shortly after forming up, 41-5831 was seen to go into a diving turn to the right and then was not seen again. The aircraft struck the ground at about a 45-degree angle and was completely demolished. The aircraft did not have a Flight Indicator installed and had been placed on the flight line as a spare for night flying. The only other known mechanical discrepancy on the aircraft was that the elevator hinges were noted as being a bit loose. Lt. McConnell was instruct-

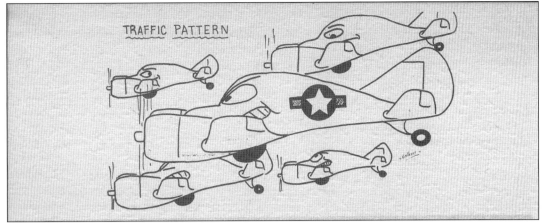

TRAFFIC PATTERN

ing his first class, having returned from the highly-regarded Randolph Field Central Instructor's School (q.v.) on June 28, 1943. The Investigating Board concluded that Lt. McConnell had suffered from vertigo and that the aircraft was not at fault. The experience of this one aircraft should obviously be weighed when contemplating the accident rate and subsequent grounding of the type at Altus.

Although the 667th TEFT Squadron, during its most intensive period of activity and as a very large unit, experienced the majority of accidents at Altus. Following the 'grounding' of all AT-9s and mass assignment to the 2508th Base Unit, a surprising total of 28 more accidents ensued with pilots from that unit, apparently most of them orientation or administrative flights. The other two TEFTs, the 1097th and 1100th, experienced two and three accidents, respectively, while the 453rd Base Unit had one.

The final AT-9 accident at Altus came on October 11, 1944 at Hat Box Field, Muskogee, OK – probably while the aircraft was being flown there from Altus for transfer to the RFC for surplus disposal. Pilot Jesse J. Beck experienced a landing accident.

Although the number of accidents involving AT-9s based at Altus at this late point in the war was unfortunate, just four of them resulted in a total of five fatalities – and two of these were a result of a mid-air collision.

Probably due, at least in part, to the high-density of AT-9s assigned at Altus, the number of surviving first-hand-accounts of flying the aircraft there is rich.

One of the instructors was none other than 1950s and 1960s TV variety show MC and comedian George Gobel, who occasionally regaled his audiences with accounts from his stint as an AT-9 instructor during the war.

Robert E. Lee, more recently of Minneapolis, MN, also an instructor at Altus – exclusively on AT-9s – described the aircraft in the July 1990 issue of *Airpower* as "...a pussy cat." He said "...it was very *stable, responsive and with a heavy enough wing loading to ride smooth. Take-offs were very easy and, if you had a crosswind, it would make a beautiful three-point take-off and skid around nicely to establish the proper crab. In the air, it handled very well. It was such a safe, honest aircraft that it could be brought to a power-off stall and, with both feet flat on the floor, with your arm wrapped around the control column (with no aileron or rudder input) would just mush down in a nose-high attitude for as long as you wished. There was no tendency to drop either wing or break into a dive. If all else failed and an emergency landing was necessary at night, this would have been one reasonable option (in Oklahoma). Landings were its only problem. I found it difficult (with my flying experience) to make a good three-point landing. The instructors often made wheel landings."*

Cadet Al Handley, Class 44-F at Altus, also recalled his experiences training on AT-9s: "...*a great airplane, you just had to fly it. A dead stick landing was done at a 45-degree angle, as there was little if any glide ratio.*"

During the second half of 1944, the AT-9s already at Altus were joined by others flown in to the station as an assembly point for transfer to the RFC for surplus action, thus accounting for a number of the odds-and-ends that showed up and that were never assigned to a unit for training there.

Amarillo Army Air Field, Amarillo, Texas

Station Field Code: None known
Known Unit Markings: None known
AT-9 Operating Units: ★Western Technical Training Command

Located almost dead-center in the remote Texas panhandle, the Amarillo station was activated in April 1942 and formally designated as an Army Air Field in May. It was actually located some 11 miles east of the city of the same name on about 1,523 acres adjacent to the civil English Field, the primary commercial airfield servicing the entire panhandle area.

The base was specifically established, at least initially, to train air and ground crews for the massive expansion in Boeing B-17 *Flying Fortress* operating units. However, starting in 1943, this was extended to include AAF basic training and technical training.

It was apparently in the latter connection that one AT-9 (41-12015) and one AT-9A (42-56900) were dispatched to Amarillo as Class 26 instructional airframes. The AT-9 arrived first, not long after having suffered a landing accident at distant Turner Field, GA July 10, 1942. It was designated Class 26 on July 15th, although there had apparently been some attempt to repair the aircraft and return it to service. The AT-9A was actually flown in and assigned to Amarillo April 20, 1943 from Pampa AAF, TX, but was condemned there May 17, 1943, possibly as the result of complications of an accident at Pampa January 25th of that year. It was probably designated as Class 26, but the record is not clear.

Arledge Field, Stamford, Texas (RFC Surplus Center)

Station Field Code: None
Known Unit Markings: N/A
AT-9 Operating Units: N/A

Arledge Field, Stamford, Texas, as it appeared around August 4, 1942. For reasons that are not clear, this rather bucolic rural field was selected as the disposition site for a number of AT-9s that had previously been stated at Douglas and Williams AAF, AZ, most arriving here to their fates around February 3-9, 1945. (USAFHRA)

Although Arledge Field (also known as Stamford-Arledge Field), about 200 miles due west of Dallas, had in fact been the site of a Contract Cadet Flying School (later the Lou Foote and still later the Coleman Flying Schools) as early as April 1, 1941 as an element of the AAF Gulf Coast Training Center (and still later, the Central Flying Training Command), it was inactivated September 8, 1944 as the ATC's pilot training program drew down.

Its role in the AT-9 story was that of one of the first of the Reconstruction Finance Corporation (RFC) Surplus Centers and, between February 2 and 12th, 1945, nine AT-9s – all formerly assigned to Douglas AAF, AZ – flew in to await their end.

Oddly, however, one AT-9 (41-5766) had been assigned to Arledge Field sometime after February 2, 1944, also from Douglas, and may have been amongst the very first of the AT-9s to go to storage. However, it was actually reassigned from Arledge to Bush field, Augusta, GA by April 16, 1945, yet another RFC concentration point.

Mr. Eugene Lyckman, who had been a teenager in Stamford in 1945, well recalled the AT-9s – and other aircraft – flying in to Arledge Field, where most were shortly thereafter demolished and sold for scrap. He told Library Director Ms. Lucile Wedeking of the Stamford Carnegie Library that he saw them when "*...most were missing wings, some tails, and the equipment inside had already been removed.*" Chillingly, he also noted that some – perhaps former combat types – had blood stains on their interiors when he ventured to peek inside a few.

It was a story that would shortly be repeated all over the country.

Atlantic Command

Station Field Code: None known
Known Unit Markings: None known
AT-9 Operating Units: Unknown

The official Consolidated Statistical Report, Section IV, Part 1, Airplane Distribution and Status issued by the Material Command on June 30, 1942, detailed the location, assignment and status of every aircraft in the Army Air Forces.

On Pages 14-16, it reported that an entity described as the Atlantic Command had assigned an amazing array of 206 aircraft, of which 192 were serviceable. For the purposes of our study, only one of these is of note: a solitary AT-9.

Efforts to further identify this organization have been fruitless, but it was *possibly* actually the Eastern Defense Command or, perhaps more likely, included aircraft assigned to the Headquarters of the Army Air Forces at Bolling Field, DC (probably the 1st and 2nd Staff Squadrons) and those assigned to the Air Materiel Command at Wright Field for test and evaluation duties, all of which existed as such as early as May 20, 1942. As a matter of interest, the array of aircraft assigned to this unusual 'organization' is described in the following table.

Aircraft Assigned to the Atlantic Command as of June 30, 1942

Aircraft Type	Serviceable	Repairable	Total
Fairchild PT-19	1	-	1
Fairchild PT-19A	2	-	2
Fairchild PT-23	1	-	1
Fairchild PT-26	1	-	1
Boeing-Stearman PT-13A	2	-	2
Boeing-Stearman PT-13B	1	-	1
Boeing-Stearman PT-17	6	-	6
Boeing-Stearman PT-18	1	-	1
North American BT-9B	1	-	1
Fleetwings BT-12	1	-	1
Vultee BT-13	1	-	1
Vultee BT-13A	2	-	2
North American BT-14	1	-	1
Vultee BT-15	2	-	2
North American AT-6	2	-	2
North American AT-6A	3	-	3
North American AT-6B	2	-	2
North American AT-6C	1	-	1
Beech AT-7	3	-	3

Cessna AT-8	3	-	3
Curtiss-Wright AT-9	1	-	1
Beech AT-10	1	-	1
Beech AT-11	1	-	1
Republic AT-12	2	-	2
Cessna AT-17	1	-	1
Douglas A-24	1	1	2
Douglas DB-7B	-	1	1
Vultee V-72 Vengeance	-	3	3
Martin B-10B	1	-	1
Boeing B-17C	1	-	1
Boeing B-17E	-	1	1
Boeing B-17F	1	-	1
Douglas B-18	1	1	2
Douglas B-18A	6	2	8
Douglas B-23	4	2	6
Consolidated B-24D	6	-	6
North American B-25	-	1	1
North American B-25A	2	1	3
North American B-25C	1	1	2
North American B-25D	2	-	2
Martin B-26B	5	-	5
Douglas C-32A	3	-	3
Douglas C-33	2	-	2
Lockheed C-36	1	-	1
Lockheed C-36A	4	-	4
Lockheed C-37	1	-	1
Douglas C-41A	1	-	1
Beech C-43	1	-	1
Beech C-43A	1	-	1
Beech C-43B	3	1	4
Beech C-43C	4	2	6
Beech C-43D	6	2	8
Beech C-43F	-	1	1
Beech C-45	3	3	6
Beech C-45A	3	-	3
Douglas C-47	2	1	3
Douglas C-48	1	-	1
Douglas C-48B	2	-	2
Douglas C-49A	1	-	1
Douglas C-49E	3	-	3
Douglas C-50	1	1	2
Douglas C-53	2	-	2
Douglas C-54	1	-	1
Lockheed C-56	-	1	1
Lockheed C-56C	1	-	1
Lockheed C-56D	3	-	3
Lockheed C-57	1	1	2
Lockheed C-60	2	-	2
Fairchild C-61	-	1	1
Howard C-70	2	-	2
Howard C-70A	1	-	1
Spartan C-71	5	2	7
Waco C-72	5	1	6
Boeing C-73	3	-	3

Stinson C-81A	2	-	2
Bell P-39F	2	1	3
Curtiss P-40	1	-	1
Curtiss P-40C	1	-	1
Curtiss P-40D	1	-	1
Curtiss P-40E	3	1	4
Curtiss P-40E-1	3	-	3
Curtiss P-40F	8	-	8
Curtiss P-40K-1	1	-	1
Curtiss P-42	1	-	1
Republic P-43	1	-	1
Republic P-43A	1	-	1
Republic P-47B	5	-	5
North American P-51	2	-	2
Douglas P-70	1	-	1
Sikorsky R-4	1	-	1

Aviation Institute, Kansas City, Missouri

(Missouri Aviation Institute?)
Station Field Code: N/A
Known Unit Markings: N/A
AT-9 Operating Units: N/A

AT-9A 42-57028 was transferred to this aviation trade school, apparently as an instructional airframe March 4, 1943, relatively early in its service life, from the AAF facility at Memphis, TN.

This transfer suggests use as a training aid, yet there are no known accidents or incidents associated with this aircraft and, even more curiously, it was noted as 'scrapped' but to the RFC April 30, 1943 – one of the very earliest known transfers to surplus status.

It appears that the 'scrapping' order was rather loosely interpreted, as the one existing photo of the aircraft shows it standing forlorn and rather shabby at Kansas City, presumably amongst other aircraft associated with this trade school. The aircraft wears some code on the nose and fuselage, which appears to be "20XX" but this must have been connected with a previous assignment.

Barksdale Field, Louisiana

Station Field Code: None Known
Known Unit Markings: [probably three-digit numbers in the 200's]
AT-9 Operating Units: ★423rd School Squadron (not confirmed) ★427th School Squadron (SP) (became 427th TEFT Squadron)

Curiously, only two AT-9As are known to have been assigned to Barksdale, according to Individual Aircraft Record Cards, specifically 42-56869 (assigned January 31, 1943) and 42-56961, which was apparently at Barksdale on Detachment from Blytheville AAF, AR. The first of these, 42-56869, suf-

One AT-9A, 42-57028 was one of the first to go to an educational institution, departing from Memphis around April 30, 1943 bound for the Aviation Institute of Kansas City, MO. It is pictured here some time later, clearly very weary and with what appears to be Field Code 203 on the nose. (NMUSAF

fered extensive damage at Barksdale in an undocumented accident, but was repaired and transferred to Roswell AAF, NM February 28, 1943. The other known aircraft with a Barksdale connect, 42-56961, suffered a landing accident there while (attributed to 'materiel failure') being flown by Louis J. Cameron, Jr. at the time, and was specifically noted as being on Detachment at the time from Blytheville. It was apparently repaired, and went to the RFC storage point at Rome, NY around September 16, 1944, with no identified interim assignment, suggesting that it remained at Barksdale between the time of the accident and retirement.

The 423rd School Squadron had been activated at Barksdale August 1, 1941 and was redesignated as the 427th Two-Engine Flying Training Squadron October 23, 1942. The organizational history of this unit makes no mention whatsoever of AT-9s; however, in fairness, it does not mention what other types may have been operated either, so it cannot be ruled out as possibly an AT-9 operating unit making use of aircraft detached from Blytheville.

The 427th School Squadron (SP) was activated at Barksdale January 30, 1942 and was redesignated as the 427th Two-Engine Flying Training Squadron October 23, 1942. The organizational history stated that "...the unit's AT-9s were exchanged for AT-10s in November 1943, a move that improved maintenance in that working with one type of plane presented a single set of problems." As the normal complement of a mixed-type TEFTS was between six and 10 aircraft, this suggests that at least this number of AT-9s had been serving alongside AT-10s there prior to November 1943, but not a single one has been identified.

Berry Army Air Field, Nashville, Tennessee

Station Field Code: None known
Known Unit Markings: None known
AT-9 Operating Units: ★8th Ferry Squadron, 4th Ferry Group ★26th Ferry Squadron, 4th Ferry Group ★308th Ferry Squadron, 20th Ferry Group

One of the greatest of unsung contributions made to the success of U.S. Army Air Forces during World War Two must surely be that of the wide-ranging and far-flung units of the AAF Ferry Command.

Originally known as the Air Corps Ferry Command, the organization was divided into Sectors to handle aircraft flowing, primarily, from the nation's airframe manufacturers, and then delivering them to their initial and, sometimes, subsequent stations.

Initially known as the Nashville Sector, this became the 4th Ferry Group on May 28, 1942, and was primarily responsible for ferrying new aircraft from the Vultee plant in Nashville and Curtiss-Wright in St. Louis.

The 26th Ferrying Squadron was activated at Morrison Field, FL July 8, 1942 but moved to Berry Field, where it was assigned to the 4th Ferry Group around August 3, 1942.

Obviously, when confronted with the prospect of having to deliver most of the 791 AT-9s built in St. Louis, it was incumbent upon the unit, and the others noted above, to not only train its ferry pilots on the type they would be flying, but to make use of some of them as light-transports to return its crews to the point of departure for yet another mission. These two functions, together, accounted for at least 12 AT-9s being assigned to Berry Field between February 20th and July 21, 1942, followed by at least 17 AT-9As between August 29 and November 11, 1942. Of these, only one was brand-new from St. Louis. The others were picked up during movements between stations, including some from Turner Field, GA, Victorville, CA, Moody AAF, GA, Columbus, MS, Kelly Field, TX, Roswell AAF, NM and a few elsewhere.

Ferrying these aircraft over long distances and essentially solo was often fraught with hazard and at least five accidents – but no fatalities – were experienced by Ferry Command crews while flying AT-9s, at least one of which was identified as type AT-9B.

Big Spring Army Air Forces Bombardier School, Big Spring, Texas

Station Field Code: None known
Known Unit Markings: None known
AT-9 Operating Units: [probably the ★365th Base Headquarters and Air Base Squadron)

By November 1, 1942, the Army Air Forces Bombardier School at Big Spring, Texas had no fewer than eight Bombardier Training Squadrons organized: the 812th through the 819th.

Most of these units were equipped with Douglas B-18s, B-18As and Beech AT-11s but, for reasons that are not clear, two AT-9As were assigned to the station in April 1943 (42-57059, from Blackland AAF, TX) and sometime after May 12, 1943 (42-57003 from Williams AAF, AZ). Of these, 42-57059 only stayed until May 11, 1943, when it was apparently replaced by 42-57003, which remained until going to surplus October 9, 1944.

We can only speculate about the reasoning for this assignment, as organizational and station records make no mention of it, but it may be assumed that the aircraft may have been used as a transition trainer or light transport by the resident Air Base Squadron to help prepare instructors who were weak in two-engine operations, prior to taking an instructor's seat on the multitude of Beech AT-11s there.

Bowman Army Air Field, Louisville, Kentucky

Station Field Code: None known
Known Unit Markings: None known
AT-9 Operating Units: [apparently the ★1077th Air Base Squadron]

Bowman Field is hailed as the 'oldest continuously operating commercial airfield in America,' but during World War Two, due in no small part to its very central location in the continental United States, the major tenant unit stationed there was the I Troop Carrier Command (from June 20, 1942) and, initially, the 89th Troop Carrier Group (from April 30, 1942).

A single AT-9A, 42-56936 was assigned to this station, ostensibly to the 1077th Air Base Squadron, from Rome, NY sometime after December 11, 1942, and remained there until going to the RFC for surplus sale December 21, 1944.

Official Army Air Forces records have not revealed the justification for this assignment but, given the preponderance of Troop Carrier activities there, it can be safely assumed that there was some connection with a requirement for two-engine transition training.

Brookley Army Air Field, Mobile, Alabama

Station Field Code: None known
Known Unit Markings: None known
AT-9 Operating Units: N/A

A single AT-9, 41-5753, was assigned to Brookley administratively on April 20, 1943 from Columbus AAF, MS. It remained only until June 1, 1943, when it returned to Columbus and, since the stay exceeded 30 days, may be safely assumed to have been undergoing what must have essentially been a complete rebuild there by the Mobile Air Depot following a known accident at Columbus July 16, 1942. Although technically 'Assigned' for administrative purposes and placed on the Brookley Property Book, other than test flights following rebuild, it almost certainly performed no other function at that station.

Bush Army Air Field, Augusta, Georgia

Station Field Code: "A-"
Known Unit Markings: None known
AT-9 Operating Units: N/A

Although an asset of the Southeast Flying Training Command for most of the war, by the fall of 1944, Bush Field had been designated as one of a number of surplus aircraft storage sites, and not long afterwards, was packed with aircraft from both CONUS stations and from overseas awaiting their fates.

And so it was with four known AT-9s. two arrived between September 2nd and 12th, 1944 (41-12200 and 41-5749), another December 2, 1944 – one from Seymour-Johnson AAF and the other from Rome, NY – followed by one sometime after December 2, 1944 (41-5748) also from Seymour-Johnson and the last on April 13, 1945 (41-5766 from of all places, Arledge Field, Stamford, TX – another RFC storage site!).

All passed to the control of the RFC between November 1, 1944 and April 16, 1945 and may be assumed to have been sold as scrap. Other than flying in, they were not flown again.

Carlsbad Army Air Field, Carlsbad, New Mexico

Station Field Code: None known
Known Unit Markings: None known
AT-9 Operating Units: Unknown

An element of the West Coast Flying Training Command, Carlsbad AAF was activated October 12, 1942 and, initially, had one training unit assigned, a Detachment of the 940th Two-Engine Flying Training Squadron, which was home-based at Roswell AAF, NM (q.v.). Not long afterwards, however, the station was designated as a dedicated bombardier school and hosted Beech AT-11s almost exclusively.

On November 15, 1944, however, a solitary AT-9, 41-5777 was assigned, apparently as an administrative action only, as it had in fact suffered an accident that same day at Douglas AAF, AZ. It was surveyed at Carlsbad November 21, 1944. The rationale for this rather strange procedure is unknown, as it should have been surveyed at the station of the loss.

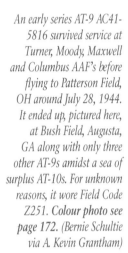

An early series AT-9 AC41-5816 survived service at Turner, Moody, Maxwell and Columbus AAF's before flying to Patterson Field, OH around July 28, 1944. It ended up, pictured here, at Bush Field, Augusta, GA along with only three other AT-9s amidst a sea of surplus AT-10s. For unknown reasons, it wore Field Code Z251. Colour photo see page 172. (Bernie Schultie via A. Kevin Grantham)

Cimarron Army Air Field, Cimarron, Oklahoma

Station Field Code: None known
Known Unit Markings: None known
AT-9 Operating Units: N/A

Some 14 miles west of Oklahoma City, this small field was home to a Contract Flying School which fell under the auspices of the Central Flying Training Command. It had been activated for training March 16, 1941.

One AT-9, 41-12150 was dispatched to this field from Altus AAF, OK via Will Roger Field in Oklahoma City sometime after September 15, 1944 but, as it passed to the control of the RFC on or about October 16, 1944, it was probably contemplated as an RFC disposal center that did not reach maturity. Ironically, photos of the remains of this aircraft were taken by the late, great aviation photographer John Kerr at Kelly AFB, TX around January 8, 1983 – and these remains were used to assemble the solitary intact surviving AT-9 now at the National Museum of the United States Air Force. How it moved from Cimarron to Kelly Field is something of a mystery.

Cochran Army Air Field, Macon, Georgia

Station Field Code: "C-"
Known Unit Markings: None known
AT-9 Operating Units: [probably elements of the 27th Flying Training Wing (Basic)]

Cochran AAF gained perhaps its greatest fame as an RAF Cadet training station, the first class having started curriculum there August 17, 1941. The last RAF Cadets graduated in March 1943, however, and the station became home to the USAAF's 27th Flying Training Wing (Basic), primarily equipped with North American AT-6 and Vultee BT-13 variants.

Cochran was unusual for large AAF training stations in having only two hard-surfaced runways. Initially assigned to the AAF Southeast Flying Training Center, by the time the solitary AT-9 associated with this station, 41-11995 arrived from Moody on June 1, 1943, it had been transferred to the Eastern Flying Training Command.

The aircraft in question was only assigned to Cochran for 36 days, returning to Moody on July 6, 1943. The reason for this assignment has not been discovered, but was probably a familiarization detachment.

This AT-9, 41-12150, started its service life at Ellington Field, TX, where is suffered two accidents before moving north to Altus Field, OK August 27, 1944, and is bears here one of the unique Altus Field Codes, 165M. For reasons unknown, it was detailed to Cimarron Field, OK for surplus disposition, where it languished until acquired for restoration by the NMUSAF – the sole surviving AT-9. (NMUSAF)

Duncan Army Air Field, San Antonio, Texas

Station Field Code: None known
Known Unit Markings: N/A
AT-9 Operating Units: N/A

Although two AT-9s, 41-5780 and 41-5846, were administratively assigned to Duncan AAF, in actuality, a Depot activity and a Division of Kelly Field, on May 15, 1942 (from Ellington AAF) and April 20, 1943 (from Blytheville AAF) these aircraft were almost certainly there for some form of undocumented modification, as neither are known to have suffered any accidents that would have sent them to Duncan for repair or rebuild around those dates. They are the only two AT-9s associated with the Depot and, considering the distance they traveled to get there, were almost certainly flown in-and-out again from Kelly.

As a personal aside, the author's late father-in-law, Woodrow Engle, worked at Duncan Field during World War Two and almost certainly saw these aircraft during the course of his daily routine there, although he was primarily involved in repairs, modifications and overhauls of North American AT-6 series aircraft.

Fairfield Air Depot, Riverside, Ohio

Station Field Code: None known
Known Unit Markings: N/A
AT-9 Operating Units: N/A

The Fairfield Air Depot had been an Army Air Corps legacy depot, just adjacent to Wright Field and on the land occupied today by the National Museum of the United States Air Force.

One AT-9, 41-12129, was administratively assigned to Fairfield October 14, 1942 from distant Ellington Field, Texas, and returned to Ellington November 12th. The justification for this cross-country trip is unknown, but given the capabilities of the Depot, probably involved some form of modification, as the aircraft is not known to have suffered any accidents prior to the assignment which would have required such a distant sojourn.

Foster Army Air Field, Victoria, Texas and the Matagorda Peninsula Bombing Range/Matagorda Island Gunnery Range

Station Field Code: "P-"
Known Unit Markings: [three-digit numbers in the 400s and 800s]
AT-9 Operating Units: ★859th Single-Engine Gunnery Training Squadron

Located six miles northeast of the city of Victoria, Texas, Foster was established as an advanced, single-engine flying school, streaming primarily fighter pilots, and was activated May 15, 1941 as a component, initially, of the Gulf Coast Air Corps Training Center. The first class started in September 1941 and, by November 1, 1942, the station was home to five Single Engine Flying Training Squadrons (the 48th, 97th, 98th and 99th), three Flexible Gunnery Training Squadrons (the 512th through 515th) and the 60th Aviation Squadron (Sep.). The station was a part of the Central Flying Training Command.

The primary aircraft types employed at foster Field and the satellites at Matagorda Peninsula and nearby Matagorda Island were large numbers of variants of the North American AT-6 and early variants of the Curtiss P-40 series.

Then, on June 1, 1943, for reasons that have not been revealed in a study of the organizational history of the station, three AT-9s (41-5804, 41-5832 from Pampa AAF and 41-12211 from Tinker AAF, OK) were assigned to the 859th Single-Engine Gunnery Training Squadron at the station. By July 6th, two of these (41-5832 and 41-12211) had been transferred outright to the Matagorda Ranges, where the 859th was garrisoned. It is possible that these may have been amongst the AT-9s modified to carry a .30 caliber machine gun in the nose, as it is difficult to understand what other function they could have carried out during this assignment. It has also been speculated that, like the AT-9 assigned to a Tow Target Squadron on the west coast, they may have been used as high-speed target tugs, but this is difficult to credit, as there were far more efficient aircraft available and equipped for this task locally. Of the three, 41-5804 was reassigned to Kelly Field, TX July 21, 1944 while the other two were finally reassigned to Altus Field, OK in May 1944 and January 1945.

Frederick Army Air Field, Frederick, Oklahoma

Station Field Code: None known
Known Unit Markings: [three-digit numbers in the 300s and 400s]
AT-9 Operating Units: ★70th Two-Engine Flying Training Squadron ★452nd Base headquarters and Air Base Squadron ★2520th Air Base Squadron

This late-blooming training station did not open until September 23, 1942 and, unlike many other training bases, it was operated under a joint-use agreement as both a military and civil airport. By November 1, 1942, the base was home to four Two-Engine Flying Training Squadrons, the 1093rd through the 1096th, but these are all believed to have operated only Cessna AT-17s and UC-78s.

Frederick AAF, Oklahoma, along with Altus, was one of the final great concentration stations for AT-9s, and the ramp view here shows at least 21 AT-9s. Oddly, only a total of 17 AT-9s and AT-9As can be accounted for assigned to Frederick, and from not earlier than around March 1943. Thus, the presence of rudder stripes on the AT-9s and the large number of AT-17s visible here is puzzling. The three-digit Field Codes cannot be discerned with certainty, but appear to be in the 600s and 900s. (Special Collections Library, Texas Tech Southwest Collection)

Initially part of the Gulf Coast AAF Training Center, it was activated for training under the Central Flying Training Command April 23, 1943 as a level-3 two-engine training airfield.

Frederick, like most of its sister stations, had four Auxiliary Fields.

The first of seven AT-9s and six AT-9As arrived on station around August 6, 1943, but apparently, the single AT-9 operating unit by that time, the 70th TEFTS, could borrow aircraft, as needed, from Lubbock AAF. The only photo located showing AT-9s at the station shows more than 16 in a lineup with a much larger number of AT-17s and UC-78s.

Of the AT-9s at Frederick, only one escaped some form of accident, while, oddly, only one of the AT-9As was bent. None were fatal, and of the total of 10 accidents, six were either ground collisions or forced landings. Only one was an in-air accident, and this occurred on September 25, 1943 about nine miles southeast of Frederick when AT-9 41-12127, assigned to the 452nd Base Headquarters and Air Base Squadron collided in mid-air with Cessna UC-78B 42-71925 while being flown by 2LT William M. Moss. The 452nd had been activated at Lubbock January 19, 1943 but was sent to Frederick to serve as the advance cadre and to set up the administrative machinery for the new station. The aircraft apparently landed successfully but was wrecked again February 11, 1944 15 miles northwest of the station when Cadet William R. Sheppard ran out of fuel. The aircraft was recovered and repaired once again, and survived the war to go to the RFC for surplus action.

Glendale (Grand Central) Army Air Base, Glendale, California

Station Field Code: None known
Known Unit Markings: None known
AT-9 Operating Units: Unknown

As noted elsewhere in this account, there were a number of AT-9s assigned to Lockheed P-38 *Lightning* units in California, Oregon and Washington states in 1942 and 1943, and the movements of these units – and the assigned AT-9s – very much reflects the nearly frantic shuffling of resources on the West Coast as the initial hysteria of the immediate post-Pearl Harbor period gradually eased.

Three AT-9s were stationed, intermittently, at Glendale as early as February 1942, and almost certainly were there incident to P-38 transition training – and at least one of them is known to have been assigned to one (the 371st Fighter Squadron) or more of the P-38 units operating there as well. Tracking the movements of just one of these, 41-12038, which may in fact have been a part of the movements of the 371st itself, is a case in point. It was posted to Glendale from March Field on August 8, 1942 and suffered a landing accident there the same day when NCO pilot S/Sgt Harry R. Morris pulled up the landing gear (instead of the flaps) when landing – an all-too-common occurrence at that stage of the war. After repairs, the aircraft was reassigned to Long Beach on August 10th, then to Santa Ana, CA September 17th – but was back at Glendale by September 21st. It then moved to Muroc Air base (possibly with a tactical P-38 unit), came back to Glendale on February 28, 1943 and then back to Muroc again on April 20, 1943 where it was apparently assigned to the 371st Fighter Squadron (TE). It suffered an accident there May 13, 1943 and was surveyed in September.

Army Air Forces Basic Flying School Goodfellow Field, San Angelo, Texas

Station Field Code: None known
Known Unit Markings: None known
AT-9 Operating Units: Unknown

Officially established August 17, 1940, this new station, located two miles southeast of San Angelo, was ready for occupancy January 21, 1941 and the first classes of Basic Training students started to arrive February 8, 1941. By war's end, some 10,000 pilots had graduated to move on to Advanced Training. The base was an element of the Central Flying Training Command.

By November 1, 1942, Goodfellow was home to six Basic Flying Training Squadrons (the 49th, 67th and 68th, 388th, 1045th and 1046th) and one separate unit, the 77th Aviation Squadron (Sep.). The station was almost completely populated with Vultee BT-13s, BT-13As, BT-13Bs and BT-15s.

Then, on February 25th and 28th, 1943 two AT-9s (41-5765 and 41-12007) arrived from Ellington Field near Houston, and remained stationed at Goodfellow until April 20th. No records have been located that explain this unusual assignment or why they were posted there.

Gulfport Army Air Field, Gulfport, Mississippi

Station Field Code: None known
Known Unit Markings: None known
AT-9 Operating Units: Unknown

This gulf coast station was home to the Headquarters, Eastern Technical Training Command and was also shared with the CONUS Third Air Force.

A solitary AT-9, 41-12147, was assigned to Gulfport AAF September 22, 1942 from Columbus AAF, MS and, nine days later, was declared Class 26 (Instructional Airframe). This aircraft was almost certainly used for instruction by an Technical Training Command element.

Gunter Army Air Field, Montgomery, Alabama

Station Field Code: "G-"
Known Unit Markings: None known
AT-9 Operating Units: N/A

Located in northeastern Montgomery, not far from the legacy Maxwell Field, until much later, Gunter was an independent base. During the war, besides USAAF Cadets (and the famed Tuskegee Airmen) its units trained numbers of British, Canadian, Dutch, and Chinese students in the Basic phase.

Although Gunter was an active Basic Training station (the first such established by the then Southeast Flying Training Command), and was home to considerable numbers of Vultee BT-13s and BT-15s, on October 16, 1942, a single AT-9 – 41-12164 – was assigned to the station from Maxwell. It remained there only a short 53 days before returning to Maxwell.

This was almost certainly incident to the accident that this aircraft had suffered at Eufaula, AL on October 12, 1942 while based at Maxwell. Gunter had what amounted to Sub-Depot repair facilities, and the 53-day stay was probably the duration of the time it took to complete the restoration of the aircraft following the damage it had suffered in the earlier accident.

Harlingen Army Gunnery School, Harlingen, Texas

Station Field Code: "FM-"
Known Unit Markings: None known
AT-9 Operating Units: Unknown

Located three miles northeast of Harlingen as of November 1, 1942, this wartime station was exclusively given over to training flexible gunners as of that time.

The units stationed there, nearly all equipped with North American AT-6 variants, included the 476th to 480th and 1047th Flexible Gunnery Training Squadrons.

Thus, when AT-9 41-5832 was assigned from Ellington on July 23, 1942 – for a scant three days – then moving on to Lubbock AAF, it must have been for some purpose which has been lost to history. Harking back to the experience of several AT-9s at Foster Field near Victoria, Texas at about the same juncture, also given over to gunnery training, for the most part, the aircraft may have been part of a short-lived target-towing experiment.

Hat Box Field, Muskogee, Oklahoma

Station Field Code: None known
Known Unit Markings: N/A
AT-9 Operating Units: N/A

Originally Muskogee, Oklahoma's municipal airport, located 2.5 miles west of the city – and a stop on various airmail routes of the 1920s and 1930s – the Spartan Aviation School opened there in 1940 and they used two arch-roofed hangars at the field.

Renamed as Muskogee Army Air Field, Spartan served as a Civil Contract Flying School for the Air Corps, Spartan providing primary training through 1944. The USAAF's 410th Bombardment Group trained at the field on Douglas A-20s in the fall of 1943.

The field closed in 1998 and only limited flight activities continued until 2000 by a company refurbishing military surplus Beech U-21s. It is now a community recreational facility with baseball fields etc.

But starting in September 1944, the USAAF, for some obscure reason, designated Hatbox Field as the final destination – and final resting place – for at least 167 AT-9s and three AT-9As, nearly all of them having been flown into Hatbox Field from temporary storage at either Patterson Field, Ohio or Rome AAF, NY, although some came direct from Altus AAF, OK and Ellington Field, TX and a few from Douglas and Williams AAFs, AZ.

All 170 of these aircraft were apparently broken up and reduced to raw materials there and, other than their delivery flights, never actually flew out of the field.

Joe D. Reynolds was 16 in 1946 and lived near Muskogee. He recalled that Hat Box Field *"…was covered with AT-9 Jeep trainers. Every one of the airplanes and engines were chopped up for scrap within a relatively short time. I remember standing at the fence watching them being chopped up."*

Hobbs Army Air Field, Hobbs, New Mexico

Station Field Code: "H-"
Known Unit Markings: None Known
AT-9 Operating Units: None Known

Hobbs AAF, in the far southeast corner of the state, was a late-starter in the war effort, with preparation of the runways there not getting underway until June 1942.

Created as a dedicated bombardier school, the first class of 80 Cadets and 20 instructors did not get started until September 7, 1942 – and it was destined to be the solitary class of bombardiers to graduate there.

An element of the West Coast Training Command, Hobbs was directed to commence work as a Boeing B-17 multi-engine pilot training school, and the first B-17s arrived in mid-December 1942. By 1945, at least 162 B-17s were stationed at the field.

It is against this background, apparently, that a single AT-9, 41-12172 was flown in to Hobbs in November 1942 from Ellington Field, TX. As it only stayed about a month before returning, it is assumed that it was engaged in transition training and perhaps multi-engine check-outs for instructors assigned to the forthcoming B-17 multi-engine courses.

Hat Box Field, Muskogee, OK as it appeared August 5, 1942. This very rural field became the final resting place and scrap-yard for the vast majority of AT-9s that survived. The first started arriving here for surplus action in September 1944, more than 167 eventually going to the smelters. (USAFHRA)

short-lived assignment, and the aircraft moved on to Blytheville, AR on June 30th. Thus, Property Book 'ownership' while there was most likely vested in the resident Air Base Squadron, the 2125th.

Key Army Air Field, Meridian, Mississippi

Station Field Code: None Known
Known Unit Markings: None Known
AT-9 Operating Units: N/A

Only one AT-9A is known to have been connected with Key AAF, and the association may be tenuous.

AT-9A 42-57099 suffered a fatal accident May 16, 1943 16 miles north of Key Field, and was assigned to Columbus AAF at the time. It is believed that a crew from Key Field was sent out to recover the remains, and conduct the Survey of the aircraft, which was accomplished at Key Field on June 1, 1943. Thus, although nominally 'assigned' there, it was as a wreck only.

Kingman Army Air Field, Kingman, Arizona

Station Field Code: None Known
Known Unit Markings: None Known
AT-9 Operating Units: Unknown

Best known as the massive grave-yard for hundreds of WWII veteran aircraft, primarily combat types, at least one AT-9, 41-5871, arrived there from Douglas AAF, AZ August 5, 1944, almost certainly for retirement and storage. It languished amidst its more muscular brethren until June 20, 1945, when it was finally Surveyed and probably scrapped.

Kirtland Army Air Field, Albuquerque, New Mexico

Station Field Code: "Q-"
Known Unit Markings: [probably Q followed by a two-digit number in the 30s, 40s or 50s and eventually into the 100s]
AT-9 Operating Units: Unknown

Best known as one of the first dedicated bombardier schools, Kirtland was equipped with at least 50 Beech AT-11s as early as January 1942, eventually reaching a total of some 150 of these excellent bombardier training twins by the end of the war. They were joined, initially, by at least 28 Douglas B-18As as well.

In August 1943, however, the station changed its major focus to that of a USAAF B-24 Pilot Transition School, specifically charged with the final stage of preparing B-24 aircraft commanders.

A total of two AT-9s and four AT-9As were assigned to Kirtland, the first, 41-12017 apparently designated as going to the station May 27, 1942, but then the order was changed and it apparently did not make the move. It wasn't until January 6, 1943 that AT-9 41-5787 arrived from Roswell, but it was condemned there on February 6, even though the aircraft is not known to have suffered any accident.

It was followed on July 6, 1943 by four AT-9As – one of them brand-new and the other three from Love Field in Dallas. They stayed only briefly, however, before proceeding on to Williams AAF, AZ July 11th. It is assumed that they were probably employed to conduct refresher training for instructors destined for the newly organized B-24 Pilot Transition School, which was just about to commence operations.

Lambert Field (Curtiss-Wright St. Louis Airplane Division), Robertson, Missouri

Station Field Code: None
Known Unit Markings: N/A
AT-9 Operating Units: ★Curtiss-Wright Plant Detachment (CPD)
It is perhaps not surprising that one AT-9A (42-57050) and at least six AT-9s returned to their 'place of birth'.

Of these seven aircraft, however, only two were actually assigned to what was known as the Curtiss-Wright Plant Detachment (CPD) or, sometimes cited as Contractor's Plant Detachment. These were the single AT-9A 42-57050, and AT-9 41-5807. Of these, the latter was crashed while almost brand-new on January 10, 1942 while being flown by Lieutenant Colonel H. W. Cook 3.5 miles south of the factory field. To his embarrassment, the Colonel had simply exhausted his fuel and, apparently, no formal accident report was filed, suggesting that the aircraft had as yet not been accepted by the AAC. The accident to AT-9A-57050 was on January 1, 1943 – a landing accident at Lambert Field while being flown by a J. H. Bates (no rank given, suggesting he may have been a Curtiss test pilot) and, as the aircraft had been accepted by the USAAF on November 26, 1942, suggests that it had been in use by the CPD for some time. It was repaired at the factory and assigned to Blytheville AAF, AR February 16, 1943.

Four of the other five aircraft returned to Lambert Field between January 15, 1942 and March 25, 1942, apparently to be rebuilt by the manufacturer, in each case following accidents, and of these two came from Chanute Field, IL, one from Scott Field, IL and one from Wright (the first aircraft 41-5804). The final aircraft, AT-9 41-12062 returned to Lambert Field sometime after March 2, 1945 from Altus AAF, OK, suggesting that Curtiss may have had an interest in re-acquiring the aircraft, as it was sold surplus there to an unknown buyer around April 16, 1945.

Las Vegas Army Air Field, Las Vegas, Nevada

Station Field Code: "Z-"
Known Unit Markings: N/A
AT-9 Operating Units: N/A
Only one AT-9 was briefly associated with the Las Vegas AAF, an element of the Western Flying Training Command, AT-9 41-11959. It was assigned there on orders dated July 11, 1942 for unspecified purposes (the station operated a wide variety of aircraft during the war, including numbers of North American AT-6 variants, Boeing B-17s, Consolidated B-24s, Douglas A-33s, Bell RP-63s, Lockheed AT-18s, Boeing B-29s, Lockheed RB-34s, Martin B-10s and Beech C-45s!).

This single aircraft may have been trucked to Las Vegas, however, and then redirected, as it was also reported to have crashed July 15, 1942 while based at Victorville when it was "...*damaged due to a sudden stoppage of both engines*" and was cited as a total loss! However, it was recommended for Class 26 (Instructional Airframe) status and was in fact allocated to the Post Schools, Alameda, CA July 22, 1942, but did not actually go to Class 26 until July 31, 1942.

Lawson Army Air Field, Fort Benning, Georgia

Station Field Code: None Known
Known Unit Markings: N/A
AT-9 Operating Units: N/A
One AT-9, 41-5824, was assigned to this Infantry Center airfield June 20, 1942 from Turner AAF, Albany, GA, and returned to Turner on June 29th.

It is assumed that the aircraft was detached to Lawson AAF for familiarization training or exhibition to students at The Infantry School.

and started to taxi "...*the horn sounded*" and the starboard main landing gear gave in slow motion. He quickly shut down the engines. The accident was charged to "Materiel Failure" and was yet another indictment of the main gear and associated controls of the AT-9 family. The aircraft was repaired and, apparently, remained at Lemoore for the remainder of its service life, going to the RFC for surplus action February 9, 1945.

This well-documented assignment leaves only the question of exactly why a single AT-9 was assigned to a BT-13A-equipped SEFTS.

Little Rock, Arkansas

Station Field Code: None Known
Known Unit Markings: None Known
AT-9 Operating Units: Unknown
The single AT-9A, 42-57018, associated with Little Rock is a small mystery.

The AAF had a presence at Adams Field, four miles east of Little Rock, but a Base Unit and the 12th Ferry Service Detachment did not become formally established until after the brief assignment.

The aircraft in question is shown as being assigned January 31, 1943, having arrived from Blytheville in distant Northeastern Arkansas. Since the aircraft actually suffered a known accident at Blytheville on February 15th, but was not formally reassigned there until February 26th, it must be assumed that the aircraft must have been at Adams Field in some connection with the establishment of the 12th Ferry Service Detachment barely a month later.

Lockbourne Army Air Base, Columbus, Ohio

Station Field Code: None Known
Known Unit Markings: None Known
AT-9 Operating Units: [probably either the 55th, 553rd or 2114th Air Base Squadron]
Yet another strange one-off assignment, for reasons unknown AT-9A 42-56952 was assigned to this element of the Eastern Flying Training Command (which became an element of the Air Service Command from October 1942) sometime after April 30, 1943, arriving from distant Randolph Field, TX. During this period, Lockbourne was conducting glider training, and the possibly (but undocumented) use of this aircraft as a candidate glider-tug cannot be ruled out. It remained in Ohio until October 1, 1944, when it passed to the custody of the RFC for surplus handling.

Love Field, Dallas, Texas

Station Field Code: None Known
Known Unit Markings: None Known
AT-9 Operating Units: ★11th Ferry Squadron, 5th Ferry Group
Five AT-9As (42-56952, 42-57120 to 42-57123) were assigned to this organization between April 20th (four) and August 14, 1943 (one), all but one formerly at the short-lived assignment to Marfa AAF

in far southwestern Texas, and thence on to Kirtland AAF, Albuquerque, NM July 6, 1943 (except 42-56952, which went to Altus AAF, OK October 28, 1943). This latter aircraft suffered an accident, however, on August 9, 1944 at, of all places, Circleville, Ohio, while being flown by Billy J. Farrington when he ran out of fuel and made a forced landing – but was listed on the accident report as having been assigned to the 11th Ferry Squadron at the time!

This unit, like many of the Ferry Squadrons, had many WAAFs assigned during the war.

Lowry Army Air Field, Denver, Colorado

Station Field Code: None Known
Known Unit Markings: None Known
AT-9 Operating Units: Unknown

A legacy installation, the Denver Branch of the Air Corps Technical School had opened on the grounds of a former sanatorium which had been improved by a WPA project in August 1937.

The installation was named Lowry Field March 11, 1938 in honor of 2LT Francis Lowry, the only Colorado pilot killed during WWI combat, and a paved runway opened April 4th.

Lowry's connection with the AT-9 is poorly understood. Starting on December 10, 1942 the first of 21 AT-9s were assigned to the station, with the last batch of eight on April 20, 1943, every single one of them having been transferred from La Junta AAF.

By June 1, 1943, all 21 had moved on to Yuma and Williams AAF, ending a relatively brief two-to-three-month sojourn.

It is assumed that the aircraft underwent some form of Depot-level overhaul prior to returning to dedicated training duties, perhaps in an effort to catch up on overdue T.O.s, which La Junta may not have been equipped to deal with.

Luke Army Air Field, Glendale, Arizona

Station Field Code: "X-"
Known Unit Markings: None Known
AT-9 Operating Units: ★66th Base Headquarters and Air Base Squadron

During WWII, Luke Field was the preeminent fighter training station in the USAAF, eventually graduating some 12,000 pilots.

An element of the Western Flying Training Command, the 'capper' organization at Luke was the 37th Flying Training Wing (Advanced Single-Engine).

On October 27, 1942, Luke field welcomed 19 AT-9s, all from Mather Field, CA, and these were assigned to the 66th Air Base Squadron. A little over two weeks later, 16 of these returned to Mather. It is assumed that the aircraft were there on Temporary Duty to facilitate Lockheed P-38 transition training.

The reasons for this brief hiatus are unknown. The aircraft were definitely flown while at Luke, as two of them (41-5835 and 41-12031) were involved in a mid-air collision 4.5 miles southwest of the field on October 26th. The two aircraft were out on a regularly scheduled dual transition flight. There was no congestion at Luke at the time, and weather was not a factor. The aircraft had been scheduled to operate both from Luke as well as from Auxiliary Fields No.1 and No.2, and air work was to be conducted at those two locations.

2LT Robert T. Blair, an Aviation Cadet, actually stationed at Mather Field, and Cadet Robert B. Longfellow crewed 41-12031, while 41-5835 was crewed by Mr. Kenneth R. Brooks, a civilian instructor also based at Mather, with Cadet William H. Blake, of Luke Field.

One of the aircraft was flying to the northeast and one southward, and neither was apparently experiencing any difficulties. They simply attempted to occupy the same spot in the sky at the same time. The Board of Officers concluded that the visibility from the AT-9 heading northeast and possibly sun blindness in the one flying south may have been the main factor. Both aircraft were complete wrecks, and no attempt had been made to use parachutes. The bodies of all four crew members eluded identification due to the resulting fires after they crashed.

Harold C. Gibson instructed during the war on Beech AT-7s, Cessna AT-8s, AT-9s, Beech AT-10s, Cessna AT-17s, Martin B-10s and B-12s, Douglas B-18s and North American B-25s in turn at Barksdale, Mather, Luke (for a special class for Cadets going to P-38s) and Douglas AAFs and recalled that "...*the AT-7 was good, but the AT-9 was the best of all.*"

the instructor described as "...*a very bad landing indeed, causing the ship to bounce.*:" As the instructor, Lieutenant Hare, took over and attempted to salvage the landing, the student suddenly applied full braking, and the ship nosed over. Fortunately, the aircraft was repaired and saw continued service at Altus AAF, OK.

The Investigating Board observed that "...*this office has had considerable reports as to the flying technique of this student; it seems that his flying ability is very limited.*" It went on to report that "...*it had just about been decided by this Command to limit this pilot to smaller type aircraft, but since then the Command has seen fit to dismiss him entirely.*"

Such were the demands on Ferrying Command that, besides older AAF pilots and some who had completed their overseas tours, joined by many WAAFs and WASPs, they were obliged to attempt to hire civilian pilots with limited flight training and who, it must be assumed, could for some reason not qualify for active service with the Army, Navy or Marines, to take on the vital task of getting the aircraft to the training stations and fighting fronts.

Mines Field, Los Angeles, California

Station Field Code: None Known
Known Unit Markings: None Known
AT-9 Operating Units: [probably the ★332nd Fighter Squadron]
One AT-9 received movement orders to Mines Field, 41-12024, arriving from Glendale (Grand Central) on July 16, 1942 – almost certainly while assigned to the 332nd FS. It remained there with the unit until November 10, 1942, when it moved with the unit to Muroc Air base, CA.

New Castle (Wilmington) Army Air Base, New Castle, Delaware

Station Field Code: None Known
Known Unit Markings: None Known
AT-9 Operating Units: ★63rd Ferry Squadron, 2nd Ferry Group ★Flight Detachment, Air Transport Command
Just as with other Ferrying Command units (q.v.), the 63rd was assigned AT-9s (two) and AT-9As (10) between July 24, 1942 and January 1, 1944, to facilitate training of ferry crews who would be flying substantial numbers of these aircraft, primarily to stations in the southeastern U.S.

At least one of these aircraft, however, 42-57125, was actually assigned to the Flight Detachment, Air Transport Command Headquarters in Washington, but apparently garrisoned at Wilmington.

One of the aircraft, 42-56922, experienced the indignity of two separate accidents while assigned to the 2nd Ferry Group. The first was at New Castle on October 20, 1943 when 2LT John B. D. Winder had his main landing gear fold on him unexpectedly – an all too common fault of the location of the flap and landing gear retraction levers which was witnessed so often in the service life of the type.

The second was also at New Castle at 0905 hours on January 1, 1944 while being handled by a ground crew consisting of Corporal Melvin V. Herrmanny and PFC Michael H. Byrnes. They had just started the engines to conduct a routine morning pre-flight check when PFC Byrnes apparently forgot which direction the throttle levers were supposed to move to close them. Instead of closing them, he opened them wide. The aircraft obediently jumped her chocks, ran up a bank and collided with the station Commanders building! The fate of PFC Byrnes was not noted, but can be imagined.

Bearing late war national insignia and an unusual, non-hyphenated presentation of the radio call numbers, AT-9A 42-56922 (with colored engine cowls) came to grief with ATC Ferry Command there January 1, 1944 at the hands of Pfc Michael H. Byrnes, who had the added ignominy of colliding with the Station Commanders office! It had served previously at Kelly Field, TX and moved to ATC control around October 20, 1943. It was repaired and sent to RFC April 3, 1945. (USAFHRA)

Naval Air Station North Island, Coronado, California

Station Field Code: None Known
Known Unit Markings: None Known
AT-9 Operating Units: Unknown

Yet another one-off assignment which has eluded explanation, AT-9 41-5775 arrived at NAS North Island from Mather Field, CA on June 22, 1942 and stayed only briefly, before being reassigned to March Field, CA July 20, 1942.

The aircraft may have been there for some form of cooperation with the major Naval aviation establishment at North Island, but other reasons cannot be ruled out.

Oakland Army Air Base, Oakland, California

Station Field Code: None Known
Known Unit Markings: None Known
AT-9 Operating Units: Unknown

Yet another brief set of assignments during the hectic period of mid-1942, this time involving two AT-9s, 41-12025, which was assigned to Oakland June 10, 1942, arriving from Hamilton Field, CA, and returning there September 20th – only to come back to Oakland once again October 8th and regress to Hamilton November 6th!

It was followed shortly thereafter, on June 19, 19423 by 41-11957, this one arriving from San Bruno, but moving on to Hamilton on July 3rd.

Ogden Army Air Field, Ogden, Utah

Station Field Code: None Known
Known Unit Markings: None Known
AT-9 Operating Units: Unknown

Yet another odd movement, and perhaps of only marginal significance, AT-9 41-12010 was assigned to Ogden from distant Ellington Field, TX on July 25, 1942 and only stayed until the 27th, when she moved on to Salt Lake City, UT.

Although Ogden became the site of the very capable Ogden Air Depot, that was not activated until January 12, 1943, will alter the hub I say of this aircraft. It is possible that some Depot-level work was being performed here more in mid 1942, but this has thus far eluded confirmation.

Olmsted Army Air Field, Connellsville, Pennsylvania

Station Field Code: None Known
Known Unit Markings: IBL125I
AT-9 Operating Units: ★487th Air Base Squadron ★496th Air Base Squadron

A single AT-9A, 42-57131, was ordered to this unusual location as a Class 26 (Instructional Air frame) on July 26, 1943, from Blytheville. The aircraft had suffered an accident at Albany, NY July 1, 1943 while on a long-distance, cross-country training flight, and was quite simply allocated to the closest organization that could make use of its remains for training.

Army Air Forces Advanced Flying School Pampa, Texas

Station Field Code: "O-" and "P-"
Known Unit Markings: O-5, 413, 620
AT-9 Operating Units: ★852nd Two-Engine Flying Training Squadron ★1102nd Two-Engine Flying Training Squadron

Two-engine advanced training commenced at Pampa in November 1942, where sizeable numbers of Beech AT-10, Cessna AT-17 and UC-78, Lockheed RB-34 and AT-9 aircraft, commencing on December 11, 1942, were heavily utilized.

The station, an element of the Central Flying Training Command, eventually acquired a total of 20 AT-9s and 20 AT-9As. Graduates included George McGovern and Jack Palance. Besides the units noted above, Pampa also was home to the 1103rd and 1104th TEFTSs as well by November 1, 1942, and it is possible that these units may have had a few AT-9s at some juncture as well. The cadre for the 1101st through the 1104th TEFTSs arrived November 17, 1942 from Lubbock, while those for the 852nd and 853rd TEFTSs arrived January 1, 1943 from South Plains. The first aircraft – 10 AT-10s – arrived November 27th from Kelly Field, followed shortly by AT-9s and AT-17s.

The base had four Auxiliary Air Fields located at Reeves, Thompson, Hoover and Laketon.

The pace of training got off to a rapid start, and the first accident followed shortly. AT-9A 42-56982 had arrived on December 18th from Kelly, and experienced a landing accident on Christmas Eve – a measure of the intensity of the curriculum. It was repaired and moved on to Randolph field June 1st, 1943. Although this was followed by 28 other incidents, all but one repairable, there was only one accident involving fatalities. This was experienced by AT-9A 42-56864, which had arrived on station December 17, 1942. On May 12, 1943, while being flown by 2LT William A. Gibbons of the 1102nd TEFTS, he collided in mid-air with Cessna UC-78 42-71574. The remains were apparently sent to Sheppard Field, TX as Class 26. One AT-9, 41-12068, which arrived January 12, 1943, experienced no fewer than four accidents, but survived to be repaired in each instance, going to Rome, NY for RFC surplus action August 13, 1944.

This AT-9A, 42-56900, was originally delivered new to Kelly Field, TX September 29, 1942 but then departed for Pampa AAF, TX December 17th, where this image was apparently taken. The aircraft is unusual in having a previously unreported Field Code, O-5, which appeared only on the red engine cowls and no anti-glare paneling at all. (Authors Collection)

Major Alan H. Conklin, USAF (Ret), was a graduate of Pampa and, in an article in the NMUSAF "Friends Journal" recalled that he learned a number of life-long lessons at the Two-Engine Advanced School. *"We learned such rules as 'Never turn in to the dead engine.' If you asked why, the answer was, 'You'll kill yourself.' In an AT-9, on final approach, power on, with half-flaps, 'Don't let your airspeed get below 120 mph.' Why? 'You'll kill yourself.'*

Fritz Schuetzeberg apparently recalled watching AT-9s at Pampa (and, he reported, also at Brady, Texas, although this must have been in a TDY status, as no AT-9s are known to have been actually assigned to Brady) as a youngster, and played on a junked AT-9 at Lockhart, Texas circa 1948. This latter aircraft is a mystery.

Pendleton Army Air Field, Pendleton, Oregon

Station Field Code: None Known
Known Unit Markings: None Known
AT-9 Operating Units: [probably ★338th Fighter Squadron, 55th Fighter Group]
The 338th FS moved about the Pacific Northwest fairly frequently while working up as a Lockheed P-38 *Lightning* operating unit, and its three AT-9s moved along with it on most occasions.

However, on deployment, from Olympia, Washington to Pendleton in Eastern Oregon witnessed only one AT-9 moving with the unit, 41-5797. It arrived there November 18, 1942 and stayed until January 31, 1943, when it returned once again to Olympia.

Army Air Forces Basic Flying School, Perrin Field, Sherman, Texas

Station Field Code: "CL" (?) or "N-" [some aircraft known with two-digit numbers and a suffix "H"]
Known Unit Markings: 25
AT-9 Operating Units: Unknown
Yet another instance of an unusual AT-9 assignment, this station in Northeastern Texas was originally created as the Grayson Basic Flying School, a component of the Gulf Coast Training Center, and welcomed it first aircraft – appropriately a Vultee BT-13 – on August 21, 1941.

The station was expecting its first Cadet class in late December 1941, after Pearl Harbor added extreme urgency to the activity, but this was after the station was renamed Perrin Field June 21, 1941, for LTC Elmer D. Perrin, who had lost his life near Baltimore, MD while conducting an acceptance test on Martin B-26 *Marauder* 40-1386.

It is not exactly clear what is being celebrated in this image, labeled only as a "Graduating Class at Perrin Field, Texas." These 27 women were all clearly WASPs, but Perrin, located near Sherman, TX was a Basic Training station, equipped primarily with Vultee BT-13s and BT-15s with Station Codes N-, CL- and I-. Although 17 AT-9As were assigned there around April 1943, all going to RFC by November 1944, their exact use and unit of assignment there is a mystery. (NMUSAF)

By November 1, 1942 Perrin was a very active Basic Flying School, hosting six Basic Flying Training Squadrons (the 508th through 511th, 1050th and 1051st) as well as the 63rd Aviation Squadron (Sep.).

Then, inexplicably, around October 2, 1942, the first of 17 AT-9As started arriving from a variety of stations, including Altus, Blackland, Moody, Frederick, Ellington, Blytheville, and Columbus AAFs. The reason for this assignment has remained unknown, despite intensive investigations. Not a single accident was noted, suggesting that whatever their mission there, the utilization must have been low.

Nearly all of the 17 aircraft assigned to Perrin went directly to RFC control on or about November 20, 1944. It is possible that the aircraft may, in fact, have been high-time aircraft that were essentially "put out to pasture" prior to surplus.

Ponca City Army Air Field, Ponca City, Oklahoma

Station Field Code: None Known
Known Unit Markings: None Known
AT-9 Operating Units: N/A

Although six AT-9s were noted as having been assigned to this station, between November 20, 1944 and January 8, 1945, it is believed that these were in actuality "final flight destinations" for aircraft which were going to be placed in surplus status with the RFC, all of which had been so declared by October 8, 1945 – including, it should be noted, the very first, hard-working "prototype" AT-9, 41-5745.

Reading Army Air Field, Reading, Pennsylvania

Station Field Code: None Known
Known Unit Markings: None Known
AT-9 Operating Units: N/A

One AT-9, 41-12121, was assigned to this northeastern station late in the war on June 28, 1944, arriving from Columbus, MS. As it was apparently scrapped there sometime after August 1st, it was probably sent there, for some reason, for surplus disposal or retirement.

Robins (Warner Robins from September 1, 1942) Army Air Field, Wellston, Georgia

Station Field Code: None Known
Known Unit Markings: None Known
AT-9 Operating Units: N/A

The three AT-9s associated with this station (41-5752, 41-11997 and 41-12269) were assigned to this station between November 11, 1942 and July 6, 1943.

Of these, 41-11997 had the briefest stay, at just 36 days, suggesting it was undergoing work or modification, while 41-12269 was there for nearly seven months and, since it had suffered an accident on November 1, 1942 at Turner, may safely be assumed to have been undergoing extensive repairs at the excellent Warner Robins depot facilities. The other, 41-5752, was assigned there from November 28, 1942 until February 28, 1943 but since there is no known accident involving this aircraft around that time, its trip there was for unknown reasons.

Rome Air Depot, Rome, New York

Station Field Code: N/A
Known Unit Markings: N/A
AT-9 Operating Units: N/A

The Rome Air Depot, for reasons that remain obscure, was selected by the USAAF to be one of the major storage and RFC surplus centers for AT-9 series aircraft.

As early as August 1944 – and possibly earlier – a total of 88 AT-9s (31 AT-9s and 57 AT-9As) started flying in to Rome, the majority from Altus AAF, OK, but others from Scott, Ellington, Pampa, Randolph, Lubbock, Turner, Blytheville, Moody, Romulus, Kelly, and Columbus AAFs. Oddly, of these 88 aircraft 23 (all AT-9s) were then diverted to either Hat Box Field (Muskogee), OK or Walnut Ridge, OK for final disposition, with two others diverted to Bush Field, GA and Chanute Field, IL.

All had passed to the RFC by October 25, 1944.

At least 31 AT-9s and 57 AT-9As appear to have ended their days at the Rome Air Depot, Rome, NY – although, inexplicably, some moved on from there to distant Hat Box Field, Muskogee, OK, before being broken up and sold for surplus scrap. Here, two young ladies of the region ground-guide an AT-9 to its final shut-down at Rome, in company with a Vultee BT-13A, Douglas C-47B-1-DL (43-16167) and, in the background, what appears to be a rare Brewster SB2A Buccaneer series aircraft. (Rome Historical Society, Patrick Reynolds)

Romulus Army Air Field, Wayne County, Michigan

Station Field Code: None Known
Known Unit Markings: None Known
AT-9 Operating Units: ★3rd Ferry Group Transition School ★19th Ferry Squadron, 3rd Ferry Group ★60th Ferry Squadron, 3rd Ferry Group

Yet another of the geographically dispersed Air Transport Command, Ferrying Division stations, the two known Ferry Squadrons of the 3rd Ferry Group operating from there briefly had two AT-9s and at least eight AT-9As assigned for familiarization training, to benefit the crews who would be flying these aircraft to their first or subsequent assignments.

Conversion must have been challenging for this Group, and it experienced six accidents involving AT-9s at the station – one in early 1942, four in 1943 and one in 1944. Every one of them involved either fuel exhaustion or some form of landing accident. That experienced by AT-9A 42-57127 may be forgiven, however, on the grounds that the aircraft lost its No.1 (port or left side) engine propeller May 3, 1943 at about 1810 hours when about 15 feet in the air, throwing it off in front of the aircraft and under the starboard wing. The pilots, 2LT Joseph T. Skully and F/O Francis B. Colby, were actually commended for immediately trimming the aircraft for straight-and-level flight ahead and into a shallow climb, cutting off the engines (when the No.1 engine, running away, exceeded 4,800 rpm, which was throwing off oil and smoke and in danger of catching fire) and making a shallow turn to the left and a perfect three-point landing. This had been the fifth (and final) touch-and-go flight that evening, while Lt. Skully was giving F/O Colby also cited as 'Cobey') dual instruction. Ironically, the accident on August 30, 1943 to AT-9A 42-57101 also involved the aircraft 'throwing' the port side propeller. These are the only known accidents involving AT-9s throwing a prop.

The first of these, on March 23, 1940, might be excused when it is appreciated that the pilot being oriented to the aircraft had only flown Curtiss P-40s and Bell P-39s previously, and had zero two-engine time. He made an excellent landing, according to the tower, but failed to ensure that the wheels were 'down and locked,' throwing up a wonderful array of sparks as he skidded to a stop.

Roosevelt Field, Mineola, Long Island, New York

Station Field Code: None Known
Known Unit Markings: None Known
AT-9 Operating Units: N/A

One AT-9A, 42-56963, is associated with Roosevelt Field and, coincidentally, if correct, thus gained the distinction of having been the most easterly assigned of all AT-9 series aircraft.

This one must have had a very strange odyssey. It had suffered a serious accident at its last training station, George Field, IL on February 10, 1943 and, by March 31st was listed as having gone to Class 26 at Roosevelt Field. However, when it was condemned June 30, 1943, the station was listed as George Field. The explanation for this is probably administrative in nature.

Sedalia Army Air Field, Knob Noster, Missouri

Station Field Code: None Known
Known Unit Markings: None Known
AT-9 Operating Units: [probably the 913th Air Base Squadron]
Yet another puzzling assignment, a single AT-9A, 42-56891 had been stationed at Altus Field, OK when, sometime after July 6, 1943, it was assigned to this obscure station.

The aircraft passed to the RFC for surplus action October 12, 1944, but there is no information on where it was or what it was doing during the preceding 14 months. It may have been an undocumented Class 26 (Instructional Airframe) incident.

Seymour-Johnson Army Air Field, Goldsboro, North Carolina

Station Field Code: None Known
Known Unit Markings: None Known
AT-9 Operating Units: ★333rd Base Headquarters and Air Base Squadron
At least two AT-9s were apparently assigned to this station as light transports and assigned to the resident Air Base squadron, 41-5749 on August 6 and 41-5748 on September 22, 1942. Both had arrived from Chanute Field, IL. They were both still resident as late as May 1944 when they were flown to Bush Field, GA for RFC action.

Sheppard Field, Wichita Falls, Texas

Station Field Code: None Known
Known Unit Markings: None Known
AT-9 Operating Units: Unknown
Created as a dedicated Technical Training Center from October 17, 1941, with extensive mechanic training courses, Sheppard is also known to have given Instructor Pilot tuition as well.

This may account for why, between June 8, 1942 and April 20, 1943, three AT-9s and seven AT-9As were assigned there, most of them having migrated there from Pampa AAF. At least two of these passed to Class 26 (Instructional Airframes) there. The survivors, however, had moved on to Altus AAF, OK or back to Pampa AAF, TX by the end of September 1943.

Stuttgart Army Air Field, Stuttgart, Arkansas

Station Field Code: "ST-"
Known Unit Markings: None Known
AT-9 Operating Units: Unknown
An element of the Eastern Flying Training Command, the five known Two-Engine Flying Training Squadrons stationed at Stuttgart AAF – the 891st to 894th and 896th TEFTSs, elements of the capper 34th Two-Engine Flying Training Group, in East central Arkansas followed after the initial task of the station, which was to train glider pilots on Waco CG-4As.

In 1943, the school was transferred to the Southeast Flying Training Command as a dedicated two-engine advanced school, and glider training halted May 19. Initially known simply as the AAF Advanced Flying School, Stuttgart, AR, it was redesignated as Stuttgart Army Air Field January 2, 1943.

The station's training units were equipped almost exclusively with Beech AT-10s (with Unit Markings in the ST300s) and Cessna AT-17s.

Oddly, only one AT-A was known to have been assigned to Stuttgart, and this was 42-57132, which arrived from Blytheville May 11, 1943. It only stayed about three weeks before returning back to Blytheville.

Tinker Army Air Field, Oklahoma City, Oklahoma

Station Field Code: None Known
Known Unit Markings: None Known
AT-9 Operating Units: N/A

Although four AT-9s and one AT-9A were assigned on movement orders to Tinker – all on April 20, 1943, and all arriving from either Lubbock or Pampa AAFs in Texas – they almost certainly were there for some form of modification at the large depot-level facilities at Tinker and were not assigned to any unit for flying. They all were then transferred to Pampa AAF on June 1, 1943.

Tucson (Davis-Monthan) Army Air Field, Tucson, Arizona

Station Field Code: None Known
Known Unit Markings: N/A
AT-9 Operating Units: N/A
One AT-9, 41-12151 had movement orders from Ellington Field, near Houston, Texas, to "Tucson" dated October 31, 1942. It returned to Ellington shortly thereafter, on November 9, 1942, and the reasons for this brief stay are unknown.

Tyndall Army Air Field, Air Corps Gunnery School, Panama City, Florida

Station Field Code: "TY-"
Known Unit Markings: None Known
AT-9 Operating Units: Unknown
Four AT-9As and one AT-9 were assigned to Tyndall between October 5 and 27th, 1942, all arriving from Moody Field, Valdosta, GA.
They only stayed briefly, and on November 3rd and 4th, departed for Blytheville, AR.
Since Tyndall was a dedicated gunnery station, it is possible that these aircraft may have been engaged in trials for the forthcoming installation of .30 caliber machine guns in the noses of at least 30 AT-9s.

Victory Field, Vernon, Texas

Station Field Code: None Known
Known Unit markings: None Known
AT-9 Operating Units: None Known
Activated in 1941 as an element of the Gulf Coast Flying Training Center specializing in primary flight training (Stage 1), this remote station about six miles south-southwest of Vernon was operated under contract to the AAC by the Hunter Flying Service and Richey Flying Service, and was almost entirely populated with Fairchild PT-19As
With the end of primary training in early 1945, Victory Field was apparently designated as a temporary storage and RFC disposition site, as between October 6, 1944 and August 12, 1945, eight AT-9s from Altus, Frederick and – surprisingly – Patterson AAFs started arriving and all had been handed over to the RFC by September 6, 1945.

Walnut Ridge Army Air Field, Walnut Ridge, Arkansas

Station Field Code: N/A
Known Unit Markings: N/A
AT-9 Operating Units: N/A
Often overshadowed by other surplus storage fields, the facility at Walnut Ridge, AR, was, in actuality, one of the largest and, because of it fairly central location and open expanses, proved nearly ideal as the final resting place for a multitude of USAAF aircraft of all types.
Surprisingly, however, only three AT-9s are known to have been consigned to Walnut Ridge, namely AT-9s 41-5794, 41-5795 and 41-5801, these arriving there from Ellington, Douglas and Rome AAFs between September 11, 1944 and March 23, 1945. All three passed to the custody of the RFC there, the first and last on September 12th and 18th. Oddly, there was no transfer date for 41-5795, although it did pass to the RFC.

Winnsboro Municipal Airport, Winnsboro, Texas

Station Field Code: None
Known Unit Markings: N/A
AT-9 Operating Units: N/A

A minor mystery at the height of two-engine advanced pilot training at Blackland Army Air Field, Waco, Texas, is why 23 AT-9s and one AT-9A were suddenly transferred to far northeast Texas to the tiny Winnsboro Municipal Airport on January 31, 1943.

It is not clear if the Winnsboro field even had a hard-surfaced runway as of that date, and there is no record of any AAF activity there whatsoever.

Then, on February 28, all but two of the aircraft returned to Blackland, the remaining two leaving for Altus AAF, OK somewhat later, on April 20, 1943.

Yuma Army Air Field, Yuma, Arizona

Station Field Code: "U-"
Known Unit Markings: U-4, U-115, U-122, U-124, U-134, U-137, U-147, U-712
AT-9 Operating Units: ★533rd Two-Engine Flying Training Squadron ★Section "A", 950th Single-Engine Flying Training Squadron (apparently redesignated as the 950th TEFT Squadron by August 25, 1943)

Located about 4.1 miles south-southeast of Yuma, the airfield formerly known as Fly Field wasn't selected by the West Coast Air Corps Training Center for development as what was to become Yuma AAF until May 26, 1942. Actual construction and revisions to meet Army requirements occupied most of the period between June 1 and December 2, 1942.

On June 2, 1942, 2LT William C. Loveless with 13 enlisted ranks arrived at what was still officially Fly Field from Luke Field, only to find that elements of the 2nd Cavalry were using the old CCC barracks, so they set up shop in what they termed "the concrete hangar" and started servicing transient aircraft.

The AAF Advanced Flying School, Yuma, AZ was formally established on June 26th and activated the following month. The first aircraft, North American AT-6Cs, started arriving August 11th and, by December 31st, at least 74 of these aircraft decorated the ramps.

It wasn't until December 18, 1942 that Cadet Class 43-A arrived from Stockton AAF, CA, along with the first two-engine trainers, Cessna AT-17Bs.

Starting in April 1943, Yuma was directed to change its remit from single-engine advanced to two-engine advanced, and the school started checking out instructors in the first AT-9s and AT-9As,

This obviously posed shot of a Cadet named Keefe at Yuma in AT-9A 42-57072 reveals what appears to be a white or light-yellow leading edge on the engine cowl, and the fact that the aircraft designation on the data block just aft of the cockpit lists the type as AT-9-A. (via Mark Nankivil)

which started arriving on May 11, 1943 from various other stations, including La Junta, Lowry, Roswell, Douglas, Stockton and Marfa AAFs. By July 11, a total of 12 AT-9s and 21 AT-9As had arrived.

Between April 17 and December 5, 1943, a total of 1,760 Aviation Cadets (from six classes, 43-F through 43-K) had completed nine weeks of advanced two-engine instruction in AT-17s, UC-78s and the AT-9s. A number of Cadets from the Chinese Nationalist Air Force were also trained on AT-9s at the station.

Yuma based AT-9s suffered a total of six known accidents and, for nearly all of them, Yuma was their final assignment before being passed to Douglas AAF for hand-over to the RFC for disposal around February 1945, although several went to other assignments.

It is worth noting that several of the AT-9s based at Yuma were detached to the Colfred Ground Gunnery Range, which suggests that at least a few of them may have been fitted with .30 caliber nose machine guns.

Bearing Field Code U-137, this AT-9A arrived at Yuma AAF by May 29, 1943, when this image was taken, from Roswell, and passed on to Douglas AAF by March 1944. It survived the war to go to surplus February 16, 1945. Note the complete absence of any anti-glare paneling. (via Mark Nankivil)

The front-cover of the Class 43-G book for Yuma AAF featured an AT-9 with white or yellow trim on the engine cowls and nose cone. The passing light aperture, located in the center of the nose cone, was usually painted bright red. The rather small dimensions of the anti-glare paneling on the engine cowl is note-worthy. (via Mark Nankivil)

THE CURTISS-WRIGHT AT-9 SERIES
POST-WAR: SURPLUS SALE AND SURVIVORS

The slide towards oblivion for the 791 Curtiss-Wright AT-9s procured by the USAAC and USAAF can be traced from an indeterminate date not long after the Allied landings in Normandy early in June 1944.

The massive Air Training Command infrastructure, by that date primarily active at the mid-Western, Western and Southwestern training stations, was systematically inactivated or consolidated, as the demands for graduated air crew waned and subsided. The vast array of dedicated training aircraft, which had been so intensively engaged completely through 1942 and 1943 were, likewise, either consolidated at certain stations for ease of maintaining minimal operations or flown, in ever increasing numbers, to Reconstruction Finance Corporation (RFC) or War Assets Administration (WAA) sites for temporary, open storage pending disposition.

A body of apocryphal legend has, since about the same time, grown up amongst the aviation enthusiast community, regarding the fate of the surviving AT-9s. Like most legends, there can be found at least some elements of fact amidst the recollections and rumors which have attended the fate of the AT-9 fleet ever since.

There is one immutable, central fact, however, that defines the AT-9 series in this context. And that is that, completely alone amongst the array of WWII era Advanced Trainer series aircraft produced in quantity for the USAAC and USAAF, *not a single AT-9 or AT-9A ever gained a United States civil aircraft registration identity.*

On reflection, this is really a rather startling fact – but, as is so often the case, is rather short of the what actually happened.

The RFC and WAA actually did advertise significant numbers of AT-9s for surplus sale, in what was termed at the time as "Class A" condition, for $1,500 "as is, where is." For the record, following is

THE AT-9 LOW-WING TWIN-ENGINE CABIN JOB

DISPOSAL COST

$150.00

Shown above is a low-wing cantilever cabin monoplane of all-metal construction, and is equipped with dual controls, retractable main landing gear, and split trailing edge flaps.   The over-all dimensions are:

Length 31' 8"
Height 9' 10"
Span 40' 3¾"

The Lycoming R-680-9 engine is used.   A Lycoming R-680-13 may be substituted

By January 1946, the Reconstruction Finance Corporation (RFC) and War Assets Administration (WAA) were advertising surplus AT-9s to qualified educational institutions on a "where is/as is" basis for a bargain $150. The exact number of takers may never be known due to the complete destruction of the records of these sales in 1972. (via Robert L. Taylor, AAA)

150

a table showing the locations of the WAA and RFC Sales Disposition Centers, and the aircraft types on offer at these locations as of early 1946:

Location	C-46	BT-9	BT-14	AT-8	AT-9	AT-10	AT-16	AT-18	AT-24	C-38	C-76	C-87
Albuquerque, NM								1				
Americus, GA						2					1	
Augusta, GA	74	1	5		10	103	1	40		1		30
Ballinger, TX						199						
Blythe, CA					15	8						
Camden, SC						191						
Cape Girardeau, MO						37						
Cuero, TX						236		4				
Fort Stockton, TX						56						
Jackson, TN		6		1		192						
Kingman, AZ												4
Madison, MS						130						
Muskogee, OK					328			55				
Oklahoma City, OK		2				1						
Ontario, CA	34					16		1				
Pine Bluff, AR						190						
Ponca City, OK					6	2		1				
Sikeston, MO		1				58		30				
Stamford, TX					86	1		44				
Tucson, AZ						1						
Union City, TN						380						
Vernon, TX					16	55		1				
Walnut Ridge, AR	406					49			1			7
West Helena, AR						3						
TOTALS	514	10	5	1	461	1910	1	204	1	1	1	41

Oddly, while this table is illuminating, it does not, apparently, reflect the entire story, as at least 57 AT-9As were located at about this same time at the Rome Air Depot, Rome, NY, and had passed to the control of the RFC between September 17th and October 25th, 1944. While 31 "straight" AT-9s had passed through Rome enroute to Hatbox Field, Muskogee, OK during about the same period, the AT-9As apparently remained at Rome and met their fate there. If this is correct, then at least 518 (including 219 AT-9As) of the 791 AT-9s built survived the war intact which, given the accident experience and "hot rod" character of the aircraft usually attributed to it by veterans, is little short of remarkable. By August 31, 1945, however, the RFC and WAA reported that not a solitary AT-9 had been sold.

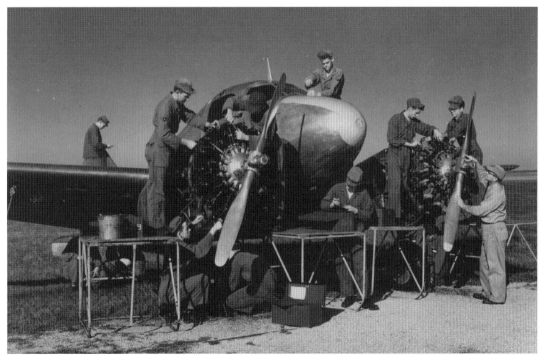

A staged photo at the world-renowned Spartan School of Aeronautics in Tulsa, OK dated October 25, 1951, the AT-9 pictured is almost certainly the very last completely intact example on earth as of the date of the photo – and the best maintained! Spartan had at least two and possibly three AT-9 ground instructional training aids. (Spartan)

In fact, the Civil Aeronautics Authority (CAA) issued Limited Type Certificate (LTC) Number LTC-31-2 covering the AT-9 and AT-9A on January 14, 1948 – nearly three years *after* the first AT-9s had been transferred to the custody of the RFC – to a Mr. Louis S. Rehr who, at the time, resided at 16 Salamanca Avenue, Apartment 8, Coral Gables, Florida. The issuance of an LTC usually meant that at least one subject aircraft had been identified and issued, usually, an Experimental Category license number. However, despite a diligent search of extant FAA records, not a single license number has been connected to any AT-9 series aircraft. This also suggests that, had such a number in fact been issued, it may have been amongst the so-called "NL-" (Limited) series, issued almost exclusively to former combat types, the CAA files for which were inexplicably destroyed by the Suitland National Records Center in 1972.

Exactly what Louis Rehr intended to do with his LTC is also a mystery, although such a request of the CAA usually meant that the recipient intended some commercial application or modification of aircraft of the specified type, or a conversion program for same.

It has been established that at least six AT-9As were sold via the RFC to civilian buyers from the batch of 15 stored at the Blythe, California site. All of these sales were consummated between February 15 and March 25, 1946, and suggests that other sales may have been similarly concluded at the much larger assemblages of AT-9s at Hat Box Field, Muskogee, OK and Stamford, TX. Unfortunately, the records of RFC surplus sales were destroyed in 1972 at the same time as the Limited license files, and no details have survived. The fact remains, however, that none of the six known aircraft, described below, were ever issued a U.S. Civil Aircraft License.

Known AT-9 Surplus Sales

USAAF Serial	Date of Sale by RFC	Buyer
42-56869	25 March 1946	George E. France1, Visalia, California
42-56910	20 February 1946	E. G. Kidwell, Los Angeles, California
42-56880	15 February 1946	H. L. Atwood, Salinas, California
42-56911	15 February 1946	H. L. Atwood, Salinas, California
42-56970	15 February 1946	Jenson Crop Dusting of Nevada, Elko, Nevada
42-57104	15 February 1946	Jenson Crop Dusting of Nevada, Elko, Nevada

Of these buyers, the only one that has been identified with precision is George E. France of Visalia, CA. He appears to have been connected with an organization at the Visalia airport which included E. L. Felt, himself a former Curtiss-Wright employee, which was engaged in the overhaul of at least six surplus Douglas C-47s for an airline in Colombia, and five Curtiss C-46s for a Sacramento operator. The AT-9A may have been included in this mix as a speculative venture, but the trail has long since gone cold.

Besides qualified civil buyers, however (preference was given to veterans), the War Assets Administration (WAA) maintained an Educational Aircraft Disposal Division at 425 Second Street, NW, Washington, DC, and advertised extensively regarding the special provisions of the surplus program directed exclusively at qualified institutions. The aircraft offered by the WAA were a mix of Basic and Advanced Trainers, as well as the ubiquitous Cessna AT-17 and UC-78 series. Their full-page ads included a coupon which could be mailed in to the agency, together with blanket information on the costs of the aircraft – "as is/where is" which were considerably less than those for more capable aircraft offered by the RFC. Cessna UC-78, UC-78B, UC-78C and AT-17 series aircraft and Curtiss AT-9s, for instance, were

---

1   In the original document, this man's last name was cited as "Franco," but research by the staff of the Tulare County Library staff, led by Librarian III Jonathan Waltmire, revealed that it was almost certainly George E. France, a well-known aviator in the Visalia area.

selling for $150, while Vultee BT-13A, BT-15, SNV-1s and North American AT-6 and SNJ series aircraft were going for $100. The following table shows the locations and types of aircraft the WAA was offering to qualified educational institutions.

War Assets Administration (WAA) Sales Centers and Sales Storage Depots and Aircraft Types as of 24 January 1946

Location of Aircraft	Vultee BT-13	Vultee BT-15	Vultee SNV-1	North American AT-6	North American SNJ	Curtiss AT-9	Cessna AT-17	Cessna UC-78
Albuquerque, NM	X			X				X
Augusta, GA	X				X			X
Blythe, CA	X						X	
Camden, SC	X			X	X			
Clinton, OK			X					
Cuero, TX							X	X
Dos Palos, CA	X							
Jackson, TN	X			X				
Lamesa, TX	X							
Muskogee, OK						X		
Oklahoma City, OK	X							X
Ontario, CA				X				X
Stamford, TX						X	X	
Vernon, TX	X	X			X			X

The sale of government surplus aircraft, as in the immediate post-WWI period, quickly became a topic of debate within the post-WW2 U.S. aviation establishment. *Southern Flight* magazine for August 1946 invited four leading aircraft sales firms to comment on the surplus glut under the monthly feature "The Operator's Forum," with the headline *Surplus Aircraft Disposal – Asset or Liability?*

Perhaps to no one's surprise, the four commentators, all of whom depended on the commissions generated by new-build aircraft sales for their livelihood, predicted disaster, and the sidebar statistical report that the magazine published to accompany the feature clearly supported that notion. It stated that the joint RFC/WAA listings published to that date described no fewer than 16,097 aircraft awaiting disposal nationwide of which – and obviously of great concern to the magazine and the commentators – 10,055 were physically located in the southern half of the country. California led with 2,782, Texas was second with 1,744 while Florida placed third with 768. Private flyers/owners constituted 66% of all buyers eligible for CAA certification. Of the 16,097 sales analyzed, 5,142 were purchased by 4,579 private fliers and the remainder went to aviation enterprises of various descriptions. Nationwide, Los Angeles County in California led all sales, with 1,753 planes purchased, while Dade County (Miami) Florida, where a thriving business in exports was blooming, was next with 365.

Although the surviving AT-9s constituted only a small fraction of this much larger picture, the fact remains that, of all of this total of more than 16,000 assorted types, the AT-9 series holds the dubious distinction of being the solitary WWII surplus type to never obtain a solitary known U.S. Commercial, Restricted, Experimental or Limited category license.

A number of enthusiasts have advanced explanations for this historical anomaly. The prevailing consensus seems to weigh towards the reputation that the AT-9 had gained during its wartime advanced training service as a "hot" airplane with poor single-engine/engine-out characteristics. Another faction points to the limited conversion capacity and relatively high operating costs compared to, especially, the Cessna UC-78/AT-17 series, which could at least carry four or five in relative comfort. However, as one Leslie R. Bowman of the Aircraft Sales Company of Fort Worth, TX pointed out, "...*the UC-78 is neither an economical airplane in gasoline and oil per mile nor a good airplane for payload with a good gas supply.*" Its primary attraction was its initial cost: $100 to $500.

Educational Uses

Besides the known surplus sales to individuals and small enterprises noted above, it is perhaps not surprising that a number of AT-9s were acquired as, apparently, instructional airframes, since the aircraft was closer to being state-of-the-art than its Beech AT-10 and Cessna AT-17/UC-78 brethren.

Besides those bailed to such institutions by the USAAF directly during the war (and which are described earlier in this account), WAA surplus sales under the Educational Institution provisions included at least three to the internationally respected Spartan School of Aeronautics in Tulsa, OK. Reportedly, one of these was almost immediately dissected into components for specific training aids applications, while one was used for line maintenance training and the third as a spares source. The older instructors reportedly cited them as "Humpback Hawks," the solitary citation located referring to this local nickname.

At least one AT-9A (42-56863), which had been amongst those awaiting disposition at the Rome Air Depot, NY, had been acquired by Penn State University by May 19, 1947, and it is assumed that it was used in some fashion by the Engineering Department there. However, a concerted effort to learn more about this aircraft was completely unsuccessful. It can be safely assumed that other AT-9s were also allocated – very inexpensively – to qualified educational institutions as well but, like the RFC records themselves, the Federal accounting for such sales was also destroyed around 1972.

And the Survivors: A Very Rare Breed Indeed

The two survivors – or what was left of them – were donated to the United States Air Force Museum. The first of these, Accession Number 1978-153, was acquired from the Spartan School of Aeronautics (where it was essentially intact but missing its doors and nose cone, with the spurious, Hollywood-inspired number "007" painted on her vertical fine!) and was airlifted to Wright-Patterson AFB by a C-130 of the 356th TAS in August 1978. This hulk served as a parts source for the second aircraft, Accession 1983-98, formerly AC41-12150.

AC41-12150 had been located around 1980, disassembled and in the possession of H. E. Babcock of Katy, Texas. It was acquired via an exchange with C. B. Thornton, Jr., of Los Angeles, California, facilitated by none other than Roger Freeman. The dismantled aircraft – photographed by my late friend John "Mad Dog" Kerr – transited Kelly AFB en route to the NMUSAF. It was found to have moderate corrosion throughout the airframe. The cockpit floor pan was borrowed from the former Spartan aircraft while two-thirds of the fuselage and one-third of the top of the starboard wing required re-skinning. Multiple components and structures had to be fabricated based on Curtiss drawings, including about 50% of the cockpit. This aircraft had, for some reason, been abandoned at Cimarron City, Oklahoma

Considering the circumstances, the remains of AT-9A 42-56882 now in the care of the Pima Air & Space Museum in Tucson, AZ are in remarkably good condition, although many parts are missing and a full restoration would be exceptionally challenging. Found by John Able in the Aldo Leopold Wilderness area, it had been based at Roswell AAF, NM and was taking part in a search for a downed AT-17 when it went down on December 30, 1942. Both crew walked out. Colour photo see page 173. (via Pima Air & Space Museum)

(where it was photographed), where it had been dropped from the inventory as surplus. Exactly how she got from that far western county in Oklahoma to Katy, Texas is a mystery, although there was apparently an intermediate owner between H. E. Babcock, given as legendary Texan aviator Lou Foote of Lockhart, Texas.

Then of course there is the AT-9A, AC42-56882, discovered at a very remote location by John Able, that was recovered via a tremendous effort by the staff and volunteers of the (then) Pima Air Museum of Tucson, AZ from the Aldo Leopold Wilderness.

The scattered wreckage was located on an approximately 30-degree slope, but the team determined that some parts – which, in spite of the severity of the crash, should have been there – had apparently been carried off as souvenirs by hikers over the years. These included the props, wheels, virtually all of the cockpit interior (although these could have been recovered by the AAF), the doors, tail wheel, and nose cone. The aircraft had gone down while based out of Roswell, NM under the command of 2LT Winston J. Bradford and Cadet Jerome Barleau aboard while engaged in a search mission for a missing Cessna AT-17, and the location of the loss at the time, December 30, 1942, was 10 miles northwest of Hermosa, NM. Miraculously, and a testament to the ruggedness of the Curtiss design, both crew members survived and managed to hike their way out. The official accident report for the aircraft gave the type at the time as AT-9B, although the data block remaining on the fuselage side of the remains reads AT-9A! Although in rough shape, and with the plan to eventually restore her, this will require a valiant effort, as many parts are missing entirely.

The recovery project was headed by Project Coordinator Lawrence V. Tagg and the challenge it represented was truly daunting. Sitting at the 8,000-foot level, the Tagg's had advised the (then) Director of the Pima Air Museum, Ned Robinson that they would like to try to recover the remains, he gave his full support to the effort. The effort required an environmental-impact survey and special-use permits but, even at that, the Taggs realized, upon examining the wreck site first-hand, that the only way to get the remains out was by helicopter. After several attempts to enlist the assistance of Arizona National Guard and active-duty USAF helicopter units, the remains were finally lifted out by a Bell 206L *Long Ranger* of the U.S. Forest Service, flown by Tom Woodworth. The extraction required seven loads and some four hours of flight time, but the remains were eventually loaded on a trailer and delivered to Tucson.

The solitary, complete survivor – itself a composite of at least two aircraft, an ex-Spartan School ground instruction airframe and 41-12150, acquired by the USAF Museum around 1978. Painted to represent an aircraft based at Lubbock AAF (probably because their archives contained only a few color illustrations of wartime AT-9s), the actual 41-12150 never served a day there, having been based for most of her career at Ellington Field, TX and Altus AAF, OK. The restoration is superb, however, and only a few small parts are missing. Colour photo see page 174. (Accession 1978-153, NMUSAF)

AT-9 COLORS
AND MARKINGS

Most observers would probably very quickly offer the opinion that, as wartime advanced trainers, the Curtiss-Wright AT-9 series offered only a very narrow breadth of colours and markings variations.

In fact, like most of their wartime brethren, the AT-9 series was subject to the same changes – and local variations – that permeated the entire Army Air Forces panoply of aircraft types as the war progressed and, in fact, considerable variations have revealed themselves upon close study.

National Insignia

Of the 791 AT-9s and AT-9As produced, all of the 'straight' AT-9s built (and approximately 25 of the first AT-9As) were handed over to the USAAC/USAAF with what is usually termed the Type 1 U.S. national insignia in four wing positions, consisting of the white star superimposed on a blue disc with a red 'dot' in the centre. This insignia had been approved for U.S. armed forces use January 2, 1921, and remained in use, officially, until the deletion of the red 'dot' in the centre August 18, 1942 with the introduction of the Type 2 insignia – although in combat theatres, the 'dot' had been removed or painted over earlier in many instances.

In actual practice, however, there are numerous instances of the Type 1 national insignia persisting in Training Command long past the August 18, 1942 changeover, as many of the operating training units simply did not possess the time nor resources to carry out an over-night change on large numbers of aircraft.

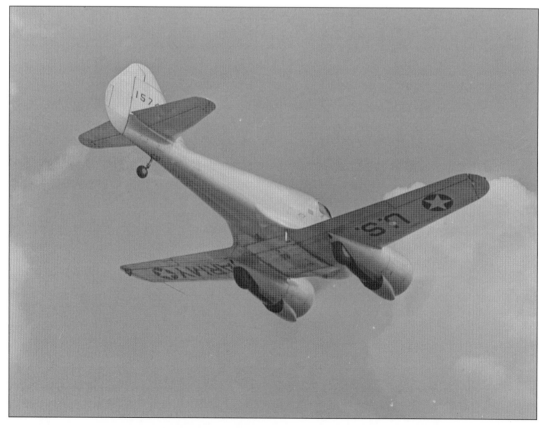

By the time this interesting view of the number one AT-9, AC41-5745 was taken on June 28, 1943, the aircraft had experienced many adventures and had amassed more than 306 hours total time – all in experimental roles. Although almost devoid of any special markings, it is unusual in still having "U.S. Army" titles on the lower main planes at this late date. (NARA RG342-FH #100415 via Stan Piet)

Similarly, when the USAAF directed the introduction of the Type 3 national insignia June 29, 1943, (the first one to have the 'wings' added to the central blue circle with white star superimposed on it) but with a thin red outline added, not a single AT-9 has been identified as having been painted with this insignia.

However, when the Type 4 national insignia was introduced September 17, 1943, essentially the same as the Type 3 but with the thin red outline deleted, most surviving AT-9s and AT-9As eventually were repainted with this insignia – but by no means all. A number of photos showing AT-9s arriving at RFC and WAA disposition centres in mid-to-late 1944 show them still bearing Type 2 national insignia, more than 18 months after the type had been superseded.

The distinctive red, white and blue rudder stripes worn pre-war by most USAAC aircraft, which were officially ordained to have been deleted effective August 1940, were in fact applied to every single AT-9 and approximately the first 25 AT-9As by Curtiss-Wright at the factory prior to hand-over to delivery crews, not being officially ordered deleted until June 1942. The leading solid vertical blue strip, which was supposed to have occupied 1/3 of the maximum rudder width, and the 13 red and white horizontal stripes, which were divided into 13 equal spacings, were interpreted in at least three different ways by Curtiss. Photo evidence shows some with the vertical blue strip some distance aft of the rudder/vertical fin hinge line, while others did not extend, for some reason, all the way to the base of the rudder. These rudder colours persisted on the all-metal AT-9s long after they had disappeared from Cessna AT-17s, UC-78s and Beech AT-10s stationed at the same training base, for the pure and simple reason that the Cessna and Beech aircraft had fabric covered rudders, which could be relatively easily removed or recovered, while the all-metal AT-9 rudders required labour-intensive efforts to scrub off the colours.

The positioning of the National Insignia on Training Command aircraft which, as noted below, employed a very necessary array of Station Codes and/or Field Numbers on all forms of training aircraft, conflicted with official guidance which, in August 1942, ordered that the National Insignia be worn on the fuselage as well. This meant that, in most cases, Field Numbers would either have to be relocated on the fuselage, or made smaller. Training Command hotly debated the subject with HQS, AAF for most of the wartime period until April 1944, when Materiel Command at last authorized Training Command to remove the fuselage stars as necessary – even though most stations did not do so.

An appropriate image for our study of the Jeep series, this view of Lubbock AAF-based Field Code 702 shows yet another variation on the amazing array of locally applied anti-glare panels used (or not used) on the AT-9 fleet during more than three-full years of intensive utilization. (Class 44-D via Mark Nankivil)

157

The large black characters (sometimes Insignia Blue) "U.S. ARMY" were also painted on the lower wing surfaces of nearly all AT-9s. It was officially no longer required after November 1942 and was officially ordered removed entirely in December 1943.

USAAC and USAAF Serial Numbers (Radio Call Numbers)

In keeping with pre-war practice, individual Air Corps serials, which were also used in modified form as individual aircraft radio call sign for aircraft equipped with radios, were permanently assigned to each aircraft built and were usually stamped, as well, onto the Manufacturers Data Plate as well. Early service Tech Orders stipulated that a radio call number was to be displayed on each AAF aircraft, but nearly all Primary Trainers without radios omitted the markings. Most new AT-9s did not carry these numbers on their vertical fins/rudders, using only the so-called Data Block on the left side of the fuselage, just aft of the cabin door to record the individual aircraft serial.

Then, with the publication of T.O. 07-1-1 dated June 1, 1942, the AAC allowed long designators to appear "...*on the fuselage*," and an unknown number of AT-9s delivered from around this date, especially those going to stations in Georgia, had such numbers painted on as well as their serials on the vertical fin. Some of these "on the fuselage", large numeral radio call numbers actually appeared on aircraft prior to the issuance of that T.O., thus rendering the date of actual implementation arbitrary. By late 1942, all new-build and the majority of the original, surviving AT-9s had their serial numbers painted on their vertical fin/rudder, although the form of presentation, due to some confusion in the field, varied rather widely and few were in actual conformance with Army Regulations.

Base Code Letters and Field Numbers

As the aircraft entered service at the initial 25 locations where new-build AT-9s were delivered, they often joined many other aircraft entering service at these locations and it became immediately obvious to commanders charged with operating the burgeoning training establishment that a simplified means of identifying these aircraft locally was necessary.

The need for a simplified system was immediate, however, and the official and permanent serial numbers were simply too long and cumbersome in most instances. Thus was born the Air Training

Command Base Code Letters and Field Number system – a subject that, unfortunately, can hardly be described as an exact science!

At first, the three major regional commands in existence at the time – Southeast Air Corps Training Center, Gulf Coast Air Corps Training Center, and West Coast Air Corps Training Center – apparently each settled on a locally designed scheme for the stations falling under their command, and apparently with little or no coordination between them. For example, the Southeast selected the letter "T" for the Base Code Letter for the multitude of aircraft assigned to Turner Field at Albany, GA, at precisely the same time that the Western Command selected the letter "T" for aircraft assigned to Mather Field, CA! This has since led many aero-historians on a merry chase, and was never resolved, sheer distance between the stations being the final 'solution,' as it were.

AT-9A 42-57038 wearing the station code A-420 for Douglas Army Air Field, Arizona, where is arrived January 5, 1943. By this juncture most of the earlier colored cowlings and special markings seen elsewhere had been surpassed, and the aircraft wore just what was necessary. (NMUSAF)

In Chapters Six and Eight, we have made a concerted effort to identify actual known and verified Base Code Letters and/or Field Numbers for AT-9s assigned to those stations or activities. These appear to have been universally painted on in black, although there is some evidence that at least a few may have been in another colour (including red at Williams AAF, AZ, for AT-9s specifically tasked with Instrument Training), although the size, location, font and stencilled examples varied widely.

However, the reader is cautioned to make use of this as a point-of-departure only, since there is ample evidence that substantial numbers of AT-9s, especially as the war progressed and the drawdown of Training Command accelerated, that many aircraft which were reassigned to new stations (including, apparently, numbers from Ellington, Blacklands and Lubbock Fields in Texas) heading for the final great concentrations at Frederick and Altus AAFs in Oklahoma, retained their old Base Code Letters or Field Numbers at these new stations for some time after arrival. Indeed, many may have retained them until the very end of their service lives, as the impetus to change them, and their comparative inactivity, rendered such an intensive effort unnecessary.

Those final two great concentrations of AT-9s in Oklahoma, however, appear to have instituted a Field Number system of their own creation that has remained virtually unique. Those AT-9s and AT-9As that were identified for continued operations were issued completely new Field Numbers with a letter "M" suffix, the significance of which has, unfortunately, eluded identification. Many of these same aircraft, as illustrated, also had portions of their empennage painted red (as were the cowlings) with the serial numbers then painted on in yellow.

Colours

In addition to the excellent colour side-views rendered for this publication by Ted Williams, throughout the text, and where positively identified, the assorted colours and special markings applied to the AT-9 fleet have been identified.

These appear to have been overwhelmingly dictated at the direction of the individual School Squadrons or Two-Engine Flying Training Squadrons which operated AT-9s, with obvious local utility. Despite intensive efforts, however, and the relatively small number of colour images of AT-9s that were taken during the war, nothing approaching a complete understanding of these colours appears possible. Yellow on the cowlings was, in varying depths and combinations, appears to have obviously predominated. Yet multi-colour cowlings are also known. A deep blue was used on the cowlings of at least one squadron, and there is reason to suspect that three other squadrons at the same station, Turner Field, GA, used red, green, and yellow to distinguish their aircraft from the others. Pride-of-place must go to the Williams AAF unit, unfortunately not identified with any certainty, which applied red-and-white "candy striping" on at least four of their unit aircraft, the significance of which has eluded explanation.

The variation in the application of anti-glare panels is striking. So far as can be determined, none of these were applied at delivery by Curtiss-Wright, and appear to have been left completely to the discretion of individual operating units or stations. Some covered the entire quadrant of the upper nose section ahead of the windscreen; others were tapered or v-shaped. Yet others extended the anti-glare flat-black or flat green panels to significant portions of the inboard engine cowlings and nacelles while some others painted the entire upper area of the cowling and nacelles aft to the trailing edge. The application of wing-walk, ant-skid/slip panels on either side of the cabin also varied enormously and, again, there is no evidence that these were applied at the factory.

There are at least two known instances of AT-9s with what appear to have been red chevrons on their upper wing surfaces – one of them near the wing tips and the other in much broader chord, at mid-wing. The significance of these is unknown, but may have been used as formation training aids.

Late in the war, some AT-9s are noted to have had portions of their lower, rear fuselage painted matt black, possibly to help protect the area from the inevitable erosion caused by FOD being thrown up by the twin props on often relatively primitive auxiliary air fields.

Tactical Unit Colours and Markings

As noted in Chapter Seven, a number of AT-9s were assigned to Lockheed P-38 units and to Tow Target units on the West Coast to aid in two-engine conversion and associated aerial gunnery training.

It is known with certainty that those assigned to P-38s operating in Oregon and Washington were camouflaged in olive drab over light grey, and it is reasonable to assume that the other P-38 units, mainly in California, followed that lead. One P-38 unit which operated an AT-9 may have applied its unit's colour codes to the nose of their AT-9, although it is not known if actual unit insignia was ever applied.

Although few in number, these aircraft were not mentioned at all in any of the formal unit histories which have survived at the USAF Historical Research Agency, although they unquestionably played a significant part in helping to prepare novice pilots assigned to these units for their state-of-the-art mounts, the P-38. Most were operating from such isolated stations that photography was virtually non-existent, not only because of the locale, but because of exceptionally strict prohibitions on photography which existed on the West Coast at or near military installations in 1942 and 1943. We know they were there; we can make assumptions about their appearance relative to their combatant brethren the P-38s, but we may never know for sure.

Interior Colours and Stencilling

For the purist, a few words regarding other paints used on production AT-9s and AT-9As as they left Robertson, MO.

Surprisingly, the engine mounts were painted with a single coat of cockpit green, rather than the 'zinc chromate' that most modellers and restoration shops would expect, and the interior areas of the wings and control surfaces received a single coat of primer.

The cockpit, so-called 'cargo area' (the rear seat area for two) and the small luggage compartment were finished with a single coat of cockpit green. The balance of the interior of the fuselage received a coat of primer.

When anti-glare panels were finally applied, the Air Corps belatedly instructed field units to apply them 'as needed' in accordance with other applicable T.O.s in force at the time, rather vague guidance which probably accounts for the wide variations found in actual practice.

The AAF did not issue T.O.01-25KA-54 entitled "Curtiss-Stenciling Instructions on Wings-AT-9" until July 1, 1942, as the result of numerous complaints from the field of damage sustained from rough handling by inexperienced ground crews. These instructions covered AC41-5745 to 41-5894 and 41-11939 to 41-12159 inclusive, and of course all subsequent AT-9s and AT-9As were stencilled at the factory prior to delivery. These involved the application, using "Paint, stencil, black, Spec.3-50" of "NO STEP," "NO PUSH" and "PUSH ON WALKWAY" stencils on the upper wing surfaces as shown on the accompanying illustration.

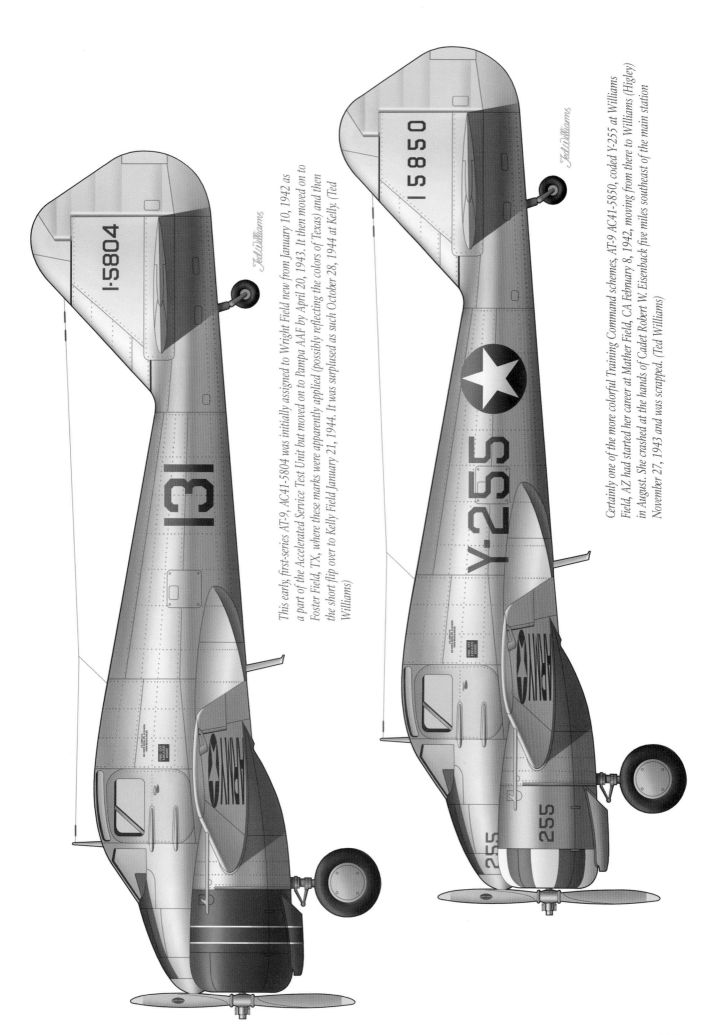

This early, first-series AT-9, AC41-5804 was initially assigned to Wright Field new from January 10, 1942 as a part of the Accelerated Service Test Unit but moved on to Pampa AAF by April 20, 1943. It then moved on to Foster Field, TX, where these marks were apparently applied (possibly reflecting the colors of Texas) and then the short flip over to Kelly Field January 21, 1944. It was surplused as such October 28, 1944 at Kelly. (Ted Williams)

Certainly one of the more colorful Training Command schemes, AT-9 AC41-5850, coded Y-255 at Williams Field, AZ had started her career at Mather Field, CA February 8, 1942, moving from there to Williams (Higley) in August. She crashed at the hands of Cadet Robert W. Eisenback five miles southeast of the main station November 27, 1943 and was scrapped. (Ted Williams)

161

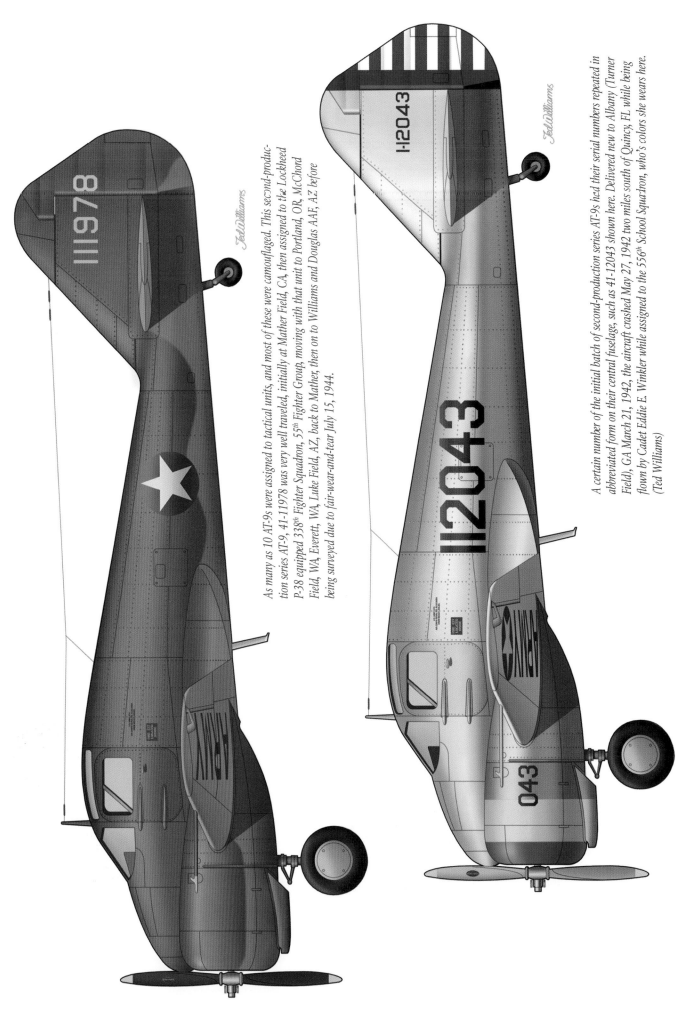

As many as 10 AT-9s were assigned to tactical units, and most of these were camouflaged. This second-production series AT-9, 41-11978 was very well traveled, initially at Mather Field, CA, then assigned to the Lockheed P-38 equipped 338th Fighter Squadron, 55th Fighter Group, moving with that unit to Portland, OR, McChord Field, WA, Everett, WA, Luke Field, AZ, back to Mather, then on to Williams and Douglas AAF, AZ before being surveyed due to fair-wear-and-tear July 15, 1944.

A certain number of the initial batch of second-production series AT-9s had their serial numbers repeated in abbreviated form on their central fuselage, such as 41-12043 shown here. Delivered new to Albany (Turner Field), GA March 21, 1942, the aircraft crashed May 27, 1942 two miles south of Quincy, FL while being flown by Cadet Eddie E. Winkler while assigned to the 556th School Squadron, who's colors she wears here. (Ted Williams)

162

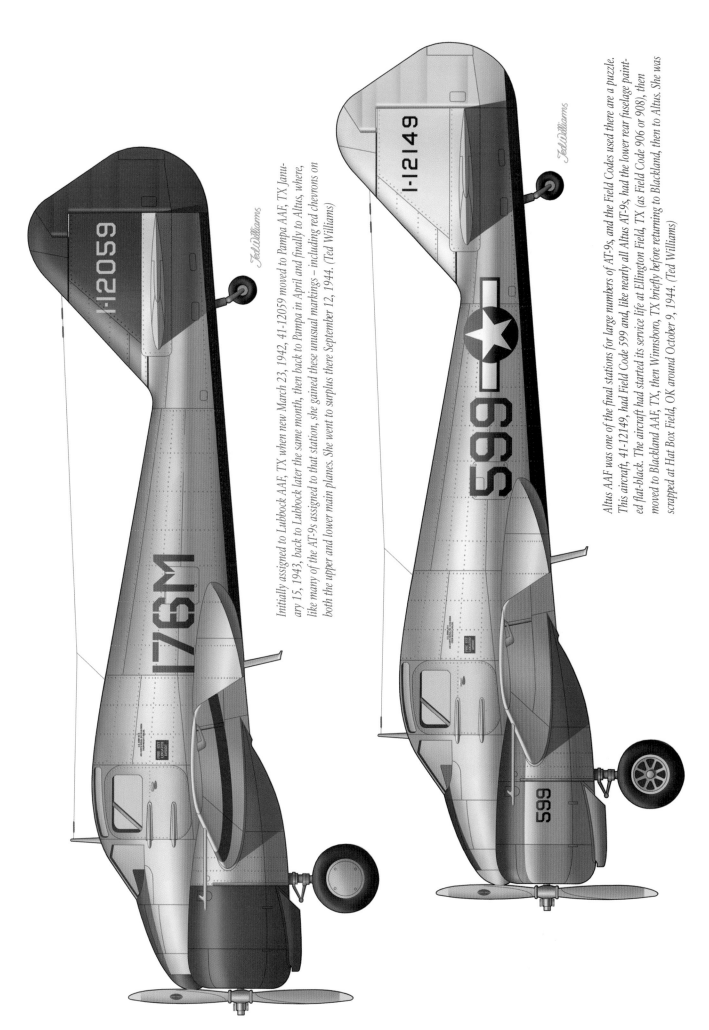

Initially assigned to Lubbock AAF, TX when new March 23, 1942, 41-12059 moved to Pampa AAF, TX January 15, 1943, back to Lubbock later the same month, then back to Pampa in April and finally to Altus, where, like many of the AT-9s assigned to that station, she gained these unusual markings – including red chevrons on both the upper and lower main planes. She went to surplus there September 12, 1944. (Ted Williams)

Altus AAF was one of the final stations for large numbers of AT-9s, and the Field Codes used there are a puzzle. This aircraft, 41-12149, had Field Code 599 and, like nearly all Altus AT-9s, had the lower rear fuselage painted flat-black. The aircraft had started its service life at Ellington Field, TX (as Field Code 906 or 908), then moved to Blackland AAF, TX, then Winnsboro, TX briefly before returning to Blackland, then to Altus. She was scrapped at Hat Box Field, OK around October 9, 1944. (Ted Williams)

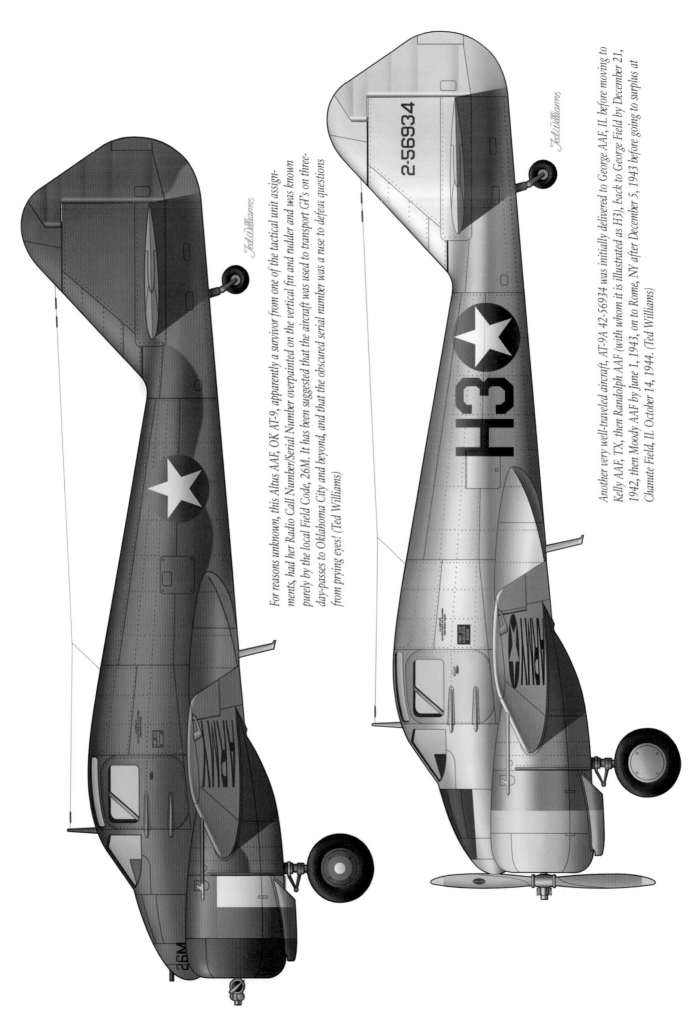

For reasons unknown, this Altus AAF, OK AT-9, apparently a survivor from one of the tactical unit assignments, had her Radio Call Number/Serial Number overpainted on the vertical fin and rudder and was known purely by the local Field Code, 26M. It has been suggested that the aircraft was used to transport GI's on three-day-passes to Oklahoma City and beyond, and that the obscured serial number was a ruse to defeat questions from prying eyes! (Ted Williams)

Another very well-traveled aircraft, AT-9A 42-56934 was initially delivered to George AAF, IL before moving to Kelly AAF, TX, then Randolph AAF (with whom it is illustrated as H3), back to George Field by December 21, 1942, then Moody AAF by June 1, 1943, on to Rome, NV after December 5, 1943 before going to surplus at Chanute Field, IL October 14, 1944. (Ted Williams)

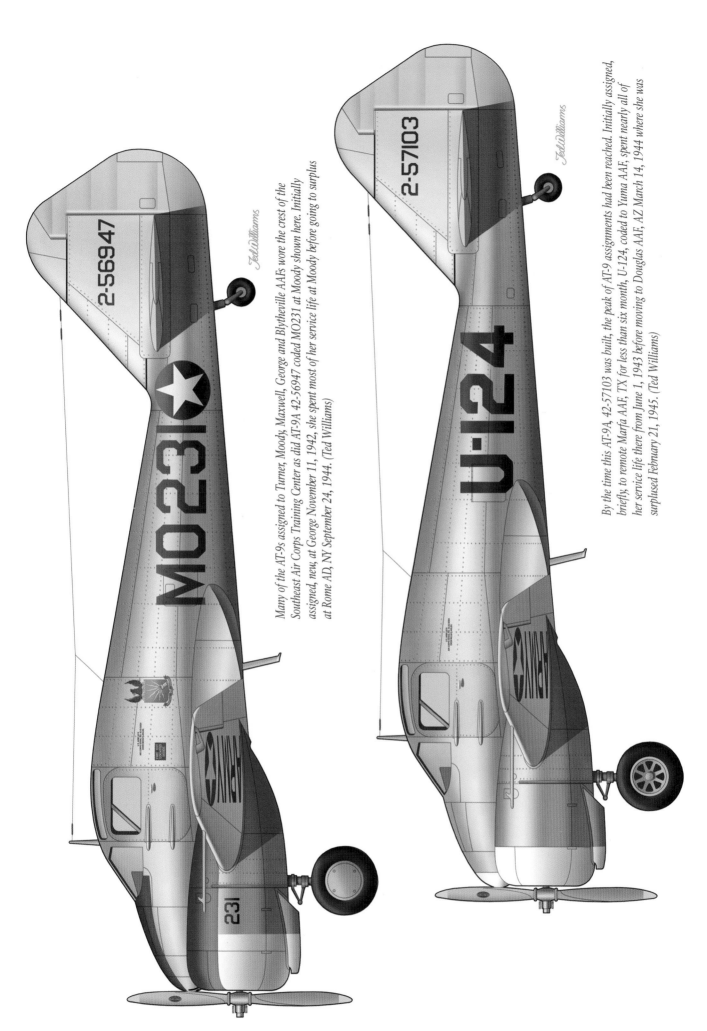

Many of the AT-9s assigned to Turner, Moody, Maxwell, George and Blytheville AAFs wore the crest of the Southeast Air Corps Training Center as did AT-9A 42-56947 coded MO231 at Moody shown here. Initially assigned, new, at George November 11, 1942, she spent most of her service life at Moody before going to surplus at Rome AD, NY September 24, 1944. (Ted Williams)

By the time this AT-9A, 42-57103 was built, the peak of AT-9 assignments had been reached. Initially assigned, briefly to remote Marfa AAF, TX for less than six month, U-124, coded to Yuma AAF, spent nearly all of her service life there from June 1, 1943 before moving to Douglas AAF, AZ March 14, 1944 where she was surplused February 21, 1945. (Ted Williams)

Although obviously a posed image, this Ellington Field-based AT-9, Field Code 21 reveals: the early 1942, low-number codes and relatively clean, yellow-cowled aircraft preparing for a dual flight. Note the unusual half-wheel cover on the port main gear. (NARA RG342-FH-K-150 via Stan Piet)

The long-suffering ground crews assigned to Training Command activities often worked in pooled or centralized organizations to meet the extremely hectic training cycles and keep the aircraft serviced, clean and ready for their exertions. Here, Field Code 66 at Ellington, an AT-9 from the second major production batch, is starting to show hard use, and has her wheel covers, and the shielded passing light aperture in the extreme nose painted red as well as the cowls. (NARA RG342-FH-K2231 via Stan Piet)

Another flight-line view at Ellington Field, TX, these AT-9s all have Field Codes in the 900s and recall the anticipation and anxiety of young Cadets approaching their mounts for another day filled with challenges. (USAAF)

A four-ship element from Ellington over the Gulf of Mexico. The lead aircraft, 41-12150, Field Number 909 moved to Altus Field, OK August 27, 1944 and went to surplus at Cimarron, OK after September 1944. It served as the basis for the sole surviving AT-9, now on display at the National Museum of the USAF at Dayton, OH. (NARA RG342-FH-K-158 via Stan Piet)

This Williams-based AT-9, Y-275, and several others like it, sported one of the most colorful of Training Command schemes, consisting of red/white "candy cane" cowls. The significance of these and unit of assignment have not been discovered. (NARA RG342-FH-K157)

An excellent color study of AT-9A 42-57038, which arrived new at Douglas AAF, AZ January 7, 1943 and was coded A-420. Moving on to Yuma by August 25, she was involved in a collision with AT-6C 41-32872 there and sent to Class 26 in November 1943. (NARA RG342-FH via Stan Piet)

An early series AT-9 AC41-5816 survived service at Turner, Moody, Maxwell and Columbus AAF's before flying to Patterson Field, OH around July 28, 1944. It ended up, pictured here, at Bush Field, Augusta, GA along with only three other AT-9s amidst a sea of surplus AT-10s. For unknown reasons, it wore Field Code Z251. (Bernie Schultre via A. Kevin Grantham)

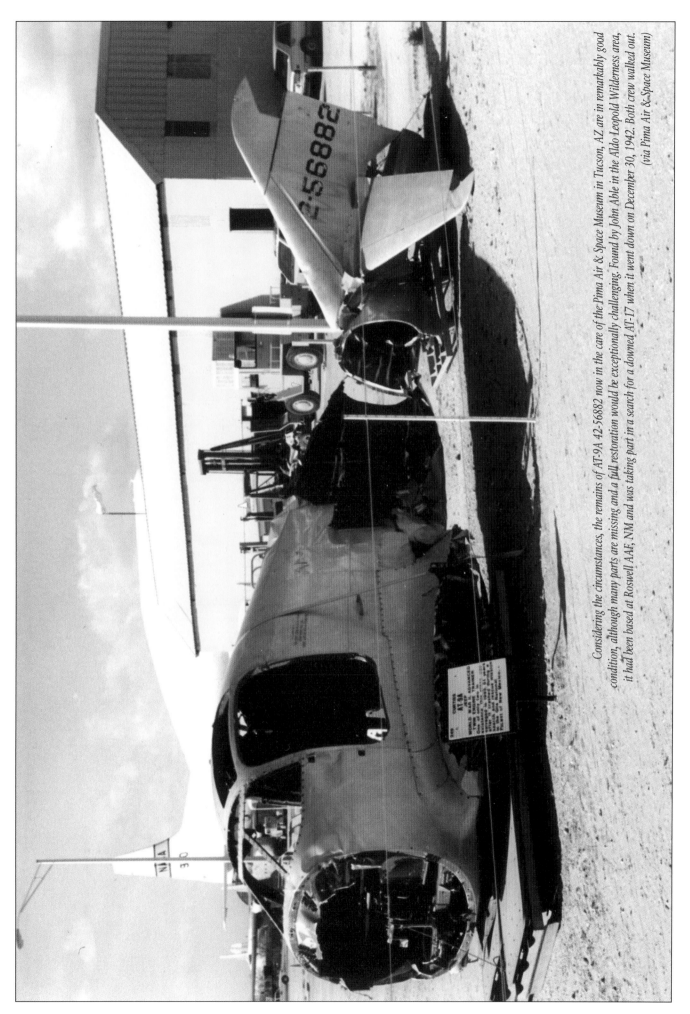

Considering the circumstances, the remains of AT-9A 42-56882 now in the care of the Pima Air & Space Museum in Tucson, AZ are in remarkably good condition, although many parts are missing and a full restoration would be exceptionally challenging. Found by John Able in the Aldo Leopold Wilderness area, it had been based at Roswell AAF, NM and was taking part in a search for a downed AT-17 when it went down on December 30, 1942. Both crew walked out.
(via Pima Air &Space Museum)

The solitary, complete survivor – itself a composite of at least two aircraft, an ex-Spartan School ground instruction airframe and 41-12150, acquired by the USAF Museum around 1978. Painted to represent an aircraft based at Lubbock AAF (probably because their archives contained only a few color illustrations of wartime AT-9s), the actual 41-12150 never served a day there, having been based for most of her career at Ellington Field, TX and Altus AAF, OK. The restoration is superb, however, and only a few small parts are missing.
(Accession 1978-153, NMUSAF)

A lineup of AT-9s at the Curtiss-Wright facilities at Lambert Field, Robertson, Missouri. (NMUSAF)